Y0-BRJ-047

Best Sports Stories 1970

Edited by IRVING T. MARSH and EDWARD EHRE

Best Sports Stories

1970 Edition

A Panorama of the 1969 Sports World

INCLUDING THE 1969 CHAMPIONS OF ALL SPORTS

WITH THE YEAR'S TOP PHOTOGRAPHS

E. P. DUTTON & CO., INC. / NEW YORK / 1970

Published simultaneously in Canada by
Clarke, Irwin & Company Limited, Toronto and Vancouver

Library of Congress Catalog Card Number: 45-35124

SBN 0-525-06616-0
FIRST EDITION

[03]

To the memory of
Bob Harron
A Great Newspaperman
A Great Friend
A Great Man

Contents

FOR THE RECORD

Illustrations

Preface

Why should the editors of *Best Sports Stories 1970,* the twenty-sixth in a series of volumes that began in 1944, attempt to gild the lily about the pieces that make up this current volume? The three sports-writing aficionados who have acted as judges in this year's contest can say it and have said it infinitely more objectively than a couple of other sports-writing aficionados who have gone through hundreds and hundreds of stories submitted by men who have pride in their craft and craftmanship.

All we can provide that our judges, the Messrs. John Chamberlain, John Hutchens and Red Smith, have not, is to present some sidelights in the summary that follows:

To tell you that Roger Kahn, the 1970 winner of the Best Magazine Story award, has now won it for the third time with his story on Willie Mays that appeared in *Sport,* and for the second time in a row, and for the first time that his victory has been unanimous. He won the award before with a story on Babe Ruth and another on Glenn Hall, the hockey goalie.

To tell you that Bob Lipsyte, the News-Feature award winner, has taken the $250 prize for the fourth time with his *New York Times* story on Dick Tiger. His last previous victory was a study on baseball rookies in 1967.

But perhaps the victory of which the editors are most proud is that of the piece under the byline of Wells Twombly, the winner of the News-Coverage award for his story that appeared in the *Detroit Free Press* on the Jets' victory in the Super Bowl of 1969. Twombly has had his efforts reprinted in our anthology many times before. But this is his first award. More, he has been nice enough to admit that his appearance in this series has helped him move up the newspaper sports-writing ladder, on whose latest rung he is columnist for the *San Francisco Examiner.*

Anyway, before you get down to the nitty-gritty of the box score of the judging, please be informed that, as in all previous years, the stories went to the judges "blind"—that is, they were identified merely by a word or two, called in newspaperese a "slug." And so, to the box scores of the judges and their comments on the stories by their "slugs":

News-Coverage Stories

	Chamberlain	Hutchens	Smith	*Total Points
Super [Wells Twombly's *The Impossible Dream*]	—	2	3	5
3rd Series [Phil Pepe's *Agee Makes the Orioles Sick Birds*]	1	3	—	4
Orange [Bill Conlin's *The "56 Scissors"*]	3	—	—	3
Frazier [Roy McHugh's *Quarry's Mistake*]	—	1	2	3
Texas [Mickey Herskowitz's *The Longhorns Silence Those "Soooooie" Pigs*]	2	—	—	2
Open [Jesse Outlar's *A Sergeant Outshoots the General*]	—	—	1	1

News-Feature Stories

	Chamberlain	Hutchens	Smith	*Total Points
Tiger [Robert Lipsyte's *The Medal*]	1	3	—	4
Betty [Stan Hochman's *Courage: A Lovely Woman*]	3	—	—	3
Caddy [Marty Ralbovsky's *A Profitable Bag*]	—	—	3	3
Wrigley [Joe Gergen's *Baseball Lives at Wrigley Field*]	—	2	—	2
Hockey [Frank Dolson's *It Was a Devil of a Weekend*]	2	—	—	2
Citation [Ira Berkow's *Citation Is Still a Ladies' Man*]	—	—	2	2
Vault [Blackie Sherrod's *Calling the Old Shots*]	—	1	—	1
Mets [Dick Young's *Dream of a Team . . .*]	—	—	1	1

Magazine Stories

	Chamberlain	Hutchens	Smith	*Total Points
Mays [Roger Kahn's *Willie Mays, Yesterday and Today*]	3	3	3	9
Sayers [Al Silverman's *Gale Sayers: The Hard Road Back*]	2	2	—	4
Lakers [Al Stump's *High-scoring Catastrophe*]	1	1	—	2
Race War [Jerry Izenberg's *Race War Is Alive and Well at Madison Square Garden*]	—	—	2	2
Dog [Don Ellis's *The Incredible Tracking Dog*]	—	—	1	1

* Based on 3 points for a first-place vote, 2 for a second, 1 for a third.

The judges commented as follows:

JOHN CHAMBERLAIN

News-Coverage Stories

1. Orange [*The "56 Scissors"* by Bill Conlin]
2. Texas [*The Longhorns Silence Those "Sooooooie" Pigs* by Mickey Herskowitz]
3. 3rd Series [*Agee Makes the Orioles Sick Birds* by Phil Pepe]

Our news coverage pros are so universally competent that there is little to choose among them from the standpoint of style. So the prizes must go to the ones who have been lucky enough to get the most dramatic assignments.

1. For first choice I like *Orange,* the story of how Kansas lost by a single point to Joe Paterno's Penn State in the Orange Bowl because Kansas had a twelfth man on the field at a critical point.

2. The No. 2 choice must be *Texas,* the story of another single-point thriller.

3. And for No. 3 I think *3rd Series,* which features Tommie Agee's catches, is the best of a number of good Met chronicles.

"Life," as John F. Kennedy once said, "is unfair," and it is certainly unfair to the sports writer who picks a dog for an assignment, unless, of course, he happens to be a genius. This year the news-coverage contests have been between men of talents, with no geniuses present. Maybe any of the contestants could have won a prize with Tommie Agee catching the ball or a Penn State quarterback improvising a play at the goal line. How will we ever know?

News-Feature Stories

1. Betty [*Courage: A Lovely Woman* by Stan Hochman]
2. Hockey [*It Was a Devil of a Weekend* by Frank Dolson]
3. Tiger [*The Medal* by Robert Lipsyte]

The features give more scope than the news-coverage story category for the exercise of originality on top of professional competence.

1. I give *Betty* an unashamed first place because the writer knows how to work on your heartstrings without mawkishness.

2. *Hockey,* the account of a strange resurgence by a team that must have been essentially mediocre does wonders with a situation that might have been treated by a less skilled writer with merely routine irony. It deserves second place.

3. For No. 3, I nominate *Tiger,* the story of a fighter from that

remarkable tribe of Ibos who have just been done in by a Big Power conspiracy.

Maybe it is my feeling for the underdog that comes out here. Other features have their points, like *Decade* [Steve Cady's *A Decade for All Seasons*], a remarkable summary of the sixties in sport; *Allie* [Gene Roswell's *Allie Hears the Last Good-bye*] and *Wrigley* [Joe Gergen's *Baseball Lives at Wrigley Field*].

Magazine Stories

1. Mays [*Willie Mays, Yesterday and Today* by Roger Kahn]
2. Sayers [*Gale Sayers: The Hard Road Back* by Al Silverman]
3. Lakers [*High-scoring Catastrophe* by Al Stump]

1. *Mays,* a nostalgic piece about Willie Mays over the years, is the best of the magazine stories. This is not only perceptive about Willie, it is also an appealing chronicle of a long-term relationship between a first-rate writer and a first-rate ball player.

2. *Sayers* [*Gale Sayers: The Hard Road Back* by Al Silverman] which I nominate for No. 2, is just as sensitive, but the writer has excluded himself.

3. For No. 3, I pick *Lakers* [*High-scoring Catastrophe* by Al Stump], which is good fun as well as being good writing about basketball.

John Hutchens

News-Coverage Stories

1. 3rd Series [*Agee Makes the Orioles Sick Birds* by Phil Pepe]
2. Super [*The Impossible Dream* by Wells Twombly]
3. Frazier [*Quarry's Mistake* by Roy McHugh]

1. Here is a story that caught the drama of a World Series game whose score, 5-0, would not seem offhand to have suggested much drama. The story's focal points are, of course, Tommie Agee's two great game-saving catches, but the other major factors, like Nolan Ryan's relief pitching, are no less well handled.

2. The cheerfully low-keyed lead to this piece caught me at once, and the rest of it held me all the way. How do you do justice to one of the great sports upsets within living memory? If you are as skillful as this writer was when he sat down to work, doubtless under nagging time pressure, you keep your cool and tell it the way it was, without melodramatics, letting the melodrama emerge on its own.

3. A first-rate account of a one-sided but nevertheless curiously exciting fight in which the loser lost because he and his strategists guessed wrong. This stark fact is enhanced by the shrewdly observed marginal material that can make the difference between a competent story and a superior one.

News-Feature Stories

1. Tiger [*The Medal* by Robert Lipsyte]
2. Wrigley [*Baseball Lives at Wrigley Field* by Joe Gergen]
3. Vault [*Calling the Old Shots* by Blackie Sherrod]

1. A truly sensitive, touching picture of one of modern boxing's most admirable gentlemen as seen for a few minutes outside the ring. You read it and you say to yourself, "Here are a couple of reasons why people like Dick Tiger and enjoy seeing him win, besides the fact of his skill and courage." The couple of things, as unobtrusively presented here, are dignity and class.

2. How could a sentimental old baseball fan, alarmed by the encroaching popularity of other sports, fail to be moved by this latter-day reminder of the era when a day at the ball park was all that any rational man (or woman or child) could ask?—and, especially, when it was the Cubs against the Mets in Chicago last summer, and a doubleheader, at that. Warmth and nostalgia and fried chicken in the fifth inning: a fine combination.

3. In my early days around newspaper offices this entry would have been called a "rainy-day piece," and perhaps the label still holds. Anyhow, a good one like this is still a work of sports-writing artistry. So it's a rainy day, and nothing big in the news to latch onto, and a writer with a self-kidding sense of humor comes up with a neat one.

Magazine Stories

1. Mays [*Willie Mays, Yesterday and Today* by Roger Kahn]
2. Sayers [*Gale Sayers: The Hard Road Back* by Al Silverman]
3. Lakers [*High-scoring Catastrophe* by Al Stump]

1. An absorbing portrait of the great Willie, on the field and—most rewardingly reported here—off the field. A finely organized piece, written with the sentiment that shies away from sentimentality, and with a friend's affection and an experienced baseball writer's perception.

2. A long, deep look at the dark peril of professional football:

the accident that threatens to end a career in a flash, the convalescence that can't be checked out until the first big test arrives with a new season, the suspense and tension that torture the player and his team until that climactic moment. The writer who saw it through with Gale Sayers of the Chicago Bears got it all down expertly.

3. I don't suppose this piece seems very funny to addicts of the Los Angeles Lakers, but just about anybody else has to be vastly entertained by the chronicle of a potentially great organization with a genius for doing itself in, thanks to sundry lapses hilariously reminiscent of the original New York Mets.

Red Smith

News-Coverage Stories

1. Super [*The Impossible Dream* by Wells Twombly]
2. Frazier [*Quarry's Mistake* by Roy McHugh]
3. Open [*A Sergeant Outshoots the General* by Jesse Outlar]

1. The story of how the Jets rose up and smacked the pro football Establishment is told about as well as a story can be told for deadline. It puts the emphasis in the right places, it is tidily organized and clearly told. Only working newspaper stiffs know how difficult it is to do this for the next edition.

2. The account of Jerry Quarry's defeat by Joe Frazier is very close to the winner. I was there, and this is the way it was.

3. The man who wrote about Orville Moody's victory in the United States Open Golf Championship had a lovely story to report, and he told it well. I could ask that next time he wouldn't strain quite so hard to bring off that General vs. Sergeant motif.

News-Feature Stories

1. Caddy [*A Profitable Bag* by Marty Ralbovsky]
2. Citation [*Citation Is Still a Ladies' Man* by Ira Berkow]
3. Mets [*Dream of a Team . . .* by Dick Young]

1. Hardly a week passes when we don't read about Jack Nicklaus or Arnold Palmer picking up another $25,000. In the piece about the touring caddies, we read about an entirely different breed of cat on the tournament circuit. A first-rate job of reporting and writing.

2. The piece about Citation gives us a warm picture of a cham-

pion who is getting on. This may be the pleasantest "mood" piece in the book.

3. "Newspaper work is knowing, not writing," Dr. John M. Cooney used to tell us journalism majors at Notre Dame a century or so ago. If he was right, *Mets* probably should get first call here, for the man who wrote it obviously knew about all there was to know about this baseball team. When you realize that he had to get it all on paper immediately after the Mets won the pennant, you wonder why I didn't vote this the best. I wonder.

Magazine Stories

1. Mays [*Willie Mays, Yesterday and Today* by Roger Kahn]
2. Race War [*Race War Is Alive and Well at Madison Square Garden* by Jerry Izenberg]
3. Dog [*The Incredible Tracking Dog* by Don Ellis]

1. The magazine category was, for me, the most difficult to judge because it offered an embarrassment of riches. I chose Roger Kahn's piece on Willie Mays as the winner, with misgivings. The winner because it is the best job of writing in this category. Misgivings because the author is my friend and I knew he was the author (he identified himself in the piece), because I get a mention in the story, and especially because this piece is half about Roger Kahn when perhaps it should be all about Willie Mays. However, it's still the best job of writing, and that seems to me to be the name of the game.

2. Right up there as a piece of writing is *Race War*. (I think I know who wrote this, though the editors are careful to give us judges no clues; I'm smug enough to think I can recognize a guy's style.) Only one thing keeps this from being best. The idea is thin. The writer has done a great job of fleshing up a feeble theme.

3. Maybe I'm the only one to give *Dog* a mention. It is an absorbing story, written with Grant Wood simplicity. So why don't I vote it best? I don't know.

As for the prize-winning photos, the action shot winner by Paul DeMaria of the *New York Daily News* tells in one quick click of the camera the story of the end of years of disappointment and frustration of a baseball team that never quit trying. All the adjectives that have been applied to the Mets of 1969 are graphically expressed in this photo of a fraction of a second of history.

And Bob Doty's feature photo winner is completely in keeping with the imaginative efforts on film of this artist of the camera. This is his fourth victory, which is more than any other photographic contributor to this series has achieved. In those four triumphs he has produced tears as well as laughter.

Move on, then, to *Best Sports Stories 1970*. Have fun, boys and girls.

IRVING T. MARSH
EDWARD EHRE

The Prize-Winning Stories

Best News-Coverage Story ———

THE IMPOSSIBLE DREAM

By Wells Twombly

From the Detroit Free Press

Play soft music and send flowers to the relatives. Let's have a little reverence. An era passed into oblivion in the third annual Super Bowl and professional football will never quite be the same.

For the first time since it was founded 49 years ago, the National Football League no longer dominates its universe.

The fun-worshiping New York Jets rose up and defeated the NFL's good gray champion, the Baltimore Colts, by a 16–7 score.

The man who turned the world upside down was brassy, sleepy-eyed Joe Namath, the hippie quarterback. He did exactly what he had been saying he was going to do all week long before the game.

He threw the ball with magnificent speed and accuracy, setting up one touchdown run by fullback Matt Snell and three field goals by Jim Turner. What's more, he treated the Colts, 15–1 in their own league this season, as if they were the Denver Broncos.

Now there will be an end to all arguments about when the American League will catch its older business rival. It happened here on a cloudy day at Miami's great steel-plated Orange Bowl. The date was January 12, 1969, when the power passed from the NFL to the nine-year-old AFL.

The Colts had no excuses. They never really got into the ball game until the final minutes of the fourth quarter when Johnny Unitas replaced Earl Morrall, the NFL's Player of the Year, who had his first bad day of the season—in the Super Bowl.

"We just didn't play our game," said Colt coach Don Shula. "It was a convincing win on their part. We didn't pay any attention to the point spread. We knew the AFL had come awfully close to achieving equality. Now I guess it's here. It's going to be a long winter."

Going into the game, the Jets were anywhere from 18- to 22-point underdogs in the betting odds around the nation. But the American League champions didn't seem to be aware of how heavily the Colts were favored although most of them had read it in the newspapers.

Namath was superb, completing 17 of 28 passes for 206 yards. Morrall had all sorts of problems, hitting on six of 13 passes for 71 yards. The Jets intercepted four passes.

Undoubtedly that latter statistic was the most surprising one. All along it has been said that the major difference between the leagues was that the AFL did not have defensive backs as good as those in the NFL.

Yet the Jets took three passes away from Morrall and one from Unitas. The Colts got close to Namath's throws a couple of times, but they never stole one. What's more, Morrall had four passes batted down in the line. Unitas had one.

This has been the AFL's season. Its clubs won 13 of 23 intra-league exhibition games. Its champions, the Jets, now have won the right to play the College All-Stars next summer in Chicago.

The Jets simply shut off the Baltimore running attack, forcing the Colts to throw 41 passes. Then their defensive backs took care of the rest. Baltimore literally lost its offense.

Namath was right about everything he said. He had indicated that Morrall wasn't as good as people said he was, and the Colts had to take Earl out of the lineup in the fourth. Joe also flatly guaranteed a Jet victory.

He insisted that Baltimore's normal brutal pass rush wouldn't bother him that much. He was right. The Colts threw him only twice, for a net loss of 11 yards.

New York stopped Baltimore's first drive of the game and then came frighteningly close to scoring when Don Maynard dropped a long pass out in the open.

The Jets looked doomed just before the first quarter ended when Namath's pass to George Sauer was fumbled on the New York 12 and Baltimore linebacker Ron Porter recovered.

If there was a time when the AFL club might have panicked, it came on the next Colt drive. But Morrall's pass to tight end Tom Mitchell bounced high in the air in the end zone and Jet cornerback Randy Beverly intercepted it.

Obviously inspired, the Jets came right back and scored.

Running fullback Matt Snell hit at the left side of the Baltimore line, where two older defenders, 33-year-old Don Shinnick and 36-year-old Ordell Braase, lurk.

The hard-throwing Namath, tossing to Sauer, got the Jets down to the Baltimore four-yard line.

From there Snell ran wide, pounding away from Colt safetyman Rick Volk. The touchdown, with 9:03 left, put an AFL club ahead for the first time in three of these Super Bowl affairs.

The Jets never blew it.

Afterward Snell, an Ohio State alumnus, was angry with reporters.

"You guys spent all week writing how great Jerry Hill and Tom Matte of Baltimore were," he said, "so go over and talk to them."

Just before the first half ended, the Jets just about stripped Morrall down to his shoulder pads. Matte had smashed 57 yards to the Jet 16. Johnny Sample, an ex-Colt, took a pass away from Willie Richard on the two.

When Morrall got the ball back, New York did it again.

Actually the Colts had decided to get overly clever. Morrall handed off to Matte, who ran right, turned and passed to Morrall, who threw downfield toward Jerry Hill. Jet safety Jim Hudson intercepted.

New York's Jim Turner kicked his first two field goals on the Jets' first two series of the third period. Jerry Logan had Namath's pass in his hands and dropped it just before Turner went into action.

Rescued from an interception, Namath gave the ball to his placekicker, who scored from 32 yards out.

The Jets came right back and Turner got another field goal from 31 yards, making the score 13–0 and causing some sweaty palms on the Baltimore bench. Shula whistled for Unitas, who missed most of the season with a sore elbow.

"I knew I was able to play," Unitas said later. "Don knew it right from the start."

But Unitas had his problems, too. After he had moved the Colts into scoring position, right after Turner's third field goal opened the fourth period, Randy Beverly intercepted a pass Johnny threw toward Jimmy Orr.

Now the score was 16–0 in favor of New York and the Jets had the ball back.

The Colts had not been shut out in 50 games, and Unitas finally averted that particular embarrassment with 3:19 left. Hill ran over from the one, but not before the Jets had stopped the Colts on the edge of the goal line three straight times.

Lou Michaels cuffed a squib kick to the Jet 45 and the Colts recovered. Unitas got them down to the 19, but on a fourth-down-and-five situation, New York linebacker Larry Granthan deflected a pass and that was it.

Sauer had a brilliant day, whirling through the Baltimore defenses for 133 yards on eight passes.

Tight end John Mackey, the man the Jets said they feared most, dropped a couple of passes in the clear early in the game and never did much damage to the Jets although he caught three for 35 yards.

"We owe this victory to Namath's ability to recognize their defenses," said Sauer afterward. "He saw so much of their film last week that he had absolutely no trouble recognizing what they were going to do."

Best News-Feature Story

THE MEDAL

By Robert Lipsyte

From *The New York Times*

Walking up the post office steps in the brilliant, chilly afternoon, Dick Tiger said: "If they ask me how much it's worth, what should I say?"

His companion shrugged. "We should try to pawn it and find out."

"I'll say a million dollars." Tiger laughed. It was the first time he had laughed. "I'll say fifty or a hundred, just so it gets there."

He stood on line at the registry window, a small black hat perched on his head, his body muffled in a fur-lined coat. He has always seemed overdressed in America, always a little colder than everyone else. Once he said it all went back to the four years he lived in England, training in drafty gyms as he boxed on the Liverpool-Blackpool circuit.

The clerk behind the registry wicket hefted the package and shook his head. "No good, you got Scotch Tape on it. Go around the corner, they'll give you some brown paper."

Another line. Tiger has always been such a patient man, waiting for bouts, waiting for return bouts, waiting for a crack at a world championship. He had won two, the middleweight and the light-heavyweight, and lost them both, and now, at the age of 40, he is picking up fights where he can while waiting for one more title shot.

"If there had been no war," he said earlier that morning, "I would be retired by now. But . . . well . . ." he smiled and spread his hands. "I'm not getting rich or investing money. Now is just for daily bread and praying the war is over. I cannot complain. I am not the only one who lost property."

A clerk handed Tiger a long strip of gummed brown paper and a wet sponge in a dish. Tiger took it to a writing desk and began to tear the brown paper into small strips, his thick fingers careful and precise. He had always taped and bandaged his own hands, rare for a champion boxer. He had done many things himself. He was always considered a very tight man with money and with intimacies. Unfailingly courteous and cooperative, but dowdy and reserved. His money all went to Nigeria, to his wife, seven children and his large family circle, and into buildings and shops. Until the country exploded into war, he was a rich man.

"Well," he said, finishing the package, "now I know there is something else I can do."

There was another wait at the registry window. Tiger studied the package. It was addressed to the British Ambassador in Washington, and inside was the medal with a pink ribbon, now grimy, he had received in a ceremony in Lagos six years ago. The medal, Member of the Order of the British Empire, had begun to grow heavy in his mind. In a letter accompanying the medal, he had written:

"I am hereby returning the O.B.E. because every time I look at it I think of millions of men, women and children who died and are still dying in Biafra because of the arms and ammunition the British Government is sending to Nigeria and its continued moral support of this genocide against the people of Biafra."

He had signed it, Dick Tiger Ihetu. He had been christened Richard Ihetu, Ibo for "what I want." Dick Tiger became his ring name in early battles against such local gladiators as Easy Dynamite and Mighty Joe Young. But bombs had fallen and blood had been spilled and babies had starved in the towns of his youth, and when he spoke of his country it was no longer with the earnest chamber of commerce pitch he had used only a few years ago.

"If you look at Africa now," he had said earlier last Friday morning, "there is fighting and trouble in every country that once was under the British Government. They were forced to give the countries independence, but they gave it with the left hand and now are trying to take it back with the right hand."

He stopped suddenly. "I am not a politician. I don't want people to say, ah, there's a dumb fighter who does not speak good English talking."

He had wanted to return the medal for some time, he said. But it was not until he read two weeks ago that John Lennon, the Beatle, returned his O.B.E. for reasons that included Britain's involvement in the Nigerian civil war, that he decided to mail back his medal.

"Okay," snapped the registry clerk, flipping the small package. "What's in it?"

"A medal," said Tiger softly.

"What?"

"A medal."

"What's it worth?"

Tiger shrugged. "I don't know. Fifty, hundred dollars?"

"No value," said the clerk, to himself. He weighed it, registered it, asked Tiger if he wanted it to go air mail. Tiger said yes.

"One sixty."

Tiger gave him two dollar bills and counted his change. He readjusted his scarf as he walked out into the bright street and smiled and shook his companion's hand and could only say, "Well . . ." and shrug and start down the steps.

Best Magazine Story

WILLIE MAYS, YESTERDAY AND TODAY

By Roger Kahn

From Sport

He is sitting on the three-legged stool they give to ball players and milkmaids, and he looks enormous and supple and strong. He has a massive flat chest and bulging arms and shoulders and the kind of muscled stomach I remember from comic-book drawings of Tarzan. Still, he is 38 years old.

"What do you do to stay in shape, Will?" I say.

"Nothin' special," Willie Mays says. "I walk a lot and I play golf now, 'stead of pool. And I don't eat too much and I never did drink, except three times, when we won pennants." A smile briefly lights the handsome brown face.

"Well, you look like you can go on forever."

"I won't lie to you," Mays says. "It gets to be work. Sometimes when I get tired and all that pressure, it gets to be work. I knew when I was 16 years old, I never did want to work for a living." Again the smile.

"You want to manage?"

"Yeah. I think I'd like to."

"What about handling pitchers? Could you do that?"

"You're a manager," Willie says, "man, you get to hire help."

It is 11 o'clock the morning after a night game and Willie will play this afternoon. The team is not going well and last night in the ninth inning, with the count 3 and 2, he guessed curve. Then Ron Taylor of the Mets threw a fast ball by him. Willie is not playing for fun today, but from a sense of obligation. He has come out early so we can talk in an empty locker room, and the conversation sweeps across a broad range. We go back a way together and when

Willie trusts you, he is warm and open and droll and humorously sly. Together, we consider divorce and alimony and child-raising and financial security and how time, the subtle thief of youth, steals from you, me and even Willie Mays.

A spring, 15 years ago, comes back in a rush and I see again the wide pellucid sky, the baked hills wanting grass and the desert winds blowing whirls of sand. I hadn't wanted to come to Phoenix. I hadn't wanted to cover the Giants. For two previous years I'd been assigned to the Dodgers. This nurtured a condition described in a general way by the late nonpareil of sports editors, Stanley Woodward. "Baseball writers," Woodward observed, "always develop a great attachment for the Brooklyn ball club if long exposed to it. We found it advisable to shift Brooklyn writers frequently. If we hadn't, we would have found that we had on our hands a member of the Brooklyn ball club rather than a newspaper reporter. You watch a Brooklyn writer for symptoms, and, before they become virulent, you must shift him to the Yankees or to tennis or golf." Woodward was gone from the *Herald Tribune* by 1954. I was shifted, under protest, to the Giants.

The ride from New York to Phoenix was interminable. We had to change trains in Chicago, wasting time, and somewhere near Liberal, Kansas, we stopped dead for 10 or 12 hours in a snowstorm.

Perhaps 50 hours after we had left New York, the train pulled into Phoenix and we stepped out into a cool and cloudless morning. Louis Effrat of the *Times* alighted with me and looked about the station. A few Indians were sleeping. In the distance lay brown hills. "Three thousand miles," Effrat shouted. "I leave my wife, my daughter, my home and travel 3,000 miles." He inhaled before bellowing, "For what?" He was making a joke, but that was the way I felt.

My outlook did not improve immediately. The Giant manager, Honest Leo Durocher, offered me tidbits on his swelling romance with a post-virginal actress, but was more devious when asked about the club. The ball players were decent enough, but I didn't know them, or they me, and I was starting from scratch, building up confidences and new sources. And aside from that, the team bored me. I was used to the explosive Dodger atmosphere, with Jackie Robinson holding forth and Charlie Dressen orating and Roy Campanella philosophizing. The Giants seemed somber as vestrymen.

While I struggled and wrote a story a day, plus an extra for Sunday, Willie Howard Mays, Jr., was struggling with an Army team at Fort Eustis, Virginia, hitting, as he later put it, ".470, or something like that." They were all waiting for him. The Giants had won in 1951 with Mays. Without him in 1952 and '53, they lost. Each day in the press room, one of the regular Giant writers or one of the officials would tell anecdotes in which Willie was always superman. In exasperation, I sat down and wrote a story for the Sunday paper that began:

"Willie Mays is 10 feet 9 inches tall. His arms reach from 156th Street to 154th . . . He has caught everything, hit everything, done everything a center fielder can possibly do."

"Look," I told Charles Feeney, the Giant vice-president, amid the amber torrents of the Phoenix press bar. "There are a couple of other center fielders, too. Ever hear of Mickey Mantle or Duke Snider?"

Mr. Feeney erupted in song. "In six more days," he choired, to the tune of "Old Black Joe," "we're gonna have Willie Mays." He may have sung it "going to." He is a Dartmouth man.

Each day Feeney warbled, amending the lyrics cleverly enough, say changing the word six to the word five. The song, like the sandy wind, became a bane.

M Day, as I came to call it, dawned like most other days, with a big bright sky. Durocher had scheduled an intrasquad game and was elaborately underplaying things. The post-virginal movie star was gone, making him somewhat irascible.

"Nothing unusual," Leo announced in the lobby of the Hotel Adams early M Day. "Just a little intrasquad game, boys, that's all." Then he walked off, barely able to keep his footing for his swagger.

The Phoenix ball park was typical medium minor league. Old stands extended partway down each foul line. A wood fence ringed the outfield. The players, Monte Irvin, Whitey Lockman, Alvin Dark, were in uniform and, as always in spring, it seemed odd to see great major-leaguers in a minor-league setting.

Willie was coming by plane, we all knew that, and in Phoenix you can see great distances. Whenever an airplane appeared, one of the writers or Giant officials leaped up with a cry, "Willie's plane." Two Piper Cubs, four Beechcrafts and one World War I Spad were positively identified as the transcontinental Constellation bearing Mays.

"Feeney," I said, "this is ridiculous."

This time he chose the key of C-sharp minor.

> "In no more days,
> "We're going to have Willie Mays!"

The athletes were still playing catch, the intrasquad game had not started, when a trim figure in slacks and a dark open-collared shirt appeared in the dugout. He was blinking at the sunlight, mostly because he had not been to sleep, and seemed to be trying to hide, to be as unobtrusive as possible. "There's Willie," someone cried in ecstasy, and the sports writers swarmed.

Mays stood next to Irvin, probably the closest friend he has had among ball players in a curiously lonely life. Irvin was very poised, very strong, very sensible.

"Hey, Willie," someone shouted, "what you got in that bag?" He had dropped off his large suitcase, but clung to a smaller one.

"Not much," Willie said. "A couple things."

"What?"

"Just my glove and my jock."

Durocher hugged him repeatedly for joy and for the news photographers. Monte, who felt like hugging him, shook his hand.

"He's shaking hands with the pennant," Barney Kremenko, one of the baseball writers, proclaimed.

"Hi, roomy," Irvin said.

"Hey, Monte."

Irvin smiled. "Roomy," he said, "how's your game?"

Willie shook his head. "What you mean my game, Monte? You talking about pool?"

"No, Willie," Irvin said. "I'm talking about your game, about baseball."

"Oh yeah," Willie said, as if surprised there should be a question. "My baseball. I'm ready anytime."

A few minutes later, when the intrasquad game began, Mays remained on the bench. Durocher, with his sure sense of drama and his always brilliant sense of handling Willie, was letting the elements cook. The game proceeded without much excitement. The most interesting thing at the Phoenix ball park was watching No. 24, striding back and forth, looking at Durocher, asking with his eyes, and being ignored.

Halfway through the game, he was sent in to hit. Willie sprang from the dugout. He ran to the batter's box. He took a tremendous swing at the first pitch. His form was flawed. There was a little lunge in the swing. But I don't believe I have ever seen anyone swing harder. Three swings, and mighty Willie had struck out.

"The thing about Snider," I told Kremenko in the press box, "is that his butt doesn't fly out of there when he swings."

"Now, listen," Kremenko began, as though I had assailed the family honor. And I suppose I had.

The first unusual thing that Willie did was snatch a sinking liner off the grass. The ball came out to center field low and hard and Willie charged it better than anyone else could have and dove and made a graceful somersault and caught the ball. "Nothing," Kremenko shouted. "For Willie that's absolutely nothing."

The next time he came to bat, I resolved to look for specific flaws in his form. I was doing that when he hit a fast ball 420 feet and out of the park. An inning later, and with a man on first, someone hit a tremendous drive over Willie's head. He turned and fled and caught the ball and threw it 300 feet and doubled the runner. Pandemonium. The camp was alive. The team was alive. And Willie had gone through the delays of a discharge, then sat up all night in a plane. I conceded to Kremenko that given a little rest, he might show me something.

Then I sat down and wrote an account that began, "This is not going to be a plausible story, but then no one ever accused Willie Mays of being a plausible ball player. This story is only the implausible truth." It ran quite long, and I had no idea whether the *Tribune* copy desk would eviscerate it, until a day later when a wire came from Red Smith in Florida. Red was the columnist for the *Tribune*, a thoughtful man, and his telegram, a personal gesture, was the first indication I'd had in a month that my stuff was getting printed and was syntactical.

That night Feeney, selecting the rather cheerful key of D-Major, honored me with the final version of his aria.

> "Gone are the days,
> "When we didn't have Willie Mays."

After Willie's debut and Red's wire, I was genuinely surprised to hear how much Feeney's voice had improved.

Willie conquered me. I had not come to praise him and sycophancy annoys me, but he brought to the game the outstanding collection of skills in our time and the deepest enthusiasm to play I've seen. He was the ultimate combination of the professional full of talent and the amateur, a word that traces to the Latin *amator*, lover, and suggests one who brings a passion to what he does.

They used to play pepper games, Leo and Willie, sometimes with Monte Irvin as the straight man. Willie has what his father, Kitty-

Kat Mays, described as oversized hands, and Durocher was one of the finest defensive shortstops. They'd stand quite close and Leo would hit hard smashes at Willie's toes, or knees, wherever. Mays' reflexes were such that he could field a hard line drive at 10 or 15 feet. And he liked to do it. He threw, and Leo slugged again. Once in a while Willie bobbled a ball. Then he owed Durocher a Coke. Durocher made great shows of cheating Willie. One morning he hit a hard smash on one hop, well to Willie's right, and Willie knocked the ball down with a prodigious lunge.

"Coke," Leo roared. "That's six you owe."

"Ain' no Coke for that," Willie said. His voice piped high and plaintive. "That's a base hit."

"Six Cokes you owe," Leo insisted.

"Monte," Willie pleaded at Irvin. "What you say, roomy?"

"Six Cokes," Irvin said, solemnly. Willie's mobile face slumped into a pout. "I'm getting the short end," the expression said, "but I'll get you guys anyway."

Sometimes Irvin hit, and then there was added byplay. Not only did Durocher and Mays stab smashes, they worked to rattle each other. Durocher seized a line drive, wound up to throw to Irvin, and with a blur of elbows and hands tossed the ball to Mays at his left. Leo has the skills and inclinations of a juggler. Willie caught the toss, faked toward Irvin, and there was the ball floating down toward Leo. Durocher reached and Mays slapped a glove into his belly.

"Ooof," Leo grunted. Willie spun off, staggering through his own laughter. It wasn't long before people started coming to the ball park long before the game, just to watch the pepper. The clowning would have done honor to Chaplin.

Willie ran and threw and hit and made his astounding catches and slowly that spring I began to get to know him. I was the youngest of the baseball writers and that helped. We had little conversations after the workouts and the exhibition games, and he always became very solemn and gave me serious answers. "Who suggested," I asked one day, "that you catch fly balls that way?" The technique is famous now: glove up, near the belt buckle.

"Nobody," Willie said. "I just start it one day. I get my throw away quicker."

"Nobody taught you?"

Willie's eyes, which sometimes dance, grew grave. "Nobody can teach you nothing," he said. "You got to learn for yourself."

On another afternoon we were talking, and Ruben Gomez, a pitcher from Puerto Rico, came up and said, "Willie. That man in New York. I forget the name. I sign a paper for him."

Willie mentioned a New York agent.

"That's him," Gomez said.

"You sign a paper," Willie said, "and you worried because you haven't got your money."

Gomez nodded.

"Well, don't worry," Willie said. "Long as you sure you signed. It may come soon, or it may come late, but long as you sign something, you'll get money." He looked at me. "Ain' that right?" I thought of leases, installment contracts and overdue bank loans, but I said, "Yes." Maybe it would always be that way for Willie, spring and youth and plenty of cash and laughter. But it wasn't, not even that spring.

Along with the Cleveland Indians, a team wealthy with pitchers, the Giants flew to Las Vegas for an exhibition game late in March. The Giant management did not want the ball players spending a night in Las Vegas. The Stoneham regime is paternalistic and the idea of a troop of young ball players abroad among the gamblers and the bosoms of Vegas was disturbing. The team would play its game with the Indians. The players would be guests for dinner at one of the big hotels. They would watch a show and seek as much trouble as they could find up until 11 p.m. Then a bus would take them to the airport for a flight to Los Angeles, where two other exhibitions were scheduled. We wouldn't get much rest.

It was a gray, raw afternoon in Vegas, and Bob Feller pitched for the Indians. Sal Maglie opposed him. My scorebook is lost, but I believe the Giants won by one run. Afterward we wrote our stories and took a bus to the hotel that invited us all. We ate well, and I caught up with Willie in the hotel theater, where Robert Merrill, the baritone, was to sing. As I joined Willie's table, Merrill began "Vesti la Giubba," the famous aria from *Pagliacci* in which Canio, the clown, sings of having to make people laugh, although his own heart is breaking.

Merrill gave it full voice and all his passions. When he was done, Willie turned to me amid the cheering. "You know," he said, "that's a nice song."

An hour later, he was in a gambling room. He was standing quietly amid a group of people close to a dice table. Monte Irvin and Whitey Lockman were fighting a 10-cent one-armed bandit. Sal

Maglie, looking like Il Patrone of Cosa Nostra, was losing a steady 50 cents a game at blackjack. I walked over to Willie. "How you doing?"

"Oh," Willie said, "I'm just learnin' the game." We both grinned.

I moved on. A stocky gruff man grabbed me by the arm. "Hey," he said. "Wait a minute."

I shook my arm free.

"That guy a friend of yours?" said the man. He pointed to Mays.

"I know him."

"Well, get him the hell away from the dice tables."

"What?"

"You heard me. We don't want him mixing with the white guests."

"Do you know who he is?"

"Yeah, I know who he is, and get that nigger away from the white guests."

If there was a good answer, except for the obvious short answer, I didn't come up with it. Very quickly I was appalled, unnerved and angry. What unnerved me was the small significant bulge on the man's left hip.

"Do you know that boy just got out of the Army?" I said.

"That don't mean nothing. I was in the Army myself."

"You bastards invited him down to your hotel."

"Who you calling a bastard?"

We were shouting and Gary Schumacher, the Giants' publicity director, suddenly loomed large and put a hand on my shoulder. "What's the trouble?" Gary said.

"This guy," the tough began.

"I asked him," Gary said, nodding at me.

I had a sensible moment. "No trouble, Guv," I said to Gary. I took my wallet out of a hip pocket and withdrew the press card. "This joker has just given me one helluva story for the Sunday New York *Herald Tribune*."

The hood retreated. I walked over to Irvin and told him what was happening. Lockman listened briefly and then, taking the conversation to be personal, stepped back. "Maybe Willie and I'll get on the bus," Irvin said. It was his way, to avoid confrontations, but he was also worried lest Willie be shocked or hurt.

Now a hotel vice-president appeared, with a girl, hard-faced but trimly built. He asked if "my assistant and I can buy you a drink, Mr. Kahn."

We went to the bar and the man explained that he had nothing against a Negro like Irvin or Mays playing one-armed bandits. It was just that the dice table was a somewhat different thing. As far as he, the vice-president, was concerned, Negroes were as good as anybody, but he had to concern himself with customers. That was business.

"We're really in the South here," said the brunette.

"I thought the South was Alabama, Georgia, Texas."

"That's it," the brunette said. "We get a lot of customers from Texas." She glanced at the bartender, and I had another drink. "We're really a very liberal place," the girl said, "even though we are in the South. We not only book Lena Horne to sing here, but when she does, we let her live on the grounds. We're the only hotel that liberal." She leaned toward me, a hard, handsome woman, working.

"Why did you invite him if you were going to crap on him?" I said and got up and joined Monte and Will in the bus.

Later Irvin asked me not to write the story. He said he didn't know if it was a good idea to make Willie, at 21, the center of a racial storm. That was Monte's way and the Giants' way and Willie's way, and you had to respect it, even if dissenting. I never did write the story until now.

In the visitors' locker at Shea Stadium 15 years later, the headline on a folded newspaper cries out: "City College Torn by Black and White Strife." The times are different and I have heard a prominent black criticize Mays as self-centered. It was the job of every black to work for a free society, he said. To the militant—a Stokely Carmichael or a Rap Brown—Willie is the embodiment of the well-fed declawed Tom.

"They want me to go out on some campus?" Willie says. "Why should I lie? I don't know nothin' about campuses. I never went to college. I wanted to play ball."

"Well, what about the whole black movement?"

"I help," Willie says. "I help in my way." His face becomes very serious. "I think I show some people some things. I do it my way." He is a good fellow, serious and responsible, never in trouble, never drunk, never in jail.

"Do you speak out?"

"Like what?"

"On schools, or full employment or whatever?"

He eyes me evenly. "I don't think I should. I don't know the full value of these things. I'm not the guy to get on the soapbox." He pauses, then announces with great assurance and pride, "I'm a ball player."

In the autumn of '54, after Willie led the Giants to the pennant and a sweep over the Indians in the World Series, our paths crossed again. I was putting together a book featuring articles by All-Star ball players on the qualities that make one an All-Star. I sent questionnaires to many like Ted Kluszewski and Bob Lemon. I telephoned Stan Musial. I went to see Willie in the flesh. He had made his classic World Series catch, running, running, running, until he was 460 feet out and grabbing Vic Wertz's liner over his head. He had taken Manhattan, the Bronx and Staten Island, too, and was in demand. At the Giants someone gave me the name of his agent.

After hearing what I could pay, the agent said Willie would let me have three to four minutes on a slow Tuesday afternoon, but while we talked he might have to sign four endorsements, accept six speaking engagements, get his shoes shined and telephone for a date. His business was being handled brusquely, although not, we were to learn, very well.

A few seconds before the appointed minute I appeared in the agent's office. Willie was in an anteroom, only signing endorsements. When I appeared he waved and smiled, relieved to see a familiar face. "Hey," he said, "Roger Kahn, is that you? I didn't know that was you. What you want to talk to me about?"

I explained.

"You writin' a book?" Willie said. "That's real good, you writin' a book."

Disturbed by gratuitous friendliness, the agent vanished and Willie held forth on playing center field. "The first thing," he said, "is you got to love the game. Otherwise you'll never learn to play good. Then, you know, don't drink, and get your sleep. Eight hours. You sleep more, you get to be lazy.

"Now in Trenton, where I played when I first signed, I was nowhere near as good as I am now, but I have my way to learn things. People tell me, 'Willie do like this, like that,' but that ain't the way."

He sat in a swivel chair, which he had tilted back. His considerable feet were on a desk. "Well, how do you learn?" I said.

"Some things maybe when you're real little, you got to be told. But mostly you got to be doing it yourself. Like once I was a pitcher and now I'm in the outfield. Watch me after I get off a good throw. I look sort of like a pitcher who has thrown.

"You got to be thinking, 'What am I doing wrong?' And then you look at the other two outfielders and think, 'What are they doing wrong?' And you're thinking and thinking and trying not to make the same mistake three times, or four at the most, and you're also thinking what you'll do if the ball comes to you. Understand?"

"Pretty much."

"You don't want to be surprised," Willie said with finality.

But on what Branch Rickey called the best catch in baseball history, Mays was indeed surprised. The Giants were playing in Pittsburgh, where center field runs 457 feet deep, a good stage for Willie. Rocky Nelson, a left-handed hitter, smashed a tremendous line drive and Willie, calculating at a glance, turned and sprinted for the wall. Nelson had hit the ball so hard that there was a hook to it. While Willie ran, the ball drifted slightly to the right.

At precisely the right instant, Willie looked. He had gotten back deep enough, a mini-miracle, but now the ball was to his right and sinking fast. He might have been able to reach across his body and glove the ball. Or he might not. We will never know. He simply stuck out his bare right hand and seized the liner at the level of his knees. Then he slowed and turned, his face a great, wide grin.

"Silent treatment," Durocher ordered in the dugout. "Nobody say nothing to him."

Willie touched his cap to acknowledge the crowd and ran down the three steps into the Forbes Field dugout. Everyone avoided Willie's eyes. Durocher was checking the lineup card. Bobby Thomson was pulling anthracite from his spikes. Hank Thompson was taking a very long drink. The silence was suffocating.

"Hey, Leo," Willie piped. "You don't have to say 'Nice play, Willie.' I know that was a nice play."

A minute later a note from Rickey arrived. "That," Rickey wrote, "was the finest catch I have ever seen and the finest catch I ever hope to see."

I finished the story by Willie with a comment that he offered in the agent's office. "You got to learn for yourself," he said, "and you got to do it in your own way and you got to become much improved. If you love the game enough you can do it." It reads right after all the years, and true, but even as I was finishing I understood that no book was likely to help a young man play center field like Willie Mays.

In Shea, we start talking about the old times. "New York was a good town for center fielders," I say, "when you were here with Mantle and Snider."

"Yeah," he says, "Mick and I broke in together, but he had a real bad body. Legs."

"How do you feel being the only one left?"

"Proud. Proud that I'm still playing."

"Lonely?"

"There's more new faces, but . . ." He turns his palms up and shrugs. "That doesn't bother me none.

"I worry, though," he says. "I get worried now that I can't do the job. 'Course I always was a worrier. I get the ball out, but I can't get it out as often as I used to."

"About old friends," I say.

"You know," Willie says. "I don't have many friends. People I know, people to say, 'Hi, Willie,' there's a million of them. My friends, I could count them on a few fingers."

I went calling in 1956, four days after Willie had taken a wife. Because he is handsome and country slick, and also because he is famous and well-paid, he does not lack for feminine attention. Joe Black, the Dodger relief pitcher, told me Willie was getting married. We played winter basketball together and after one workout, Joe said he hoped Willie knew what he was getting into.

"I'm sure of that," I said.

"I mean I hope he doesn't get hurt."

"What's the girl like?" I said.

"The girl," Joe said, "is older than Willie and has been married twice before."

A number of people counseled Willie against getting married, but he doesn't like to be told how to run his life, and each bit of counsel was a shove toward the altar. Then, in February, he gathered Marghuerite Wendelle, stuffed her into his Lincoln, and set off for Elkton, Maryland, where one can marry in haste. On the way, he picked up a $15 fine for driving 70 in a 60-mile zone.

He set up housekeeping in a tidy brick home not far from La Guardia Airport. East Elmhurst was one of the early colonies open to the black middle class and I remember the white taxi driver looking at the clean streets and detached houses in surprise. "Colored people live here?" he said.

Mrs. Mays received me with a cool hand, tipped with pointed fingernails. She was a beautiful woman, who stared hard and knowingly when she said hello. It was midday, but Willie hadn't come downstairs. "Just go on up," Marghuerite Mays said. "I have to go out to the beauty parlor."

I found Willie sitting in an enormous bed, gazing at morning television, a series starring Jackie Cooper and a talking dog. Willie was wearing tailored ivory pajamas. "Sit down," he said, indicating a chair. "What you doing now? How come you don't come around? You okay?"

I had left the newspaper business and gone to work as a sports writer for a newsmagazine. The salary was better and the researchers were pretty, but the magazine approached sports in an earnest, sodden way. One of the supervising editors had been a small-town sports writer once and then become a sports writer on the newsmagazine. The change of fortune downed poorly. He alternately tried to relate great events to his own experiences, perhaps covering a play-off game between Bridgeport and Pittsfield, or he demanded scientific analyses of the events and men. A great story on Mays, he told me, would explain in complete technical detail how Willie played center field.

In the bridal bedroom, I told Willie I was fine. I was wondering how to swing the conversation into a technical analysis. I asked what had made him decide to marry.

"Well," Willie said, "I figured that's it's time for me to be settling down. I'm 24 years old."

"You figure being married will affect your play?"

"I dunno," Willie said. "How am I supposed to know? I hit 51 home runs last year. Man, if you come to me last spring and tell me I was gonna do that, I woulda told you you were crazy." Willie shook his head and sat straight up. "Man," he said. "Tha's a lot of home runs."

On top of the TV set rested three trophies. The largest was a yard-high wooden base for bright gilt figurines of ball players running, batting and throwing. It bore a shiny plaque which read: "To Willie Mays, the most valuable player in baseball."

"What are you hoping to do this year?"

"I dunno," Willie said. He frowned. "Why you askin' question like that?" he said.

I stopped and after a while we were talking about marriage. "You hear some people say they worried 'bout me and Marghuerite," Willie said. "Same people last summer was saying I was gonna marry this girl and that girl. But they was wrong then, like they're wrong now." He thumped his heart under the ivory pajamas. "I'm the only guy knows what's in here."

They didn't know what to make of my story at the newsmagazine.

They cut out chunks of it, and devoted equal space to the picture of a 2-to-5 favorite winning a horse race. Willie's love song was not newsmagazine style.

The marriage went. I like to think they both tried. They adopted a son and named him Michael, but some years later they were divorced. "Foundered on the rocks off the Cape of Paradise," is how the actor Mickey Rooney likes to put it, but there is nothing funny about the failure of a marriage or having to move out from under the roof where lives your only son.

In Shea before the game against the Mets, Willie is talking about the boy. "He's with me, you know," Willie says.

"How come?"

"He was with Marghuerite, but when he started gettin' older I guess he missed me and we kind of worked something out.

"Michael is ten years old," Willie says, "and there's a lady who keeps house and she looks after him when I'm away. A real nice boy. I send him to a private school, where they teach him, but they're not too hard with him."

I think of the ironworker's son with a boy in private school.

"I've made a deal with him," Willie says. "He needs a college degree in times like these, and the deal is I send him to good schools, put it all there for him, and after that it's up to him to take it."

"You think he will?"

"He's a real good boy."

Two men have come into the Mets' clubhouse to see Willie. Paul Sutton is a patent attorney and David Stern is a vice-president of Sports Satellite Corporation. Willie hopes that these men and a Salt Lake businessman named Ernie Psarras will build his fortune up to seven figures. For now Willie is concerned about filling the house he is building on an acre, in Atherton, down peninsula from San Francisco. He stands to greet Sutton and Stern and says, "Hey, what about the furniture?"

"We're seeing about it," David Stern says.

"Man," Willie says. "I got to stay on you guys."

"Willie doesn't like to pay retail," Stern explains.

"I don't like to pay," Willie says, and he laughs.

Larry Jansen, a coach who pitched for the old Giants, approaches and asks Willie about a doctor or a dentist. Willie gives him a telephone number. Willie owns the keys to the kingdom in New York.

When the Giants moved to San Francisco after the 1957 season, I lost touch with Willie. I read he was having problems. He moved into a white neighborhood and a Californian threw a soda bottle through his living room window in protest. It was a good thing for the Californian that Willie didn't grab the bottle and throw it back. With that arm, he would have cut the man in half. Later, at least as we got word in New York, some San Francisco fans felt disappointed in Willie. They didn't appreciate him as we had; a number said they preferred Orlando Cepeda.

I was paying less attention to sports and writing more about other things, but I knew Willie was not disgracing himself. He kept appearing in All-Star Games and driving homers into the high wind over Candlestick Park. But I wondered if the years and the franchise shift and the divorce had dampened the native ebullience.

It was 1964. Forces that would explode into Black Revolution were gathering and an editor asked me to spend a few months in Harlem, "a part of New York that white New Yorkers don't know."

"I don't know it," I said.

"You've been there," the editor said.

"Sure. Whenever I took a taxi to the Polo Grounds, I'd ride right through."

This time I got out of the taxi. I went from place to place on foot, trying to grasp the bar of music, the despair, the life and death, the sour poverty, the unquenchable hope of a black ghetto. It was different than living in a press box.

To shake off the gray ghetto despair, a man can stand a drink, and one evening I walked into Small's Paradise, with my new blonde wife on my arm. Across the bar a major-leaguer was drinking hard, although he had a girl with him. She was quite young, a soft off-tan, and wore an enormous round black hat. The athlete and I raised glasses to each other's ladies. Suddenly Willie walked in.

It was a cold day in January, but his stride was bouncy. Willie wore a beautifully tailored topcoat of herringbone charcoal. He has unusual peripheral vision and he covered the bar with a glance. Then he bounced over with a smile.

"Buy you a Coke?" I said.

Willie shook his head. "How are you? You okay? Everything all right? What you doing around here? Who's the girl over there with . . ." And he mentioned the other major-leaguer's name.

"I don't know."

"You sure you okay, now?" Willie said.

"Fine." I introduced him to my wife.

Willie put an elbow on the bar and placed a hand against his brow and fixed his gaze at the girl. "Who is that chick, man?"

None of us knows what happened next. Willie was around the bar quickly, greeting the other ball player, talking very fast to the girl. Then he bounced out of the bar, calling, "See ya, man." Five minutes later the other major-leaguer was drunker and the pretty girl in the big round hat was gone. "That," said the blond on my arm, "has to be the smoothest move I've seen."

You don't judge a man's vigor only by the way he pursues fly balls.

Back at Shea, Willie is asking if he'd given me enough to write an article and I tell him I think so.

I find his father sitting in the dugout. Kitty-Kat Mays has his son's big grin and says sure, he'd like to talk about the boy. Kitty-Kat is smaller than Willie. He has a round belly. He was a semi-pro around Fairfield, near Birmingham, Alabama.

"I was down there, Mr. Mays, when Bull Connor was the police commissioner."

"Things are a lot different now," Kitty-Kat says.

"You still live there?"

"No. I'm up here. I've got a good job."

The man knows baseball and I ask when it first struck him that his son was going to be a superlative ball player. Kitty-Kat screws up his face, and I can see that he is going backward in time. He says, "Well, you know we lived right across from a ball field, and when Willie was eight he had to play with older kids."

"I mean even before that."

"Soon as he started walking," Kitty-Kat says, "he's about a year old, I bought him a big round ball. He'd hold that big round ball and then he'd bounce it and he'd chase it, and if he ever couldn't get that ball, he'd cry.

"I knew he'd be a good one, with those oversized hands." Mr. Mays extends his own palms. "I was pretty good, but my hands are regular size. Willie gets those big hands from his mother."

Willie emerges, taps his father's shoulder, and goes out for batting practice. He does not take a regular turn in rotation. He hits for three or four minutes, then sits down. That way is a little gentler on the legs.

He doesn't dominate the series. The Mets do. In one game Ron Swoboda hits a 430-foot home run to left center field. Willie sprints back, the way he can, but this is not the Polo Grounds. He has to pull up short. He is standing at the fence when the ball sails out. In his time and in his park, he would have flagged it.

Later, he crashes one single to left so hard that a runner at second couldn't score, and then he says he wished he'd hit it harder. He hits a long double to left that just misses carrying into the bullpen for a home run. He leads off the ninth inning of a close game with a liner to left that hangs just long enough to be caught. The Giants lose three straight and, in the way of losing teams, they look flat.

When we say good-bye in the clubhouse, Willie seems more annoyed than depressed. The last game ends with the intense frustration of a Giant pitcher fidgeting, scrambling and walking in the winning run. "What can you do?" Willie says. "You got to play harder tomorrow."

For an aging ball player, he seems at peace with himself. He went through money wildly in the early days, borrowing from the team, spending August money by April. "You're really okay financially?" I say.

"Oh, yes," Willie says. "Very good." His face was serious. "I ought to be, I've been working a long time."

Back in the Arizona spring we wore string western ties and we worried about flying DC-3s and we ate in a restaurant where a man dressed like a medieval knight rode a charger and pointed with his spear to show you where to park. Who would have thought then that the Giants would leave New York, and that my old newspaper would fold, and that in another spring, my hair showing gray, I would sit in a strange ball park and ask Willie Mays about legs, fatherhood, investments and fatigue?

Driving home, while Willie flew to Montreal, the spring kept coming back. I saw in flashes a hit he made in Tucson, a throw he loosed in Beaumont, how Leo made him laugh, and I could hear how the laughter sounded. The racists were appalled that year. A Cleveland coach snapped at me for praising Mays and one writer insisted on betting me $20 Willie wouldn't hit .280. We made it, Willie and I, by 65 percentage points.

All this crossed my mind without sadness. Once Willie was a boy of overwhelming enthusiasm. He has become a man of vigorous pride. I don't say that Willie today is as exciting as Willie in '54, but what he does now is immeasurably harder. Playing center field at 38 was beyond the powers of Willie's boyhood idol, DiMaggio, or his contemporary rival, Mantle. Willie stands up to time defiantly and with dignity, and one is fortunate to write baseball in his generation.

I guess I'll look him up again next trip.

The World Series

AGEE MAKES THE ORIOLES SICK BIRDS

(World Series Game III)

By Phil Pepe

From the New York Daily News

A city that has seen Joe DiMaggio and Willie Mays play center field—and figured it had seen it all—now has seen Tommie Agee. Not once, but twice. Agee went to his right, then went to his left, and came up with a pair of spectacular catches that will rank among the greatest in World Series history.

The two catches saved the Mets five runs, exactly their margin of victory as they blanked the Orioles, 5–0, in Shea yesterday and took a 2–1 lead in the best-of-seven Series to crown baseball's 1969 World Champion. With their aces, Tom Seaver and Jerry Koosman, ready to pitch games four and five, the Mets figure they can wrap it up in five and avoid a return trip to Baltimore.

Rookie right-hander Gary Gentry, just a week past his 23rd birthday, got credit for the victory with saves going to Nolan Ryan and Agee. Gentry departed with the bags loaded and two out in the seventh, and Ryan came in to wrap up the four-hit shutout.

The Mets have caught the Orioles in a batting slump or, depending on your point of view, the Met pitchers have silenced Oriole sticks. The Birds have scored five runs and made only 12 hits in three games. Over the last 22 innings, Met pitchers have held them to one run and six hits.

It was obvious this would be Agee's day right from the start. After Gentry retired the Orioles in the first, Tommie led off for the Mets and drilled Jim Palmer's 2-1 fast ball over the center wall. It was his first hit in the Series and emphasized the reason manager Gil Hodges likes to have Agee leading off. It's an old

Casey Stengel idea, hoping to grab a psychological advantage with a big hit to start the game.

Four times during the season Agee led the game with a homer. The Mets won three of those games. Having given the Mets the lead in this important third game, Agee was determined to keep the Orioles from taking it away. He was to get his chance in the fourth.

By then the Mets had jumped out to a 3–0 lead, the second and third runs coming from a most unexpected source. Gentry had driven them in with a double over the head of a rather surprised Paul Blair in center.

Gary's big blast came after Jerry Grote walked and Bud Harrelson singled with two out. Then Gentry jumped on Palmer's first pitch, a high fast ball, that landed at the start of the warning track some 10 feet in front of the 396-foot sign slightly to the right of center. The hit was Gentry's first since August 3. He had failed to hit in his last 28 at bats and had driven in one run all year.

Buzzing the ball for three innings, Gentry had retired the Birds without a hit. Then, after he got Blair looking to start the fourth, Frank Robinson lashed a rocket to left. At first, Cleon Jones seemed to back off to play it safe. Then, as if realizing the Orioles were hitless, he dashed in and tried a shoestring catch. Left-field ump Hank Soar ruled Cleon had trapped the ball and Robby was on with the Birds' first hit.

When Boog Powell followed with a hit through the right side, the Orioles were in business. But Gentry threw hard stuff and buzzed a third strike past Brooks Robinson and faced lefty-swinging catcher Elrod Hendricks.

Playing Hendricks to pull, Agee was over in right center and deep, but Ellie crossed him up by hitting the ball hard the other way. With a crack of the bat, everybody was running—Agee to left center and the two Oriole base runners tearing around the infield.

After going full speed for about 40 yards, Tommie caught up with the ball near the fence, reached out backhanded and caught the ball in the webbing of his glove about waist high. It was a catch that veteran press-box observers were rating over Mays' back-to-the-plate grab of Vic Wertz's drive in the 1954 Series, Al Gionfriddo's steal against Joe DiMaggio in the 1947 Series and Sandy Amoros' one-hand grab of Yogi Berra's opposite field shot in the 1955 Series.

It was a catch that electrified the crowd of 56,335, including the distinguished gray-haired gentleman sitting in Commissioner Bowie

Kuhn's box to the left of the Mets' dugout. The man's name is Joe DiMaggio.

It was a catch that Agee almost didn't make. "The ball," he said, "almost went through my webbing."

It was a catch that saved at least two runs and protected the Mets' 3–0 lead.

It was a catch that brought the inevitable press-box crack, "I'd like to seem him do it again," a parody of a line Charlie Dressen once delivered after Willie Mays made one of his unbelievable grabs against the Dodgers. In this case, the quipster had to wait just three more innings to see Agee do it again.

The Mets upped their lead to 4–0 in the sixth when Grote cracked a double to left to deliver Ken Boswell, who had singled and moved to second as Ed Kranepool grounded out to the right side.

Gentry was still firing zips when the Birds came to bat in the seventh. Hendricks drove deep to center and Davey Johnson did likewise. Then, with two out and nobody on, Gentry was bitten by wildness. He failed to find the plate against Mark Belanger. He also walked pinch-looker Dave May, then loaded the bases by throwing four off the plate to Don Buford.

With Blair, the tying run, coming to bat and Gentry obviously tiring, Hodges reached into his pen for smoke-thrower Nolan Ryan, the 22-year-old right-hander who was the hero of the third play-off game against the Braves.

Everybody in the park knew what Ryan was going to do—throw bullets. Blair looked at the first lightning bolt, then swung and missed at the second lightning bolt. Now the Mets were one strike away from getting out of the inning.

But Blair hit the next fast ball and it went out faster than it had come in, heading for the alley in right center. Three runners took off and so did Tommie Agee.

This time he didn't have to run very far. This time he did not have to reach across his body. This time he had only to dive headlong with his glove outstretched and scoop the ball just before it hit the running track. Tommie Agee had done it again, had saved three runs, had taken the heart out of the Orioles' attack.

Kranepool's smash over the center-field wall off Dave Leonhard in the eighth made it 5–0 for the Mets as Ryan went out to pitch the ninth.

Hendricks and Johnson, the first two Bird hitters in the ninth, kept the ball away from Agee and flied to right, but Ryan walked Belanger after having him 0-2. Clay Dalrymple batted for Leonhard and stroked one up the middle that Al Weis smothered, but he couldn't get the ball to Harrelson in time to force Belanger. When Buford followed with a walk, Hodges also walked—to the mound.

The bases were loaded. The tying run was in the on-deck circle and his name was Frank Robinson. In the Mets' pen, ace relievers Tug McGraw and Ron Taylor were warmed and ready to go, and Hodges had to know the Orioles possessed the firepower to wipe out a 5–0 lead in a hurry. They had done it many times during the season. Once, against the Tigers, they had belted three straight homers, a double and a single to turn a 5–2 defeat into a 6–5 victory.

When Hodges returned to the Mets' dugout, he came back without Ryan. It was up to the kid from Alvin, Texas, to pitch the Mets out of one more jam.

Again Ryan threw two lightning bolts to get ahead of Blair, 0-2. The situation was the same as it had been in the seventh, but this time Ryan didn't need Tommie Agee. Instead of smoke, Ryan crackled a curve ball over the plate and the game ended with Blair's bat on his shoulder. The man had made the right move once again.

Long after Blair watched the third strike snake over the plate, they were still talking of Agee's catches, comparing them with Amoros' and Mays' and Gionfriddo's and comparing them with each other. The consensus was: both great.

Tommie Agee, who had done it all for the Mets all season, but had done little in the first two games of the Series, was the man for the Mets yesterday. They asked him if he liked the home run or the catches better.

"The home run meant only one run," Tommie said. "The catches meant more. I think I'd rather have caught the two balls than hit the home run."

Naturally, he'll take the catches and the homer. At the plate he was Batman. In the field he was Robin. Because of Tommie Agee, the Orioles today are sick birds.

THE METS GO INTO ORBIT

(WORLD SERIES GAME IV)

By Lou Chapman

From the Milwaukee Sentinel

Forget about sending the astronauts to Mars. The New York Mets could do it—naturally, or rather, supernaturally. They're already out of this world.

The amazing Mets had angels in the outfield Wednesday, a gremlin on the base paths—and Tom Seaver on the mound.

Just to make it look real for a change, the Mets allowed the Baltimore Orioles to carry them into the 10th inning before "pinch-ing" them, 2–1, and grabbing a 3–1 stranglehold on the World Series.

The angels worked overtime for the Mets this trip, invading enemy left-field territory in that fateful final inning as Jerry Grote caught reliever Dick Hall's pitch off the end of his bat and sent a high fly to left.

Don Buford, in that sector, was fooled, broke late for the ball, and it dropped in for two bases as shortstop Mark Belanger vainly scooted back in short left for an attempt at a "forward pass" catch.

Al Weis drew an intentional pass and left-hander Pete Richert was called in to face Seaver, who was lifted for pinch hitter J. C. Martin. Rod Gaspar, meanwhile, had been sent in to run for Grote.

Martin bunted Richert's first pitch down the first base line, and both the Oriole hurler and his catcher, Elrod Hendricks, charged for it. Richert picked it up, threw—and lo and behold, here comes that gremlin.

The errant peg hit speeding Martin on the wrist and ricocheted between first and second as the rocketing Gaspar orbited home to launch a wild greeting party in front of the Mets' clubhouse.

The maneuver also created tremendous delirium among the 57,367 faithful in the stands—an all-time Shea Stadium high.

One of the Orioles before the game denied his team was "spooked," but there aren't too many around giving the Birds a ghost of a chance in Thursday's fifth game.

Baltimore lost its manager as well as the ball game, their field leader Earl Weaver being thumbed from the premises in the third inning by plate umpire Shag Crawford for protesting too vigorously on his strike calls.

At any rate, Weaver was spared the agony of sitting in on the Mets' latest feat of magic.

Seaver's sleight of hand on the mound was highly creditable. The right-hander's six hitter was indicative of his consistently fine performance all season which had given him 25 victories.

But would you believe a defensive stunt by Ron Swoboda in right? Swoboda, who will never win any prizes in fielding, turned in a sensational diving backhand catch in the ninth inning that in reality made his club's "unreal" triumph possible.

The Orioles, their prestige torn to shreds, got back a remnant of their pride in the ninth when they placed runners on first and third with one out and Brooks Robinson as the hitter.

Brooks slashed a drive in Swoboda's sector and the Mets' right fielder, as he described it later, made a "do or die" dive for the ball. He snared it backhanded inches out of the dirt.

Frank Robinson, on third at the time, had the presence of mind to keep "cool" and tag up to score the tying run. The Mets had grabbed a 1–0 lead in the second on Donn Clendenon's second homer of the series.

Swoboda's maneuver prevented at least one run from scoring. Seaver, then recovering his composure, got Elrod Hendricks to send a routine fly to right for the third out.

In that inning, Frank Robinson singled to left with one out and Boog Powell moved him to third with a hit to right.

"It wasn't a gamble," Swoboda said later. "It was a do or die play. There's one chance in a thousand that I'm going to catch it, but I had to go for it. If I don't get to it, two runs score. I had to try and keep the runner at first. I had to give it the effort.

"I dived backhand," Ron continued. "With an open glove, you have more area. Backhanded, the glove is narrower."

Seaver emerged victorious against three Oriole pitchers—starter Mike Cuellar and reliever Eddie Watt as well as Hall.

Cuellar, the only Oriole winner with a tenacious six hitter in the opener, wasn't nearly as effective this time, although he had limited the Amazins to seven hits in as many innings.

Watt managed to hold the Mets at the pass for two innings before retiring for a pinch hitter. Hall, however, deserved a better fate—but then you've got to be on the alert for angels, too.

Seaver confessed later that he had "run out of gas in the ninth and 10th."

"I knew the 10th was going to be my last inning," he added.

The Oriole strategy set up Tom's removal by intentionally walking Al Weis, the No. 8 hitter, after Grote, the lead-off man in the 10th, delivered the key "double."

The Mets apparently aren't running out of that old magic, but Baltimore is running out of time. Dave McNally, the pitcher with the best percentage (.800) in the American League, makes a last-ditch effort for his club Thursday against Jerry Koosman, who took the second game in Baltimore.

THE METS COMPLETE THE MIRACLE

(World Series Game V)

By Robert L. Burnes

From the St. Louis Globe-Democrat

The amazing New York Mets, everybody's darling but nobody's pennant favorite, completed the incredible, the impossible, the unbelievable Thursday afternoon at Shea Stadium.

The doormat of the league since their birth in 1961 until they came alive under Gil Hodges this season, the Mets completed the miracle by whipping the stunned Baltimore Orioles, 5–3, to win the World Series, four games to one.

They did it with a flourish, too. They pulled out all the stops, using the long ball, which is not their cup of tea, on homers by Donn Clendenon and the improbable Al Weis.

They even resurrected the old shoe polish routine, patented in 1957 at Milwaukee by Nippy Jones, for a key run. They used a favoring wind to left which seemed to blow harder when they were at bat. They used the indecision of losing pitcher, reliefer Eddie Watt, to provide an insurance run.

And they went with starter Jerry Koosman all the way, even though he was rocked for three early runs as the Orioles, infuriated at their own futility, came out fighting at the outset.

Thus the Mets had to come from behind, a caper they had not previously employed in the Series.

But after spotting the Orioles those three early runs on homers by pitcher Dave McNally and Frank Robinson, Koosman shut them out the rest of the way, restricting them to one additional hit, a harmless two-out single in the sixth by Boog Powell.

When Dave Johnson flied to Cleon Jones to end the game, the frantic crowd of 57,397, largest ever, for the third time in three weeks made a disaster area of Shea Stadium. They wreaked havoc on the premises when the Mets beat the Cardinals to clinch the division title, again when they whipped the Braves in the play-offs and now again on this day to be remembered in Met history.

Home plate, the bases, the pitching rubber all went in a matter of seconds. Umpires Lee Wyer and Larry Napp had to fight their way through throngs grabbing at their clothes. Huge chunks of green grass were torn up. Even the white foul lines went as souvenirs.

One of the first of the wild faithful on the field dashed immediately to the mound and held up a sign which read simply "What Next?"

There isn't any next. The Mets have done it all.

The Orioles, thoroughly beaten in all facets, couldn't even get a draw in arguments with the umpires. There were two prominent ones, both on hit-by-pitch situations, and the Orioles lost them both. They both affected the scoring.

Before the game two of the Orioles had made statements which in the early going appeared significant.

Brooks Robinson said, "We're gonna break out of it today; we're disgusted with ourselves. I've never seen our team this mad."

Boog Powell had clapped pitcher McNally on the back and said, "We're going to get you two runs today, I promise, two whole runs."

McNally answered, "I hope I'm around in the 15th inning when it happens."

He did better. He delivered the two runs himself in the third inning. Mark Belanger had singled to right and with the Mets half expecting a bunt, McNally swung away and lofted a homer on the first pitch to the Baltimore bullpen.

Moments later, Frank Robinson delivered only his third hit of the Series but it was a king-sized home run over everything in left center. Cleon Jones took one look and didn't even move.

That made it 3–0 and for a while that looked decisive because the Mets were suddenly flat.

Things began to come alive in the sixth inning. Frank Robinson apparently was hit by a pitch but umpire Lou DiMuro said nothing doing, it was a foul tip. Robinson went to the dugout for prolonged treatment, then returned and struck out.

This was another break which went against the Orioles. Powell delivered the last Baltimore hit and Brooks Robinson lined to left.

Had the claim bitterly fought by Robinson and manager Earl Weaver been allowed, it could have meant an additional run.

By contrast, the Mets won their similar claim leading off the bottom of the same inning. Cleon Jones tried to tightrope away from a low pitch but it appeared to hit him on the foot. DiMuro again shook his head. But Hodges strolled out of the dugout, baseball in hand, apparently the one which had just been used. DiMuro looked at it, detected shoe polish and waved Jones to first.

This same routine won a key game for Milwaukee against New York in the 1957 series. Another Jones boy, Nippy, showed the ball to umpire Augie Donatelli who awarded him first base because of the evidence of shoe polish. It started the Braves to a three-run inning and a 7–5 triumph for Warren Spahn.

The Mets cashed in immediately. Clendenon, the winner of the automobile from a national magazine as the outstanding player of the Series, crashed a clout into the second deck of seats in left. It was his third homer of the Series, one short of the record. Now the lead was only 3–2 and you could see all the early inspiration seeping out of the Orioles.

Al Weis, one of the unheralded players who became a star in this Series, tied the score in the seventh with a windblown homer into the left-field seats. It was the first homer he had ever hit at Shea Stadium but that's the way the happy Mets did it in this Series.

In five earlier years in the American League, Weis had hit a total of four homers but one of these was at the expense of McNally, his victim Thursday.

Weaver gambled a futile pinch hitter for McNally in the eighth. When the Mets came to bat, you knew they were going to finish it off and they did.

Cleon Jones lashed a double against the left center-field wall off reliever Watt. The home-run king, Clendenon, tried twice to bunt, then took a shot at right field and just missed but wound up grounding to third.

Now it was Swoboda's turn. He seldom bats against right-handers but he whipped a drive down the left-field line which Don Buford tried to backhand into a catch but missed. Jones came racing home with the go-ahead run.

Jerry Grote bounced sharply to Powell who fumbled, then found Watt was late coming off the mound to cover. Grote beat both of them to the bag, and when Watt bobbled Powell's throw, Swoboda kept right on going and scored from second with an insurance run.

That was it.

In the clubhouse, Hodges said, "This is the most exciting moment of my life . . . this is greater to me than the Dodgers' World Series victory over the Yankees in 1955."

The most poignant moment of all, though, was reserved for George Weiss. He had built many championship Yankee teams, then became the first general manager of the Mets. He, Bing Devine and Johnny Murphy put together the team which won it all in its ninth year of life.

Now in his 80s, Mr. Weiss came into the clubhouse in tears, congratulated everybody.

Other Baseball

DREAM OF A TEAM . . .

By Dick Young

From the New York Daily News

In the most momentous accident since Columbus set out for India, the Amazin' Mets last night clinched the National League East. The rest will be easy.

Winning the division is the tough part. You must play 162 games, and you must have it. From April through September you must have it. Then comes a short series with the winner of the other division in your league. This is three-out-of-five. Anybody can win three-out-of-five, especially anybody who has Seaver and Koosman on his side.

Where did it all begin, this miracle of Flushing Meadow, this happy happening which could wind up in the utter delirium of a World Series? Who knows? Did it start that distant day the Giants and Dodgers were uprooted from New York, thus making room for the sprouting of a deplorable little weed that got its name in a contest like some orphan?

Did it start with Bill Shea and Branch Rickey, back in those Continental dream league days, or with Mrs. Payson and Don Grant, or with George Weiss and Casey Stengel? Was that early hopeless laughter necessary for today's genuine joy, or did it all really start a short time ago, when Gil Hodges came up from Washington and said, gentlemen, this is a baseball, and this is a cutoff man, and the idea is to hit the cutoff man with the baseball?

Did it start with the teaching of the championship fundamentals Gil Hodges had learned in Brooklyn, or did it start that day in Florida when Ron Swoboda decided to go to the john in the middle of the game, and when he got back somebody else was up there hitting for him? That day, Gil Hodges, the new manager, got across the message that this is a team, and no individual is bigger than it. Nobody.

Wherever it began, who would have guessed it? Who would have guessed it on Opening Day, when the Amazin' Mets, given an expansion club on which to perpetuate their first getaway victory in history, were beaten by Montreal, 11–10? Tom Seaver, knocked off in five; would you believe that? Would you believe that club would win a pennant? Would you believe half a pennant?

Then, things began to happen, little things at first, things which only later became perceptible, things that a man looks back upon in September and says, how about that? Like the month's time that began in late April, when Koosman and McAndrew and Nolan Ryan could not pitch. A sore shoulder. A pulled groin muscle. Finger blisters upon blisters. How can a team lose three of its five starters for a month and survive?

The Mets did. They didn't burn up the league, but they survived. Tug McGraw came out of the pen to start. Cal Koonce relieved and relieved. Tom Seaver found the groove. The Mets held their own.

Then other amazin' things began to occur. On May 21, in Atlanta, the Mets reached .500 for the first time in their eight-year history. Newsmen ran down to the clubhouse expecting to sip the happy stuff. There was no champagne. Tom Seaver, who had pitched it, sat calmly at his locker.

"We do not celebrate five hundred," he said, aloofly. "We are the new Mets. Come back when we move into first place. We will have champagne."

The Mets lost their next five games, and downstairs Tom Seaver looked at the newsmen guiltily and said, sorry about that, fellows. "The next time we get five hundred," he said, "we'll celebrate."

The Amazin' Mets took off on an 11-game tear, biggest in club history. They soared to .500 and beyond and did not stop to celebrate. They made the deal for Donn Clendenon at the trading deadline, and he came through big. He beat Pittsburgh with the boos of his old fans nipping his earlobes like a mighty frost. He banged 11 ribbys on that trip. The Mets won 6-of-8 and moved up.

When they got home, the slumping Cubs were waiting at Shea, five in front. Kooz won the first game, and Seaver had his perfect game broken up by Jimmy Qualls the next night, and the Amazin's were just three down and the guys were beginning to say ridiculous things in the clubhouse, like they could win the whole thing.

They took 2-of-3 from Chi at Shea, then went out there and took 2-of-3 under intimidation of the Bleacher Bums, and the singing started on the Met airplane: "East Side, West Side . . . the Mets are going all the way."

Back home and, gulp! Houston. Gulp! Doubleheader. First game, 16–3. Second game, 11–5. Next day, shutout by Tom Griffin. Six games down. Damn Texas. Damn Sam Houston.

On to Houston. Gulp! Three more beatings. Damn the Astroturf. Damn the Astrodome. Damn the Alamo. August 13 and nine and one-half games down. The Mets is dead. Met jokes are revived on the Johnny Carson Show.

Then came one of those quirks of fate a man always needs in the dark hour. Along came San Diego. If ever a team needed San Diego, it was the Mets. The Mets were playing lousy ball. For four straight games, they didn't score more than three runs per game, but they won all four. Resurrection.

The Giants came in. Marichal was at his best, and Tommie Agee beat him in the 14th with a homer, and the next night Jim McAndrew threw a two-hitter at Gaylord Perry. The Dodgers were swept 3-for-3, and the gap was down to two and one-half when the Cubs came into Shea for the last time. There was no way the Mets could knock the Cubs out of first place. It was only a two-game set.

And yet the Mets did. They won both, and the Cubs departed Shea Stadium a half-length in front and knocked out. The world has rarely known such a dispirited first-place team.

The Mets were in first place in spirit. The next night they were there in actuality, in the cold, incontrovertible type of the newspaper standings. That night some of the boys broke out four bottles of bubbly they had stashed away, unofficially, in a corner of the clubhouse, and Tom Seaver poured for the newspapermen.

It was September 10, forevermore known as Met Day, the day the Mets reached first place.

BASEBALL'S NOT-SO-JOLLY GREEN GIANT

By Ron Smith

From True

In a game against the Washington Senators last spring, Mickey Lolich of the Detroit Tigers—the brassy southpaw whose World Series pitching shrank the St. Louis Cardinals' confidence to the size of an umpire's heart—was standing on the mound at Tiger Stadium trying to decide what kind of a pitch he was going to throw to the Senators' cleanup hitter.

Two innings earlier Lolich had thrown a slider over the outside corner of the plate. Reaching out, the guy had pulled the ball into the left-field seats for a home run. Six days earlier Lolich had thrown him a curve ball low and away. That time the ball didn't stop flying until it landed in the center-field seats.

This time Lolich decided on a fast ball high and tight ("I got the pitch where I wanted it," said Lolich afterward, still visibly shaken). With two runners on base, Lolich rocked into a stretch and lurched forward. The ball rifled toward the plate. Then it rifled toward the left-field seats. Hooking near the foul line, the ball cleared everything, fence, seats, roof, and landed on an unfinished highway outside the Stadium, more than 600 feet away. Awestruck press-box veterans said it was the longest homer they had ever seen, and maybe the longest ever hit.

The man who hit it was Frank Oliver Howard, and when he really meets a pitch you don't need a tape measure, you need an aerial survey. American League pitchers say he is so strong that someday he will bunt a ball and the stitches will fly off. In the Era of the Pitcher, when the home-run hooligan has nearly vanished and mediocre moundsmen ring up scoreless innings like a supermarket checkout, Howard has emerged as baseball's Number One fence wrecker and window breaker.

At 6-foot-7 and 272 pounds, Howard looks as if he should be brought to home plate by a gantry. He is 32 years old and has legs like trees, massive shoulders and a chest that is slabbed with muscle. He is literally and figuratively the biggest thing in power hitting—a thoroughly likable, thoroughly stubborn, moody, at-times hot-headed man who hitherto has spent most of his major-league days either being laughed at or booed. He can hit a baseball out of sight but sometimes the people around him wish he would go out of their sight.

Mostly this happens when Howard is trying to catch fly balls. Clomping about in the outfield, he catches hell from the crowds more than he catches anything else. And as a base runner he is right out of the Marx Brothers. As a batter he not only is at his best but often his worst. His strikeouts run 100 per year, and he is so eager to swing that one coach had to plead with him to wait at least until the pitcher threw the ball.

"They've made a joke and a freak out of him for years," said Gil Hodges, the New York Mets' manager and a longtime Howard booster. "I'm glad to see that he has finally shown up the wise guys."

Show them he did. In a season when his batting brethren seemed helpless, Howard hammered 44 homers to lead the big leagues. He batted in 106 runs for a team which, were it only a little better, would be awful. He also had a .274 batting average for the finest all-around slugging performance of the year. At times he not only was spectacular, he was downright incredible. While pitchers overwhelmed hitters, Howard aimed for the streets with a 40-ounce bat (baseball's biggest) and put together the greatest week-long home-run binge in the game's history. He walloped 10 of them in six successive games, scattering home-run records that had stood for decades, and caused mass evacuations in bullpens from Boston to Anaheim.

Right-handed Dean Chance of Minnesota, whose sweeping side-arm fast balls have been known to make batters perspire, once struck out Howard with three straight slow curves. A writer asked if Chance had found the perfect way to pitch to Howard. "Hell no," blurted Chance. "I threw him slow stuff so I'd have plenty of time to run and hide before he swung."

Such comment is typical of the awe and wonder in which Howard is held. Four seats in D.C. Stadium—three in the upper deck in center, one in left center—have been painted white to mark the spots where Howard homers have landed. Last year he hit so many mammoth drives that he graduated out of normal conversation and into a special frame of reverence.

"The guy ain't human," said Cleveland catcher Duke Sims. "Every time he comes to the plate I keep looking behind to see where it is you wind it up."

Human Howard is. Ordinary he is not. He wears a size 15 shoe. His suits are 48 extra long and he has difficulty finding white shirts (38-inch sleeves) that fit. He has a voice like the anvil chorus and when he talks he is painfully sincere. His hair is short and the color of a pumpkin. He is handsome but on his forehead are the high-tension lines of a worrywart. Indeed he has had plenty to worry about.

"I've seen him fooled, catch a pitch with one hand on the bat, and still drive it 450 feet," Leo Durocher once said. "Then he starts pressing and lunging and looks like the worst bum you have ever seen. With his power and potential, you've got to be patient."

Frank Howard has exhausted many patiences, including his own. He has battled with fans and front offices alike. Managers say he will not listen to advice. He argued violently with Walter Alston of the Dodgers and got himself traded from Los Angeles to Washington. Said George Selkirk, the former Senator general manager: "Baseball got along nicely before Frank Howard, and will get along when he goes."

Selkirk said this last spring when he was trying to sign Howard to a contract. It was not a happy time for him. Howard has the bargaining instincts of a used-car peddler, and the Senators did not want to pay the $50,000 a year to which Howard figured he was entitled. "He's an incomplete player," said Selkirk. "His salary demands are preposterous and he knows it."

Howard said he didn't know any such thing and told the newspapers he would quit before he played for less than he was worth. "Let him quit," crackled Selkirk. "Personally I think it would be nice to see someone out in left field who can throw, run and field." Howard eventually signed for $48,000, but not before being publicly branded as ungrateful, unreasonable and unyielding.

One day late last summer, though, Howard was standing by a batting-practice cage before a game and saying that if he is un-anything he is unshakable.

"Nobody wants to look like a big dummy out here," he said. "I know what the fans call me. A lummox. Two left feet. Hell, I've been booed as loudly as any man who ever played this game. I've heard the whispers. Howard's a donkey. Howard should hit 60 homers, Howard this and Howard that. I've lived with adversity. That's why I cherish everything I have earned. It all seems so much sweeter to me now because I have worked to become the best at what I do. And I've done it my way. If I had listened to other people I'd be out of baseball by now."

Over the years Howard has been the target for a barrage of catcalls, second guesses, and just plain horselaughs. Fans find him hard to take and executives turn purple trying to deal with him. But doing things his way he has won the respect of the players, and their affection as well.

Teammates ride him unmercifully. They say Blue Cross has an automatic cancellation clause if he slaps you on the back; that bat boys can only communicate with him by telephone; that he clanks when he walks; that when he falls asleep on airplanes, as he does all the time, he either has to bend his knees or put landing lights on his feet.

This is fine with Frank. "Nobody takes a bigger riding than I do," he said. "But to me it's a compliment." And it is. Howard knows that as long as the players are on you they are with you. The time to worry is when they don't talk to you. So far this hasn't happened. Nor is it likely to happen, although he sometimes does things that would frighten and bewilder a Hun.

"I've seen him crush a batting helmet with one hand," said Bob Humphreys, the pitcher. "He was mad at himself for popping up with a man on third."

Another time, in Chicago, Frank was having his troubles. He had gone to bat 22 times without a hit. Coming back to the bench he whirled and began smashing at an iron door with his fists. The door didn't quiver and neither did Frank. But he had aggravated a strained right elbow. That winter doctors cut chips out of the elbow. Howard's throwing arm, once like a rifle, now is like a popgun.

There are locker-room theories and Freudian theories, two for a quarter, about Howard's hara-kiri habits. Some people say that he tries too hard. Others that he is constantly striving to prove he not only is very big but very good. Still others say his outbursts and attitudes are simply the actions of a man subjected to chronic frustrations for most of his career.

Probably all are right. Being both big and full of muscles he has been set apart from the start. When he first came up, the baseball crowd took one look at his caveman physique and said he would hit homers by the inningful. He did not. Batting coaches were ordered to work on him. They made plenty of suggestions, hoping to find out what was wrong. All they found was that Howard goes for suggestions the way he goes for a cut in pay.

"This guy is murder," moaned Pete Reiser, a Dodger coach and one of the men who tried to tinker with Howard's stance, if indeed not his psyche.

"Here is a man who could be great if he would only listen and not be so stubborn. You talk and talk to him about the importance of learning the strike zone. You think you are getting through to him. Then he goes up to the plate and starts swinging. He swings and swings and swings. Someday a pitcher with a good move is going to throw over to first base . . . and Frank Howard will swing at it."

To be sure. Howard loves to swing, to swing hard, to swing at anything. Last year he kept swinging and baseballs kept disappearing. "He even fouled them off longer," said Mayo Smith, the Detroit manager and a man who saw a lot of Howard in that one wondrous week when Frank single-handedly had pitchers in a state of near-collapse. Even the cynics had to concede that what Howard did might never be done again.

Frank started the spree in the sixth inning of a Sunday game in D.C. Stadium when Mickey Lolich threw him the slider. In the seventh inning the Tigers brought in Fred Lasher, a right-hander who throws submarine balls. Howard lashed a Lasher low ball into the fourth row of seats of the upper deck.

The Senators moved to Boston and a two-game series. Howard blasted one into the net above the wall at Fenway Park off Ray Culp. Later in the game he arched a shot into the center-field bleachers off Lee Stange. The following day he greeted José Santiago with a first-inning homer that traveled to the screen in left center.

Next the Senators were in Cleveland and the pitcher was Sudden Sam McDowell, a powerful left-hander who openly bullies, badgers and browbeats hitters into submission. McDowell only throws a fast ball. If that doesn't work he throws a faster one. He tried to slip one over the inside, in on Frank's fists. Throwing fast balls in on Howard is a little like bleeding in front of a shark. Frank's hands blurred as he pulled it into the stands 450 feet away.

Two innings later Frank was standing at the plate again. But not for long. McDowell knocked him down with a fast ball. Frank got up and belted the next pitch over the gate in the runway in left, about 480 feet from lift-off.

Detroit was the next disaster area. After grounding out twice while battling Joe Sparma on 3-and-2 counts, Frank got a low curve outside. Instead of pushing it to the opposite field, as the book says, he reached out and pulled it across his body and it was gone. The following afternoon he got two more off Lolich, including the one that some people say was hit as hard as any baseball has ever been hit.

Statisticians poking through the wreckage announced that home runs in six successive games had tied a league record. But 10 homers in six games was three more than anybody had ever struck. They also were the most homers for a single week's work. Babe Ruth once hit nine in a week but the Babe needed nine games to do it.

Back in Washington, Howard was summoned to Selkirk's office. "Congratulations on a great streak," said the general manager. "It hasn't gone unnoticed."

Howard knew what was coming next. He held up his hand. "You don't owe me a penny," he said. "I signed a contract. You gave me the money I wanted."

"You'll have to let me do this in my fashion," said Selkirk.

Selkirk's fashion was to rip up Howard's contract and sign him to a new one for $55,000. Afterward Selkirk told the writers, "That was the first time I ever saw a ball player try to turn down money. But I wasn't surprised. That's the kind of man Howard is."

The malcontents who make a living in baseball are many and Howard has met his share of them. With some it is liquor or women or cards. With others it is showing up for a game like a guy who goes to the office and spends eight hours looking at the clock. But Howard never stops trying.

At the plate he has none of the idiosyncrasies—Willie McCovey's deep scowling or Rocky Colavito's shoulder shaking—that you associate with sluggers. He does not even have a good home-run swing. Howard's swing is long and disconnected. It is a sandlot swing, like a lumberjack whacking away at a tree. The ball is not jerked out of the park with timing and grace. It is mangled by raw force.

At the All-Star Game a reporter asked Dick Williams, the Red Sox manager, if he thought the American League would beat the National League. "I don't know if we can beat them," said Williams, nodding toward a locker where Howard was pulling on his uniform, "but I'd sure like to fight them."

Size and strength alone do not account for Howard's success, though. If they did he'd be out of a job and King Kong would be wearing a cap. Not endowed with great natural ability, he makes it mainly on pride and a willingness to pay what he considers the price.

Clearly, hard work is Howard's only hobby and he's as much a cutup as Calvin Coolidge. It is almost Holy Writ that home-run hitters drive Cadillacs; Howard arrives at the ball park in a station wagon. On the road if you are looking for Howard the last place you look is the bars; the first place is the movies. His tastes run to gunfire, and teammates say he has seen every Indian that John Wayne ever killed.

When he's not hitting homers he is selling paper boxes for a mill in Green Bay, Wisconsin. This is where he lives in the off-season with his wife Karol and their children—Tim, eight, Kathy, seven, Danny, six, Mitchell, five, and Mary Beth, two. With his money he could live where he likes. He says he likes Green Bay and he does, although the winters there would stop the Russian army. He is Green Bay's best-known commodity—Vince Lombardi excepted—but has trouble getting tickets to see the Packers play. "There's a long waiting list for season tickets," said Karol Howard, "and Frank is not a man who asks for favors."

Obviously he is not. For a guy who likes to win, going from the Dodgers to the Senators is like going from the penthouse to the outhouse. But looking back, Frank is certain he did the right thing when he asked to be traded and wound up playing for a last-place team.

"If I had stayed with Los Angeles I'd be out of baseball," he said.

This was one day in the backyard of a house in Silver Springs, Maryland, that Howard rents during the season. He was wearing sandals and bermudas and lying on a patio lounge like a beached whale soaking up the sun.

"Leaving a contending team was a gamble. But when you are making $25,000 and you think you can make $50,000 you are shortchanging yourself. Anyway, I didn't like the idea of depending on a Koufax or Drysdale to win a championship for me. I wanted to see what I could do on my own. I think that's being more of a man."

Being a man is important to Frank. When he was 14 he was working a jackhammer in the streets of Columbus, Ohio. The city was paying him one dollar an hour, which he was gratefully accepting. The son of a 6-foot-3, 220-pound railroad worker, Howard had to scuffle from the start. "There was always food on the table," he said, "but if I wanted money I had to earn it."

When he was eight he shined shoes. He set up pins in a bowling alley. He caddied on a golf course. It was the kind of a life that has given him his outlook, and some of his problems, about baseball.

"I was always independent," he said, "always on my own. I've taken care of myself since I was a kid. I learned a long time ago not to put faith in what other people told you."

Frank Angelo is an equipment man for the Washington Senators. He has been in the Senator's clubhouse since the days of Walter Johnson and he is one of Howard's biggest boosters.

"You know why I like No. 9?" Angelo asked, referring to Frank's uniform number. Clubhouse people seldom use names when they can use numbers. "Because after a game he sits around in the locker room and drinks beer, and he talks about baseball. Not about stocks and bonds. About baseball. The old-timers used to do that."

This was shortly before a game with the New York Yankees and Angelo was pointing around the clubhouse saying, "Some of these guys, after a game, they leave so fast you look around and ask yourself, 'What the hell, did those guys change clothes in the dugout or something?' Not Howard. No. 9 is the last guy out."

That night, against the Yankees, Howard ran for a fly ball off the bat of Joe Pepitone. It was a long run and the ball was slicing away from him, toward the foul line. Still on the run, Frank put his glove out the way a guy sticks his hand out the door to see if it's raining. The ball plopped into his glove. Then it plopped out. By the time Frank got the ball back into the infield Pepitone was standing on third. The crowd was standing, too. It was booing loudly.

Late in the game Howard came to the plate with a man on second and the score tied. Dooley Womack gave him a breaking ball up high and Howard tomahawked it. The ball didn't stop sailing until it landed in the left-field seats.

The Senators were ahead and Frank was jogging around the bases while the fans cheered. Frank did not tip his cap to the crowd, the way a player is supposed to do when the crowd is cheering him. He simply circled the bases and headed for the dugout, to the people whom he trusts.

Howard has had to swallow a lot of pride, a lot of embarrassment. He has done it because he knows that sooner or later he is going to get his pitch and he will do his thing—hit homer after homer. He also knows there are plenty of players who would have caught that fly ball in their back pocket, except that most of them are still in the minor leagues trying to learn how to hit.

Howard has known for a long time that he is not a great athlete.

In high school he played baseball and basketball and even then he was not the best player. Sometimes, when he goes to Columbus to see his mother, he says he can look in the eyes of the kids he grew up with and see what they are thinking. They are thinking, "How in hell did Howard get to the big leagues?"

He got there mostly because his size helped him win a basketball scholarship to Ohio State University. It was not a full grant, and Howard had to work after school and in the summer. He joined construction gangs. He laid stone, mixed mortar and carried a hod. In basketball he averaged 21 points a game and was picked on the second team All-America with the likes of Elgin Baylor and Guy Rodgers.

In baseball he hit .366 and home runs were jumping off his bat. The scouts came out in platoons. They talked about sums of money so vast that Frank thought they were putting him on. They were not. To his astonishment, the Dodgers offered him $108,000 to sign a three-year contract. Somebody asked Walter O'Malley, the Dodger president, if he thought Howard would make good. "If he doesn't," said O'Malley, "you are going to see the damnedest unemployment since the bank holiday."

Most people, if they got $108,000, would head for the French Riviera. Howard bought a new home for his parents. Playing at Green Bay in 1958 he met a small, brown-haired girl named Karol Jahanski at a pizza parlor. Karol is 5-foot-1 and six months later she and Frank were married. Frank bought a home in Green Bay for himself and Karol, and then bought another house for Karol's parents.

Working his way up, Frank needed only two years in the minors. In Cedar Rapids, Iowa, they measured one of his homers at 550 feet. In Victoria, Texas, a Howard homer was recovered in a city park, some 600 feet from home plate. By the time he got to Vero Beach in 1960 for spring training with the Dodgers, some people were saying Frank should not stop at the National League but go directly to the Hall of Fame.

Three years later the same people were saying Howard was a bum. He started fast enough, hitting 23 homers in 1960 and being named Rookie of the Year. Next he hit .296 but the homers had dwindled to 15. He was hearing boos for the first time. Frank didn't have to be hit over the head to know why. "If a guy 6-foot hit .296, they'd say he had a hell of a year."

By 1964 his batting average was practically invisible (.226) and he was being platooned. He batted mostly against left-handers and he did not like it. Neither did Walter Alston, the manager. Alston wanted Frank in the lineup every day but thought he went for too many bad pitches—a notion obviously shared by the National League pitchers.

That winter Howard was sent to the Senators in a seven-player deal that brought pitcher Claude Osteen to Los Angeles. Frank was happy as a cricket. But in Washington the news was greeted like a tax hike. There were jokes in the newspapers about how the Senators had traded for a toy—the Frank Howard doll; you wind it up and it strikes out.

At first it was almost that bad. Howard hit 21 homers. Deciding he couldn't hit what he couldn't see, Frank bought a pair of glasses and began wearing them on the field. So the following season he hit 18 homers and heard boos like few men will ever hear.

Howard tried everything. In the spring of 1967 he even tried listening. Gil Hodges, one of his closest friends and then the Washington manager, suggested that Frank spread out at the plate. Frank said he would sink or swim with it for a month. Four weeks later he was searching for a life raft. He was batting .200 and homers were something he could vaguely remember.

Frank finally compromised. He stayed with the spread. But doing things his way, he moved himself closer to the plate. Whether that little move was magic, or whether he simply was learning to live with the spread, no one will be certain. What is certain is that Howard suddenly was slapping homers at a startling pace—and with startling results.

Once, in Chicago, he pounded a line drive that never climbed more than 15 feet above ground before slamming into the centerfield seats. Next day somebody kidded Tom McCraw, the White Sox outfielder: "I thought you could have caught that ball if you had leaped for it."

"Sure I could," said McCraw, "but I would have wound up sitting in the stands with it."

Howard kept swinging and pitchers kept ducking. By the All-Star Game break he had 24 homers. One night, running out a double, he injured his leg in a thundering, lumbering, hell-for-leather slide into second. The slide tore up half the infield. It also tore up the muscles in his thighs. Howard missed several games and finished with 36 homers. He spent the winter selling paper boxes and telling Ken McMullen, the Senator third baseman, on the telephone: "I used to get some satisfaction in just knowing I'm not the worst who ever wore a uniform. But now I've got a chance to show I belong with a lot of good players. I could get close to the great ones."

He got closer than close. These are not very good times for batters, and last year the pitchers were so far ahead of the hitters that the shutout totals looked like the Dow-Jones index. But Howard acted as if he hadn't heard about it. He surprised the pitchers and the skeptics, but not the people who had been rooting all along for him.

"What you have here," said Jim Lemon, the Washington manager, last year, "is a guy who is just coming into his peak years. It has taken him a little longer to develop. But right now nobody is more dangerous at the plate. The next four or five seasons are going to be great ones for him. And it couldn't happen to a better person. Here's a guy who really likes baseball, who appreciates what the game has done for him. Now he's done something for the game."

What he's done has cost him. Doing things his way, he has had to work hard and wait long to find success. He's been the butt of booing and bad jokes. Thousands of words of wisdom have poured through his ears. Second guesses have followed his every move. But though he lost the battles he is winning the war. Even now there are signs that the fans are warming to him. Sometimes there are banners in the ball parks. "Hit it here, Howard," they say. It isn't much but it's a beginning.

If it doesn't work out Howard will know why. Consider the time when I asked him how tall he was, just to get it on record.

"I am 6-foot-7 in my stocking feet," he said. "I give the impression of being bigger because I have always stood straight. I know a lot of big men who stoop. I don't. I stand tall."

AN ARMY COOK DID IT ON A PASS

By Joe Heiling

From The Houston Post

It wasn't so much the seventh straight defeat. Or Willie McCovey's two homers. Or the excellent National League pitching; those things happen, right?

What must have hurt the American League, way down deep, was that an Army cook was the guy who laid the wood to them in the NL's 9–3 triumph in the 40th All-Star baseball game Wednesday.

The cook, a PFC in the Army Reserves, is completing his two weeks of summer military encampment at Camp A. P. Hill, Virginia. In civilian clothes, he answers to the handle of Johnny Bench and he catches for the Cincinnati Reds.

The 21-year-old Bench, on a pass from his duties in the kitchen, slammed a two-run, 400-foot homer off the Yankees' Mel Stottlemyre in the second inning to establish the beachhead for the NL's seventh straight victory.

It was a glorious day for the Nationals. A crowd of 45,259 returned to Robert F. Kennedy Stadium after the previous day's rainout and their first cheers went out to Bench.

Which proves once more, only in America. Just the day before, he went through President Richard Nixon's reception line at the White House.

Today, after the game, Vice-President Spiro T. Agnew entered the clubhouse to shake his hand and that of the other conquering heroes.

Thursday, at about 2:30 a.m., the bugle will sound for PFC Bench and he'll rub the sleep out of his eyes, rush to the mess hall and begin preparing eggs and bacon and other Army delicacies for a company of some 120 men.

As they say, fame is fleeting.

Bench's homer and the record-tying pair by the hulking Giant McCovey, produced five of the NL's runs.

The 6-foot-4, 210-pound McCovey connected off "Blue Moon" Odom of the A's with one aboard to trigger a five-run third inning. Then he put the slug on Denny McLain, the Tigers' flyboy right-hander, for a solo shot the next inning for the final NL run.

McLain was scheduled to start for the American League. He had piloted his plane back to Detroit, however, to keep a dental appointment, have caps put on nine teeth and fly back to the game site.

Only his plane was stacked up in traffic over the airport and Stottlemyre got the nod instead.

That may have not been the turning point, but it wasn't far off.

Stottlemyre yielded an unearned run the first inning when Matty Alou singled and scored as Frank Howard failed to flag down Hank Aaron's high fly ball to shallow left.

Howard started in on the ball, slowed up, surrounded it, came on again and with a last-gasp stretch had it hit off the fingertips of his glove for an error.

"I saw it all the way," said the genial giant of the Senators. "I just butchered the play, that's all. What else can I say?"

This presented southpaw Steve Carlton of the Cardinals with a 1–0 lead and Stottlemyre with a severe case of heartburn.

The next inning, Bench backed a single by Cleon Jones of the Mets with his first home run in All-Star play. He also contributed a single and had Carl Yastrzemski of the Red Sox rob him of a possible second homer with a great leaping catch at the fence in the sixth.

Bench may drop shells in the eggs tomorrow just thinking about Yaz's steal.

It was the biggest thing that happened to the downtrodden AL except for Howard's tremendous 460-foot blast to center in the second and a blast by Bill Freehan of the Tigers off Carlton, the winner, in the third.

The AL was to score once more off the Cards' Bob Gibson in the fourth on a walk and singles by Sal Bando and Freehan.

Otherwise, the Dodgers' Bill Singer, Jerry Koosman of the Mets, the Astros' Larry Dierker and knuckle-balling Phil Niekro of the Braves were completing a six-hit victory.

Sudden Sam McDowell of Cleveland and Boston's Ray Culp helped the AL finish in a blaze of glory by striking out six of the final nine NL hitters.

McDowell blew the ball past four of the players he stared down at. Unfortunately for the AL, they were finishing up the game, not starting it.

Those solid blows were the most boisterous of the NL's 11-hit attack, although the Braves' Felix Millan was to double in two runs in that big third inning and Carlton was to double across another before the Senators' Darold Knowles restored order.

McCovey's long shots marked him as only the fourth player to slam two homers in a single All-Star Game. He shouldered his way right up there with Arky Vaughan (1941), Ted Williams (1946), and Al Rosen (1954).

He enjoyed the sight of them, but not much else.

"My biggest thrill?" he repeated the question. "Nope."

Then McCovey expanded on his feelings about the All-Star Game.

"When guys vote you to the All-Star team," he said, "it means they have a lot of confidence in you, and if you come through, you are doing what they want.

"I feel satisfied that I came through for the league. Other than that, it doesn't mean a lot. It hasn't helped the Giants any."

McCovey hammered a fast ball and a change-up for his two homers.

"The first one might have been a sinker that didn't sink," he smiled. "He's [Odom] supposed to throw one. I've faced McLain twice before—in two other All-Star Games—and Odom last year."

Bench came within a glove—the one on Yaz's left hand—of getting a piece of the action with McCovey.

"I started off from the plate in a trot," admitted the polished young Redleg. "I thought it was gone," but he made a great catch.

"Yes, I was most excited today. My first one got us ahead and on that second ball, well, I hoped it would go out for personal reasons. I would have liked to have a share of that record."

Yaz snatched that prize from him with a well-timed leap in front of the left-field fence, gloving the ball just over the top of the wire.

On the other side was the National bullpen, and Mike Ryan, a catcher for the Phillies, had his mitt up for the grab. The ball never reached him.

Bench wasn't certain he would be allowed to play in the All-Star Game after the postponement. So Johnny called his captain and asked if he wanted him to return to camp. Luckily for the NL, the answer was no. Bench's homer opened up the game as the National tied its record for runs in one game and ran its series edge over the AL to 22–17–1.

He also chipped in a single in the fifth as Odom had the dubious distinction of matching a mark of yielding five hits in one inning. Blue Moon joined Sandy Consuelo of the White Sox (1954) and Tex Hughson of the Red Sox (1944) in the record books. "I offered to work overtime in the kitchen to make up for the time," Bench said of his sales pitch to his captain. "I'm sure they will take me up on it."

But Bench will have a lot of pleasant thoughts as he works his 24-straight-hour shift, cooking breakfast and preparing salads for later meals.

Does he ever get any complaints about his Army chow?

"No, not really," grinned PFC Bench. "Well, maybe a few. But nobody's perfect."

The American League will be glad to learn this fact about Johnny Bench.

MANTLE'S ROAD TO FAME: PAIN, STRUGGLE, FRUSTRATION

By George Vecsey

From The New York Times

The retirement of a player as great as Mickey Mantle should inspire only a recitation of great deeds and enjoyable moments, yet his story must include frustration and unfulfillment along with the glory. Mantle never enjoyed his 18 years in New York the way many other stars have enjoyed their careers, and injuries and personal struggles were equally responsible.

For many years he seemed on the verge of becoming a happy, healthy star—he was certainly a hero to millions of fans—but injuries and temper delayed that process. Then in the closing years, after he had achieved many great things on the field and developed a relative maturity to appreciate them, he was cheered every time he poked his head out of the dugout.

However, Mantle understood that the cheers were for him as a descending star and he had never wished to be the central figure in a tragic-opera situation. When fans in Houston gave him a standing ovation last summer after he had struck out in the All-Star Game, he talked of being "tired" and retiring. The one glorious year of being whole and happy had never quite come.

The intermingling of pain and joy began in Mantle's first season in the major leagues. Born in Spavinaw, Oklahoma, on October 20, 1931, he needed only two years in the minor leagues before joining the Yankees in 1951—a powerful, fleet young man who could not miss being a star if a boyhood case of osteomyelitis, a bone disease, remained arrested.

That first season saw him twist his right knee on a drain pipe while playing right field in the second game of the World Series. For the rest of the Series he was in the hospital—in the bed next to his father, who was suffering from Hodgkin's disease, which would eventually kill him.

The records show that Mantle's best years were in 1956–57, when the Yankees won pennants as usual and he was twice voted Most Valuable Player. He batted .353 in 1956, hit 52 home runs and drove in 130 runs, leading the league in all three categories, the so-called "triple crown." In 1957, he batted .365 with 34 homers and 94 runs batted in. When the Giants took Willie Mays to San Francisco after 1957, Mantle was clearly New York's biggest sports hero.

But Mantle never was at home in New York, preferring to settle in Dallas with his wife and four sons and rent homes or live in hotels during the season. And even in the best of summers, New York was not his scene. The fans saw him heave his batting helmet in disgust when he struck out and he heard as many boos as cheers.

"Me and the fans really had a go-around those first couple of years," he recalled recently. "I didn't like them and they didn't like me. But it's gotten better since then."

When fans did approach Mantle, he often did not seem to know how to react. Whereas many stars would chat with their fans—while trotting toward the sanctuary of the clubhouse—Mantle would often bolt frozen-faced through them, occasionally scattering youngsters like the halfback he wished he had been. And Mantle's reaction to the press was inconsistent and occasionally rude, although he was a funny and loyal friend to his teammates, who liked and respected him.

After the first decade, Mantle began to cope with many things, running bases, playing center field and swinging the bat with a new understanding, coupling wisdom with his physical skills.

"It seemed like I was finally getting the hang of it," he once said.

Then the injuries struck again. He tried to play the 1961 World Series with an abscess on his right buttock that oozed blood through his uniform, visible to players and fans. In 1962 he pulled a right-thigh muscle while running to first base and fell to the ground "as if he had been shot," as one reporter described it. Mantle recovered in a month from the hamstring, but he had bruised his left knee in the fall and he wound up playing only 123 games that year. Yet the Yankees won the pennant and he was voted Most Valuable Player for the third time.

The games diminished to 65 in 1963 as he broke his foot when his spikes caught in a wire fence in Baltimore. He also had knee cartilage removed in the off-season.

By 1964 it was commonly accepted by players and fans that Mantle was playing mostly on courage. Players saw him pull himself up stairways using his powerful arms to supplement his wobbly knees, and they marveled that he could play at all.

"Every time he misses, he grunts in pain," one opposing catcher said. "You think he's going to fall down."

In 1965, as the Yankees fell from first to sixth place, Mantle suffered back and neck spasms, shoulder and elbow aches and he pulled his left hamstring and missed 21 games. He had a chip removed from his right shoulder before the 1966 season, yet he insisted on opening the season in left field—to minimize his throwing. He later strained a hamstring and bruised his left hand.

By 1967, Mantle moved to first base and played in 144 games, suffering only minor aches. His average fell to .245 and his pride was hurt, but he did not quit.

"I need the money," he sometimes said, laughing as if it were a joke. But friends whispered that he needed his $100,000 salary because of poor investments, so he played on. Last year he appeared in 144 games again, this time batting only .237.

As he grew older, Mantle became extremely popular with the New York fans and he had always been adulated by fans in other cities. Last year many clubs asked if they could honor Mantle on the Yankees' final appearance in their town, just in case it was his final performance. Mantle usually said he did not want a fuss made over him and he refused the honors. He still will be honored many times, of course, but as a retired hero rather than as a future hero or a declining one, two roles he never thoroughly enjoyed.

JIM BOUTON, RELIEVER

By Jack Mann

From the Washington Daily News

Jim Bouton pitched an inning of relief for the Seattle Pilots Friday night, and two innings Saturday afternoon. That's the way it is these days for Jim Bouton, 30, who started 37 games for the Yankees in 1964.

They were three pretty good innings for a guy who throws only one pitch. Bouton got almost everybody out and he got Frank Howard, on a one-two pitch, to pop up.

The trouble with Howard is that some of his pop-ups land in places where nobody can catch them. This one landed in the bull-pen when it came off the wall. That wasn't bad.

What was bad was that Bouton's hat never fell off. It hasn't fallen off for a long time. It probably never will again.

The hat fell off when he labored in the vineyards of Auburn and Kearney and Greensboro and Amarillo. He is not a very big man, so he had to throw very hard to throw very fast. He knew he had to make it as a fast-ball pitcher or not at all.

Bouton came right over the top with the ball and the maximum effort made the fingertips of his right hand touch the ground as he followed thru. He needed all of it, all the time.

And the hat fell off. It was still falling off when he won 21 games for the Yankees in 1963, and won half enough games to win the World Series in 1964.

Then he lost the fast ball. Nobody believed he had lost it in 1965, when he went 4-15. He was lousy, but so, suddenly, were the Yankees.

By opening day, 1966, at Minneapolis, the truth was evident. He threw three consecutive change-ups to Jim Kaat, a pitcher, and the third one beat him.

"I couldn't throw the curve," Bouton said yesterday. What he meant was that he could throw it, but unaccompanied by that fast ball that hummed and darted, it didn't fool anybody. He was Jim Bouton, fast-ball pitcher, and he had lost his fast ball.

Two years ago the Yankees tentatively gave up on him and for the rest of the year, Bouton got knocked around in Syracuse. Last year they gave up on him unqualifiedly and shipped him to Seattle, which was still minor league.

Bouton didn't give up. "I thought about quitting," he said. "We talked about it a lot, but my wife is great. She just said, 'Whatever you want to do.' "

Bouton wanted to pitch. He began throwing knuckle balls. "What could I lose? I was 0-7 in a minor league. I had thrown a knuckler as a kid, and I found out I could still throw it. After a while, I was getting it over."

After a while he was 4-7. Maybe, he feels, he can still make it for a few years as a knuckleballer. And if he can't, he feels, it's no great tragedy. "I guess I'd sell real estate, or something," he said. "I know I won't work in an office. I'll have to combine something to make a living, with something I really want to do."

There are other things to think about. There is Kyong Jo Cho.

"Oh, sure," Bouton said, "we could have had more children. But with the population situation what it is, I don't think anybody has the right to have as many children as they can, where there are already so many children in the world that nobody is taking care of."

Michael Bouton will soon be six and Laurie is almost four. For the past year, suburban New Jersey has been getting used to the fact that they have a middle brother named Kyong. "His mother was Korean," Bouton explained. "His father was an American soldier. It is not an advantage to have white blood in Korea."

The Koreans, after several centuries of being whipping boys for the Japanese—being given in Japan the menial equivalent of Negroes in the American South—have finally found somebody of their own to be prejudiced against.

"We didn't specify a Korean kid," Bouton said. "We just told them we wanted a boy, and the age, and one with an aggressive personality.

"We did say we didn't want a child with a Negro background. You know I don't have anything against Negroes, but my wife and I had doubts about what kind of America it's going to be 10 years from now."

He had doubts about what kind of America it is right now. When Bouton came to the Yankees in 1962, he was brainwashed like all young Yankees about what not to say to newspapermen. He decided to make up his own mind and found that he even liked some of them. He horrified the senior Yankees by socializing with reporters.

He learned from the experience of a reporter his own age that adopting a Negro orphan could lead to unforeseen heartbreak and be a failure.

Kyong Jo Cho was on the way, so Jim Bouton went to Berlitz. "I learned how to ask him if he wanted a cab to his hotel," Bouton said, "but I didn't learn how to ask him, 'Where does it hurt?' So I took a cram course, and now a lot of kids in the neighborhood know how to say, 'Where did he go?' in Korean."

It was, in a sense, a waste of time. Kyong has steadfastly refused to speak a word of Korean. He came to Bouton a few weeks ago and complained that all the kids were calling him Kyong.

"He said he wanted an American name," Bouton said. "I asked what he thought about David. My wife and I had thought about that and we were hoping he would ask. He said that would be fine."

David Bouton is a lucky kid.

THE LAST OF THE AUTOCRATIC UMPIRES

By Bob Addie

From The Washington Post

The name of Ed Hurley came up twice recently. The first time was in the recent World Series between the Orioles and Mets, when Baltimore manager Earl Weaver was ejected from the fourth game by umpire Shag Crawford. The second time Hurley's name came up was Wednesday, when he died in Boston.

Quite a few baseball graybeards remembered that the last time anybody was thrown out of a World Series game before Weaver was in 1959, when Hurley chased the late Charley Dressen, then a coach with the Los Angeles Dodgers.

The Dodgers were playing the White Sox in Chicago in the sixth game of that '59 Series when first base umpire Hurley turned to the visiting dugout and motioned to Dressen.

"Our bench was yelling at plate umpire Frank Dascoli," Dressen explained, "and Hurley told us to shut up. We had some words and he ran me."

There was an amusing sequel. Hurley pointed to the Dodger dugout and told Dressen: "Go out through your dugout. I don't want you crossing the field and showboating in front of the crowd."

At the time, the only exit to both clubhouses was through the White Sox' dugout. It wasn't until a few years later that another exit was constructed from the visiting dugout. Hurley, in his anger, apparently forgot that Dressen could not leave through his own dugout unless somebody knocked down a brick wall.

That is exactly what Dressen attempted to do in pantomime while the enraged umpire kept shaking his finger. Eventually, it dawned on Hurley that Dressen would have to cross the field to leave the game and the umpire motioned the coach to go that way. Dressen took his sweet time.

Dressen always claimed that Hurley never forgot a previous argument. When Dressen managed Washington in 1956, it got dark during the fourth inning with the Senators leading the Detroit Tigers, 4–1. Hurley called time and a few moments later called the game. It was, of course, no victory for the Senators and the game had to be replayed.

The irony was that a few moments after the game was called, the sun came out and stayed out. The fiery Dressen yipped at the umpire's heels for at least 10 minutes. Hurley was never one to run away from the fight.

"How," asked the infuriated Dressen, "could you call a game because of sunshine?"

"I'm calling it because of thunder," answered the umpire, and Dressen's appeal was lost.

Hurley was regarded as a fair umpire, but he was often accused of having "rabbit ears." In baseball that means that an umpire is supersensitive about criticism in the form of vocal complaints from the bench.

Hurley could have been among the last of the autocratic umpires. They are all fading into a pattern now and few arrogate to themselves the supreme power the old-timers used as their badge of office.

The late Bill McGowan, a Washingtonian, was among the great ones. He, too, brooked no questioning of his judgment. But McGowan was a gregarious soul. He loved baseball and all those associated with the game and he particularly delighted in the off-duty company of players.

On one occasion McGowan made the train trip back to Washington from Philadelphia with the Senators. Umpires carry huge bags for their equipment and McGowan had just recovered from an illness. Pete Runnels, the Washington infielder, solicitously insisted on taking care of McGowan's bags, even to ordering a taxi at Union Station here and personally loading the heavy luggage.

The next night Runnels questioned a call of a strike and immediately was bounced by none other than McGowan.

"You're ungrateful," protested Runnels. "Did you forget what I did for you last night?"

"That's outside of business hours," blandly replied McGowan. "Now scoot."

In the old, rowdy days, the umpires had to run the game and thus was built up the legend and tradition of infallibility. The late Bill Klem, noted for his sharp tongue, once was reflecting on his 45 years in the National League, and remarked: "I never missed a call."

There was Tim Hurst, who heard the complaints of a fellow umpire and coined the phrase: "You can't beat the hours."

There never has been a question of "conflict of interest" with these athletic judges, and the umpires can boast with truth that no member of their arduous profession has been involved in malfeasance, misfeasance or nonfeasance in this century.

Hurley died a bitter man. He was retired against his will four years ago, because he was 58. He always protested he could have umpired "for at least 10 more years."

BASEBALL LIVES AT WRIGLEY FIELD

By Joe Gergen

From Newsday

You remember baseball. The sport with the caps, the long socks, the funny britches and the kids. Most of all, the kids. It supposedly expired along with quaint old places like the Polo Grounds (now that's a funny name), Braves' Field and Sportsman's Park. And, of course, Brooklyn. You remember Brooklyn.

Coney Island, the Cyclone, Steeplechase Park and . . . Ebbets Field. You remember Ebbets Field. The little kids with the gloves in one hand and immense brown paper bags—containing breakfast, lunch, dinner and a late-night snack—in the other, standing outside the bleacher entrance two hours before game time. They couldn't miss batting practice.

But that was the past. Just ask Lou Harris or George Gallup. Americans' tastes have changed. They've come a long way, baby, to get where they've got to today. Nobody wants to waste a day at the ball park anymore. Too slow, too dull, too bad. They want action, speed, violence and Pete Rozelle.

The people in Chicago are trying to tell Mr. Harris something. They went to great lengths Sunday to prove him wrong. It's a shame Mr. Harris couldn't have been there to see. But then there's no guarantee they would have let him into old Wrigley Field. Unless, that is, he presented himself at the gate before 10 A.M.

You remember Wrigley Field. It's the biggest baseball joke of all. Brick walls, ivy in the outfield and perpetual, everlasting sunlight. Day baseball they call it.

There were 40,484 persons in a 36,667-seat park who remembered baseball Sunday. They were, as the expression goes, hanging from the rafters. You remember rafters. "They've got enough seats," one observer said, "just not enough rafters." The surprising thing about the majority of the fans is that they have very short memories. They also have very short legs. It's two of the occupational hazards of being 10 years old.

They stood on Waveland Avenue two and one-half hours before the start of Sunday's doubleheader (twice the boredom, according to the now generation) with the gloves on one hand and those brown paper bags, filled with hidden delights, clutched firmly in the other. They jabbered among themselves and fidgeted, waiting their turn to get inside. They managed to keep the boredom from showing.

By 11:30 A.M., an hour before the start, all the grandstand and bleacher seats were occupied. You remember the bleachers. It was the place where you took your shirt off and let your hair down. People take their clothes off and let their hair down elsewhere nowadays.

The crowd was liberally mixed. Some wealthy, many shabby; some white, some black; all enthusiastic. It was the kind of crowd Walter O'Malley found increasingly distasteful as Ebbets Field grew older and seemingly smaller. They get a more sophisticated class of people in Los Angeles. What difference does it make if they cheer the radio. Sunday, those at Wrigley Field, roared at real people doing real things.

The kids, with eager faces and hot little hands, lined up three deep by the dugouts, straining to touch the uniforms on their heroes. You remember heroes. Ushers came around and occasionally ushered the kids away but, to their credit, they did it lackadaisically. Two little girls beckoned to Ernie Banks, who has a lease on the building. One of them presented him with a green and purple Easter bunny. Ernie went into a soft-shoe routine to the tune of "Easter Parade." The other presented him with a pie. American apple, naturally.

"They love the Cubs," Ernie philosophized. "Look at those people. It's just like Ebbets Field." What a beautiful thing to say. "I think baseball is meant for small parks like this," he said. "It's a personal game. You've got to feel close, get involved. These people would sleep here if they could. So would I."

Ernie's spirit, fortunately, is not a personal thing. It's contagious. It's what made 25 strangers stop and talk to each other on a busy corner of Michigan Avenue Saturday. They were standing in front of a television showroom and the Cubs and Mets were battling to a draw into the eighth inning. Fortunately, the Cubs broke the tie or they'd still be there arguing strategy.

It's the kind of spirit which prompted a family of 10 to set up shop in the lower grandstand Sunday and start distributing a chicken dinner on paper plates in the middle of a fifth-inning rally.

And it's the kind of spirit which prompted a police officer, whose work was growing with the crowd Sunday morning, to smile his broadest smile. "This crowd is beautiful," he said. "I wish I could go inside. That is really fun."

Surely, you remember fun.

Football

THE "56 SCISSORS"

By Bill Conlin

From the Philadelphia Daily News

All-America tackle Mike Reid says he didn't see anything that happened after Joe Paterno sent in a play labeled the "56 Scissors."

"I was down on my knees facing the crowd, praying," Reid said, a tear running down his right cheek.

It was third and goal on the Kansas three-yard line. Twenty-two seconds remained in the most incredible Orange Bowl game in its 35-year-old history. Mike Reid was praying and Chuck Burkhart, the quarterback people laugh at, was holding up his hands for quiet while 77,719 fans blew their minds at the drama of it.

Less than a minute before, Burkhart arched a long pass from his 49-yard line. Halfback Bobby Campbell made a great over-the-head catch to take the ball away from little Jayhawk safety man Tommy Anderson. Campbell churned to the three-yard line and suddenly there were cracks in the 14–7 Kansas lead.

Two shots at the middle by fullback Tom Cherry were hurled back by the Kansas defense.

"We decided on the Scissors on third down because we wanted to come back with some counteraction," Joe Paterno said after the 15–14 victory. "We felt they were set up for it."

Burkhart was supposed to fake another hand-off to the fullback, then stick the ball in halfback Charley Pittman's belly for a cutback over tackle. For years it has been a stock Penn State play.

But Chuck Burkhart, the ugly duckling of college quarterbacks, never went through with the 56 Scissors. What Chuck Burkhart did is typical of the kind of leadership Paterno teaches at Penn State.

As Burkhart made his first fake, he saw that All-America defensive end John Zook was jamming up the area where Pittman would cut. As Charlie came past, the 190-pound junior quarterback from Montour High School did a magnificently daring thing.

He kept the ball himself, pausing in the thunderous traffic while Pittman was dumped by Zook. Then he tucked the ball under his left arm and rolled left into the end zone. Few people saw what really happened or who scored the touchdown. That's how well Burkhart hid the ball.

State trailed 14–13 with 15 seconds left and everybody knew that Joe Paterno would rather be tortured by the North Koreans than settle for a tie.

He told Burkhart to go for two points and run the "18 Flip," a sprint-out to the right, with Campbell and All-America end Ted Kwalick flooding the right corner of the end zone.

The pattern was covered. Burkhart's pass to Campbell was batted away by right safety Dave Morgan and delirious Kansas rooters stormed the end zone, engulfing their heroes.

Alone in the middle of the field, resting on the goal line like a patch of doom, was a small red flag. Kansas, incredibly, was guilty of having 12 men on the field.

The ball was moved to the one and a half-yard line. While the crowd was being herded off the field, Paterno pondered what to do. He decided on a quick pitch to Campbell sweeping right end. No, he reasoned that was too obvious. Let's go to their power, right at Zook.

"I changed my mind," Paterno said. "I decided the 50 Sweep to the left would be better."

Fullback Tom Cherry, whose assignment was to blast Zook, improvised by taking out defensive back Bill Hunt when he charged up to force the play wide. Sophomore guard Charley Zapiec, from La Salle High (Philadelphia) threw the key block on Zook.

"I didn't knock him down, but I held the block long enough to let Bobby cut into the end zone," Zapiec said. "I knew Bobby was going to get in and we were going to get him there."

"Joe never goes for ties," Campbell said. "I just knew there was no way they were gonna stop us. We gave them the ball four times in the first half and all the highest scoring team in the nation got was seven points. It was a game where the momentum kept shifting. They took it away from us when we couldn't go in with four shots from the five. But we're the better team. We didn't play a typical game for us."

Except when it counted and the clock was running and this team of togetherness completed its 11–0 season without anybody in a blue and white uniform thinking it could possibly end any other way.

Burkhart doesn't know why he improvised on the Scissors play.

"It wasn't in my mind before the play or when the play began," Chuck said. "But when I saw them pinching to the inside, I remembered what coach Paterno told me once in practice. To take it myself if it looked like the play couldn't go. But even then . . . it was mainly instinct. I'm not even sure I thought about it when it happened. I just did it. It's my first touchdown all year."

Paterno says all Burkhart did was remember a casual bit of advice he gave him during practice on the Scissors play.

"The only coaching involved was that I said he could probably make it a better play if he rolled out when there was a defender between the hole and the halfback.

"They say he can't throw, he can't run, he can't do anything a great quarterback has to do," Paterno said. "He's been terribly maligned, because all he's done is win the last 31 games he's started in football and all he did was score the big one for us tonight. Is this my greatest thrill?"

Paterno pondered it for a moment. "This team has been the biggest thrill that's happened to me in my life, except perhaps for my wife and family and my mom and dad. My players have been a great inspiration to me personally. They've never cracked in the face of adversity and they proved how big they are coming back against a great football team and great odds tonight."

Penn State tossed the vaunted Kansas runners around like rag dolls most of the game, holding Donnie Shanklin, Junior Riggins and All-America quarterback Bobby Douglass to a game total of 76 yards.

Douglass was dropped eight times for 54 yards, including two straight superhuman efforts by Reid in the dying moments when Penn State desperately needed field position and the ball. And when Kansas finally punted with 2:06 to go, Neil Smith tipped the ball, which took a crazy bounce to the State 49. Then Campbell made his great catch and all hell started breaking loose in the Orange Bowl.

"At half time we thought we were going to blow them out of here," Paterno said. "We made the drive we wanted to make and when we got it to the five with first down, we thought we could knock it in by running the middle. From the films, we felt Kansas could be hurt inside on the goal line. I might do it another way now."

It was a tremendous victory for Eastern football. Nobody who saw one of the great games in Orange Bowl history is going to say Penn State beat a patsy.

"Even if we lost it 14–7, we've still made Eastern football look good," Paterno said. "People say who did we play. Well, we've won 11 games this year and nobody's licked us in the past 19 and we've played teams from every section. We knocked off North Carolina State last year and they beat Georgia in a bowl game. We knocked off Miami and they played in a bowl game. People knocked us this year because some teams we played weren't having the years people expected of them. But we still played them and beat them. I feel we have as much claim to be No. 1 as Ohio State."

It's a question that will be debated until the head-knocking starts again next fall. But everyone who has followed Paterno and his kids through a captivating season knows that Eastern football can be proud of this team. No finer group of young men and athletes have ever been put together during the cynical days of big-time football.

ALLIE HEARS THE LAST GOOD-BYE

By Gene Roswell

From the New York Post

The fans finally got what they wanted.

They got Allie Sherman fired and they got it with the power of song, with the "Good-bye, Allie" serenade that had become almost a lynch chant wherever the Giants played and lost.

Allie, immersed in the scholarly cryptics of football, closed his ears and his mind to it, but Giants' owner, Wellington Mara, couldn't.

Mara heard it at Yankee Stadium from once fiercely loyal fans now fiercely critical. He heard it at road games and he heard it louder and longer at all five exhibition games this season away from New York—five losses, including the creaming by the Jets that rubbed Giant noses in the dirt.

"Sure it bothered me," Mara said yesterday at the hastily called press conference in which he announced that Allie had been asked to "step aside" and that Alex Webster had been signed to a two-year contract as the new head coach.

"It was an indication to me," Mara said, "that we weren't doing what we should. It was an indication that the fans weren't happy."

What the Giants weren't doing was winning. In the last five years of Allie's eight as head coach, the best they could do was three 7–7 seasons. The other two were utter disasters, 2–10–2 and 1–12–1.

The fans forgot Allie's first three years, his '61, '62 and '63 Eastern Conference champions. They remembered the losers, the breaking up of the Huff-Robustelli-Modzelewski defensive axis, the endless flow of mediocrities thereafter, the futility, the humiliations, the defeats.

They forgot that Allie once was the "Boy Genius" of football, a young man who came to the Giants as a backfield assistant to Stout Steve Owen after five years as a left-handed second-string quarterback with the Eagles under Greasy Neale.

They forgot that it was Allie, the kid from Brooklyn College, who converted a rookie named Charlie Conerly from a single-wing tailback to a T-formation quarterback on the Giants.

They forgot a lot of fine things about Allie—about his three years and three play-offs in the Canadian League, about his replacing Vince Lombardi as offensive coach on the Giants in '59 when Mr. Football went to Green Bay, and they forgot that Mara gave him a 10-year contract in '63, after he produced three straight title play-off teams in New York.

Memories dim quickly for losers in the cruel world of sports, although it cannot be said that Mara didn't give Allie enough time. Five years without a winner is a lifetime even in tolerant New York.

So the fans, driven by their frustration, sang "Good-bye, Allie" and Mara's heart broke. It was Wellington's father, old Tim Mara, who took the Giants from the sandlots to the Polo Grounds and it was his late brother, Jack, who built them into a dynasty at the Stadium.

"I grew up in those games," Mara said yesterday. "I've been in and around it for 45 years, ever since I was old enough to hang around. I'm a fan too.

"I know that if a team doesn't win games, it doesn't fulfill its function for fans."

Mara struggled with this burden for a long time. He is a quiet man, loyal and compassionate, and his faith in Allie seemed endless. He understood that success and failure go in cycles and he wanted desperately for Allie's turn for the brass ring to come up again.

But the fans wouldn't wait. They sang "Good-bye, Allie" at the drop of a punt. The song spread like a Beatles hit. They sang it in Green Bay last month when the Giants lost their exhibition opener 22–21 because of fumbles and such.

They sang it in the Yale Bowl in the tragedy of boo-boos against the Jets, and the chorus swelled with losses to the Eagles at Princeton, the Vikings in Minneapolis and last Thursday night in Montreal to the Steelers. It was becoming the national anthem of football.

The sight and sound of Canadians derisively singing "Good-bye, Allie" in a baseball park as the Giants floundered against a weak Steeler club was too much for Mara. It was the tune that broke his own sound barrier.

Mara couldn't sleep after driving home to White Plains at 2:30 A.M., following late arrival at Kennedy on the Giant charter flight from Montreal. The accumulation of years of disappointment and chagrin welled up inside him.

After the Jet debacle, it was apparent to anyone familiar with Mara's deep sense of pride in the Giants that he was close to a turning point. He looked so grim and sick at heart even close friends wouldn't approach him, and it was rumored that he laid it on the line to Allie the next day.

Then more defeats, particularly the one to the Eagles, where Mara sat alone staring forlornly out of a window in the gym locker room while Allie spoke to the press.

So there was Mara, tossing and turning in bed in the wee hours of yesterday morning, agonizing over an 0–5 preseason record, worried about opening the regular schedule against the Vikings in the Stadium September 21, and the refrain of "Good-bye, Allie" in his head.

"I made the decision about Allie between three and six o'clock that morning," Mara said. "I called Allie at 7:30 and asked him to come up to my place after he got the kids off to school.

"He came some time after 8:30 and we talked for an hour and 20 minutes. We were both unhappy over the necessity for such a talk, but . . .

"When you come to a decision and you think it's right, then that's the time to do it. I guess I felt like President Truman when he dismissed General MacArthur."

How Allie really took the news is hard to judge.

Reached at his home in Scarsdale late last night, Allie confessed that he was surprised but declined to expand further.

"I was too busy with my family," he said. "I haven't given any thought to anything else.

"I have to think things over. I have no calendar date for the first time in a long while.

"My association with Wellington Mara was a good one and a happy one. I wish Webster, the coaches and the players luck."

Allie's first move on arriving home was to pick up his three children—Randy, 15, Lori, 12, and Robin, 10—at school before the news spread.

Mara couldn't tell if Allie was surprised, but must have surmised that he was.

"I always told him I'd lose confidence in myself before I lost confidence in him," Mara said.

"But we all know it's due some time or other in this game. How many coaches die on the job? You always think it won't happen to you, but it does.

"When Allie came in, I told him I wanted to talk to him, that I thought we had reached the point where both of us would become a couple of highly paid spectators."

Mara apparently was eliminating himself along with Allie. He also was referring to the five years at approximately $48,000 per remaining on Allie's contract as well as to a phrase in his statement to the press.

That portion of the statement read:

"Although I will continue to be the chief executive officer of the Giants and, as such, will continue to have the ultimate responsibility for all decisions, I will appoint an experienced football man to assist our new head coach in the evaluation, selection and procurement of players."

He further stated that it "may not be possible to make such an appointment until after the current football season . . ."

Mara seemed to be talking himself out of control of player personnel selections in which he always played a prominent part.

Mara's next call was to the man he had chosen to be his new coach. It was a shocker. Alex Webster, Big Red. The burly back who symbolized all the Giants stood for in their rugged glory years between '55 and '64, Webster's 10 seasons with the club.

Alex Webster, who left football after he left the Giants because he was beat up and tired, up to here with a game that had occupied every minute of his time and every ounce of his energy.

"I never saw my wife or kids," Alex said yesterday. "I wanted to get away from football, but after a year I found I couldn't. I was the color man on a football program, but that wasn't enough."

Alex returned as a rookie backfield coach in '67 under Allie, a man who had cut or dealt away most of his old teammates and pals, a man with a different way of life.

But they got along well in their new relationship. Yesterday, Webster said he considered Allie his friend.

The job offer from Mara stunned Webster. "Are you kidding?" he asked after his arrival at Giant headquarters in Columbus Towers following Mara's hurry call. "I was on my way to New York anyway," Alex said. "I was visiting a young friend in a hospital. When I got the call, I didn't think anything of it.

"When he told me what it was about, I couldn't say anything for a while. A lot of thoughts flashed through my mind. I've been with Allie one way or another for a long time. I've always admired his ability and I learned a lot from him."

Still, Webster took the job. Alex Webster, 38, family man from Sea Girt, New Jersey, son aged 15 and daughter Debbie, 12, wife Laura still in shock.

Alex Webster, the uncomplicated good fellow, friendly as a St. Bernard, straight-shooting and straight-talking. No record as a coach, no record as an intellect. Just Alex Webster.

How did Mara ever come to select a Webster over a Norm Hecker or a Jim Trimble, men who had experience as head coaches in the NFL? Or Ken Kavanaugh, in his 15th season as end coach and one-time great with the old Chicago Bears?

"Because I thought he was the man for the job," Mara answered. "Because I felt for the moment I had run out of answers and wanted a fresh viewpoint.

"I had not considered an outsider at all. That would have been giving up on the season. A new man would have to start from scratch. It would take him a month to know the problems—and by then the season would be shot."

Webster seemed to take on a new dimension yesterday in his meeting with the news media.

"It's a helluva responsibility," he said of the appointment. "I've only been coaching two years, but my background in football goes back a long way."

It is the only rebuttal he will have for the football critics who are sure to descend on Mara for his selection of a relatively green and untutored coach for the No. 1 job on a team which is in serious distress.

"The biggest asset I've got is my assistants," Alex said. "Hecker, he did a great job with the defense at Green Bay and as head coach at Atlanta. Trimble was headman with the Eagles. Tunnell, Rosey Brown, Kavanaugh, they're all good men. It'll be their baby. I'm going to let them handle their departments. Let them go all out, and I'll coordinate. On Sundays, on the sidelines, I'll make the decisions."

If Webster had apprehensions, he didn't show them.

"A change is good at times," he said. "I never was tough, it's not my personality, but I have my own ideas as to how a man should play and I'll expect a lot more out of them."

Obviously, Alex has some iron in him and there will be some changes. He will continue to handle the backs and he let it be known immediately that Tucker Frederickson was his best back.

"The big thing we have to do on this team is find the right combination," he said. "Sure, on defense we need instant help, but man, where do we go to find it?"

The suggestion that his friendliness of the past might impose a strain on his new relationship with players, especially men he had come up with, was no problem, he said.

"I can't be as friendly with the guys," Alex conceded, "but then I can't be unfriendly either. It's not my nature. I don't see how I can change my personality.

"When I was a player, I always went out to win. As a coach, it'll be the same. If a player doesn't produce, I don't see any use paying him.

"I haven't been out of football long enough to forget what it's like as a player. I think I can relate to them."

The best part of it, Mara must have had in mind, was that the singing would stop in the stands. How could any fan be mean to Big Red?

THE MOST HATED WINNER IN FOOTBALL

By Leonard Shecter

From Look

The day in 1966 when Al Davis, who now runs the Oakland Raiders with a small, iron fist, was appointed commissioner of the American Football League, he leaned over the shoulder of the young publicist who was typing the announcement and penciled two words atop the paper. "Think you can work these in?" Davis asked. The words were 1. Dynamic. 2. Genius.

Al Davis' immodest assessment of himself is not precisely mirrored in the world of professional football, where winning, by whatever means, is usually the only measure of a man. Indeed, even though Commissioner Al Davis' slashing attack on the National Football League helped the upstart AFL force a merger, even though his Oakland Raiders won 25 of 28 games in the last two seasons, not including two division titles and a league championship, even though the Raiders are favored to take another championship this season, Al Davis is the most hated man in professional football.

In his dedicated, single-minded pursuit of pro-football's only goal, Al Davis has, his legion of detractors say, lied, cheated, manipulated, maneuvered and, wearing spikes, marched up and down the backs of his hired hands. And last season, lady football columnist Elinor Kaine elected him "Super Rat of the Year."

To all of this, dynamic Al Davis, 40-year-old football genius, tanned, flat-bellied, with blond hair that is disappearing in front and hanging shaggily over his collar in back, bats his big blue eyes, smiles a large-toothed Bugs Bunny smile and says, "I want to win. That's it, all of it."

Growing up in Brooklyn helped turn Al Davis into a gut fighter. ("When your gang met my gang, and I got out in front to fight the other guy, I had to win," he says.) He had openmouthed admiration for the success of the Yankees, the ruthless methods of Vince Lombardi and Paul Brown. In the end, he was able to slam the savage dogmas of athletic success right back into the teeth of the men who practiced them best. "We knocked hell out of the NFL," Al Davis says of his reign as AFL commissioner. "Al Davis will do anything to win," football establishment people were saying, not without admiration. This admiration turned to howls of anguish though, when they found Davis stomping around on their toes.

Winning is all Al Davis knows and is probably the only thing he enjoys. A humorless man, he laughs only at conquest. "Tell him a joke," says a man who used to work for him, "and you'll get a blank look. But if a general manager on another club calls him up and congratulates him on some fast deal he put over, he'll laugh like hell."

Davis' sense of competition is so finely honed that he was bitterly disappointed when peace was declared between the warring AFL and NFL. And not only because he thought the terms, under which the AFL had to pay some $20 million in reparations, were too harsh ("We didn't have to give 'em nothin'," he says, the Southern accent he cultivates—because it's easier to "tahk" Southern to football players—evaporating under the stress of emotion), but because he hadn't had time to implement his elaborate schemes to humiliate the NFL even further.

One of them involved the infiltration of NFL baby-sitters—the men who guarded college football players during the draft to make sure they would be available for signing—so that he could, with one masterstroke, send them all traveling to the wrong place at the wrong time. "All of a sudden, they would have all found themselves in Hawaii," Davis said. He laughed.

That's Al Davis and big think. Al Davis and small think involves his firing employees for largely imagined disloyalty. A secretary in the commissioner's office got it because Davis decided she had given one of his Oakland players information about whether his name appeared on a waiver list. Then there was the publicity man (Davis is hell on publicity men) who innocently told Don Klosterman, Houston GM, that a player he had conditionally traded to Oakland was doing very well indeed. This led Klosterman to demand a player in payment and Davis to can his publicity man as a spy.

So working for Davis can be a grinding experience. "I used to go to work every morning with a knot in my stomach," says a man who has escaped the Davis salt mine. "I never knew when the next attack was coming."

"Davis' theory is that people are motivated by fear," says Bob Bestor, who resigned as Raider business manager to do publicity for the Oakland Seals hockey team. "He thinks people perform better if they're afraid."

Davis admits it. Sitting in his cold, impersonal office, which is decorated in black and silver, the team colors, Davis pointed a finger and said, "What do I mean by fear? People in an organization have to have the feeling that there's someone there who, if they don't move in the right direction, will chop. Are you with me?"

It's all perfectly clear, of course, although it should be noted that Davis is something of a semantic escape artist. He has, for example, described himself as a top assistant or next under Weeb Ewbank in Baltimore at age 24. What Ewbank, now coach of the New York Jets, says is: "He was in my scout group. We had 40 scouts."

This sort of thing inspires a good deal of the scorn that is heaped upon Davis. He is charged with trying to make himself larger than life. He says that he played basketball, football and baseball at Syracuse University, where he took his degree in English. Yet the Varsity Club at Syracuse has no record that Davis lettered in any sport.

Another example. Davis gives his height as 6-foot-½ and his weight as 200. "He is no more than 5-11 and 190," says Lee Grosscup, author, former quarterback and another Davis ex-publicity man. "He wants to be thought of as an athlete. But he isn't even particularly well-coordinated. And he may have the skinniest pair of wheels in America, which is why he never takes off his pants where anyone can see. Then there's the Al Davis handshake. It's done with the fingers held apart and rigid so his little hand will seem bigger. Also notice the way he dresses. He still wears those suits with the big padded shoulders. The players call him 'El Bago.' "

Finally, there's the matter of his odd title, managing general partner. Dictator would be more apt. "In order to run an efficient organization," Davis says, "there has to be a dictator." Despite the record of dictators all over, he is quite serious. But he is not precisely a general partner.

Wayne Valley, who with E. W. McGah is a general partner (there are 23 limited partners), says Davis will own "less than 15 percent" of the club if he remains at his post for ten years, which means he has seven to go. "He wanted to be an owner," Valley says. "Davis is very image conscious. He felt being an owner was a step up from being commissioner. Anything else would have been a step down."

Although it may be easy to ridicule some of Al Davis' mannerisms, he doesn't take any steps down. Valley, a large, tough, self-made real estate and construction millionaire, who in his own way is probably as hard to work for as Davis, makes the point when he says, "If I said Al Davis is lovable, I'd be a liar. But you don't have to love him; just turn him loose."

The first time Al Davis was unleashed on pro football, he pulled off an extraordinary turnabout. Appointed coach and general manager of the Raiders in 1963, Davis took a team that had won three out of 28 games, and in a single season came in with a 10–4 record. If the New York Mets had won a pennant in their third season, it would have been no greater upset.

Says Jim Otto, the All-League center who was there at the start, "It was terrible. We practiced on lots with rocks and broken glass. There was no organization, no leadership. Then Davis came in, and he went out and got it done, all of it, the whole shebang."

Long-haired, modly dressed Grosscup, who is making a living as a model and college-football color man on TV, is hardly a Davis booster. Yet when it comes to the game of football, Grosscup rates Davis highly. "He has developed a brilliantly conceived offense that is so complex and so effective it's frightening," Grosscup says.

Daryle Lamonica, the Oakland quarterback, agrees. "His knowledge of the game is shocking," Lamonica says. "This is my third year as a starter, and I'm just beginning to grasp the overall picture. I'm throwing to at least four men, often five. This means our whole offensive line has to be involved. Every lineman has to know what every back is doing. It's a terrific offense."

It is in this area that Davis apparently feels he can afford modesty. Sitting in one of his black-plastic office chairs, wearing a bulky sweater, he succeeds in looking large and rather boyish: "Let me say this. Football is complex, but you don't have to be smart to understand it. You just have to have that kind of mind."

Asked when he knew he going to run a football team for a living, Davis says, "When I was six." This could well be, for his life has gone in a straight line in that direction. The son of a successful garment manufacturer, Al Davis was born in Brockton, Massachusetts, moved to Brooklyn and talks about his early life with great reluctance. "Al's a complex guy," says Don Klosterman, who worked with Davis for the Los Angeles, later the San Diego, Chargers. "It's hard to figure out what he's thinking. His mind is a labyrinth. One minute, he's very concerned about his image. The next, he doesn't seem to care." (The kind of thing that probably throws Klosterman is Davis saying this: "I don't want this in the story. I really wish you wouldn't print it. You follow me? But when I got out of public school, I won the American Legion medal for all-around kid.")

Davis' first job was assistant coach in football and head coach in baseball at Adelphi College on Long Island, New York. It was while he was there that he met and married Carol (he calls her Ca-ROL-ee) Segall. They have a redheaded son Mark, 14, named after General Mark Clark. Davis didn't meet the general until he went to The Citadel some years later, but it was shortly after he was drafted in 1952 that Davis sort of took over the army. Assigned to special services at Fort Belvoir, Virginia, where the commandant wanted to build a football team, Davis waded in with his customary vigor.

He took over two barracks, and in one of them he had his own room with a sign over the door that read "Off Limits To Players." He was a private, but he had a car and driver, and was the only enlisted man who always wore an officer-type, peaked hat. Everywhere he went, recruits scrambled to salute him. "He had a good deal, but so did his players," a man who served with him recalls. "They slept until noon and ate the best food on the base. He built a hell of a football team."

When Davis left Fort Belvoir, it was only a step ahead of a congressional investigation into the coddling of athletes. When he remembers this, he laughs. "You know how generals are," he said. "They want to win. This general gave me carte blanche. I also had very good contacts in the Pentagon that could move people. You follow me?"

After his stint as a scout in Baltimore, Davis went to The Citadel as an assistant (for which he apologizes—"What was I, 25?") and recruiter. With Davis beating through Pennsylvania for young talent, The Citadel promptly chalked up its best record in 13 years. The University of Southern California was the next stop, and several Citadel football players went with him. This was noticed by the NCAA, which put USC on probation. It did not prevent USC from winning.

The negative effects of college recruiting have never intruded upon Davis' moral sense. "Recruiting isn't the worst of it," Davis said when the subject came up over a glass of ice water in an Italian restaurant in Oakland. (Davis drinks little, smokes not at all, eats no breakfast, works out with weights in a black-and-silver office gym every day and substitutes water for tea and coffee.) "Fifty percent of

All-Americans are on the downgrade in their third year because they're failures. They can't go home because they've reached a peak too early."

An odd looked crossed Davis' face as he said this, a strangely empty look. "And how about if you're 40 and you own the goddam team? And you're not sure what you want to do?"

If Davis has time for a problem, this seems to be it, a recurring doubt about where he goes from here. He would be lost if he weren't leading something. Even his leisure reading is devoted to things military, and he sprinkles his conversation with references to obscure battles. ("Did you know we were blobbered at Archangel?") And once he was asked if he would have liked to be President. "No," he said. "I'm not interested in inflation. I'm interested in the power behind the scenes. Secretary of State."

Davis went from USC to the Chargers, where he was soon tearing at the NFL. Among the college stars Davis lured into the AFL fold despite NFL blandishments was Lance Alworth. "Lance and I became close friends," Davis said. "That's the first thing you do. Anytime you're selling, there's got to be warmth. My father had died a week before I went to see Lance, and he's very close with his father, and somehow there was a lot of warmth."

In 1963, when Davis was 33, he was asked to come to Oakland as general manager and coach. Oakland had no stadium. There was bickering among the owners. The team was demoralized. It did not seem like a very good job. Davis leaped to take it. With one condition. He demanded absolute control. "I'm not running a school to teach owners football," Davis told them.

As his success mounted, Davis began to use a lot of words Vince Lombardi used in Green Bay before he defected to Washington. "Pride," Davis says, "and a little poise. Dedication and loyalty. Sacrifice. And yeah, love."

What helped the Raiders a lot more than rhetoric was Davis' knack for picking up players other teams didn't want and getting good performances from them. The Jets let Art Powell play out his option, and he was an All-League end for Davis in 1963. "Powell was a bad guy," Davis said with only a slight snarl. "He got into the end zone for us. He helped build our new stadium. A real bad guy.

"Ben Davidson was with three clubs. They said he was a dog. I picked Ike Lassiter up off the street. Bad guys. All they could do was win." (Lassiter: "I told Davis I could play if the coaches didn't jump on my back all the time. They left me alone and I played.")

Another Davis strong point is a talent for spotting a player in the wrong position. Billy Cannon was switched from the backfield to tight end and made a major contribution. Hewritt Dixon was a tight end for Denver until Davis turned him into a fine running back. "Davis can turn an ordinary player into a great one by making a few adjustments," Lamonica says.

Not that Davis overlooks the rewards of small think here too. He rejoices in spreading misinformation about injuries to his players. He employs a network of spies so that if a linebacker in Boston has a boil on his tail or a tackle in Denver is angry with the line coach, Al Davis knows. He has, for some time now, been scouting the NFL teams involved in the merger, but when they tried to scout Oakland, Davis barred them from his field. If there's an edge, Davis will have it.

"Edge? Me?" Al Davis said before a Jets-Raider exhibition this summer. "I don't look for an edge. If I did, before this game with the Jets, I'd have arranged a ceremony, the city of Oakland giving the Jets a thank-you trophy for winning the Super Bowl. Then I'd have had one of the guys on our team say, 'Those bastards are collecting our trophy.' " Al Davis laughed.

Then there was the shelter caper. At five o'clock on the frigid morning the Raiders were playing the Jets for the AFL championship in Shea Stadium, a work crew talked its way onto the field and erected a weather shelter over the Oakland bench. "We'll build one for the Jets later," they said as they left. Only the fact that it blocked the view of fans in the stands prevented Davis from getting away with it.

There is a delicious duplicity to this stunt, which is why many people count Davis a charming rogue. Others don't find him that charming.

"It was a high school trick," snarls Weeb Ewbank, in a relatively mild reaction compared to, say, Sid Gillman, the San Diego general manager, who screams that Davis coaches offensive holding. "I never listen to anything Al Davis says," Gillman says.

Still, Davis did turn Oakland's fortunes around—the club is beginning to make some real money in its new stadium—and this was so impressive that when Wayne Valley proposed him as the man to do battle with the NFL while the war was at its peak in 1966, there were no demurrals. The only question about Davis' four-month regime as commissioner—for which he is still collecting on a reported $250,000, five-year contract—is just how influential he was in bringing about the quick settlement. There are those, including Commissioner Pete Rozelle, who insist that peace was near even before Davis became commissioner. Indeed, there had been talks, but there was no action until Davis waded in, went to top NFL stars, shoved money at them and induced them to play out their options and jump to AFL clubs.

Among the defectors were Roman Gabriel and John Brodie, quarterbacks for Los Angeles and San Francisco. A lot more were preparing to jump. "One of these days Pete Rozelle [then commissioner only of the NFL] is going to wake up in the morning and reach for his drawers—and they will be gone," wrote Larry Merchant in the New York *Post* of the Davis modus operandi. Sure enough, Rozelle woke up one morning and found the leagues merged—with himself as commissioner.

"I didn't want to be commissioner," Davis says. "No way. It's a desk job."

"He thought he ought to have it," says Valley, who calls Davis The Genius. "He felt hurt. But the guy is in the right place, running a shop."

Davis came back as managing general partner and ran the shop with a vengeance. Losing to Green Bay in the Super Bowl and to the Jets last season for the AFL championship were his only two serious defeats. And one other. The noisy resignation of John Rauch, his coach.

"Al always said he didn't want the owners telling him how to run the club," Valley recalls. "When he came back, I kidded him about it. I said I suppose you want your coach to have the same right. He didn't laugh. Al hasn't much of a sense of humor."

The only surprise about Rauch's departure was that it was so long in coming. Dictator Davis does everything but take tickets, and a coach is almost certain to resent the hot breath on his neck. "Davis is a hard worker, and he'll do anything to win," says Rauch, who is now coach of the Buffalo club. "I respect him for that. But I don't think he is the greatest coach in the world. I mean here we were preparing for a championship game and a Super Bowl game, and he's got 15 reasons why I'm not a good coach. All he wanted was to run the show himself from behind his desk."

Wayne Valley isn't sure that's the right way to do it. "Who are the geniuses in this game?" he says. "Lombardi. Brown. How can you tell? They put their guts on the line. They're judged as coaches."

Davis disagrees. He believes that Lombardi, who had one year as a losing general manager at Green Bay, could have had better results if only he had paid more attention. "Instead, he let his coach run the team and he played golf." Al Davis doesn't play golf.

In fact, he is bugged that he failed to keep Rauch pacified. He went to great lengths to do so.

Lee Grosscup tells of the time the Raiders played in Miami, and a columnist wrote a kind piece on Davis.

"Does he flatter me too much, Bob?" Davis said to Bob Bestor.

"He lays it on you, but it's a good column."

"Well, listen. Don't you think it makes the coach look bad?"

"He doesn't even mention him."

"I know. Listen, that's what I'm worried about. I tell you what. Why don't you go down to the lobby and buy all the papers so the coach can't get one. And let's send Grosscup out to the airport to buy them up there."

"And that's what I did," Grosscup said. "There I was, athlete, author, big man, lugging 25 newspapers under each arm just to please The Genius."

It is possible that Rauch would have been better off if he had fought Davis less and listened to him more. At least this is the policy of John Madden, the 33-year-old assistant Davis has elevated to head coach. Lowering his 260-pound bulk into a chair too small for him, Madden explained how he feels about working with Davis.

"I'd say he comes to about 50 percent of the practices," Madden said. "But you don't say, 'Oh, hell, here he comes.' It's a pleasure to see him. If I have an idea I want to use, I have to sell it. It's the same way with Al. He doesn't tell me, he sells me."

In which case Davis must sell football a lot better than he does himself. He'd have a terrible time working up a list of people who were anything more than acquaintances. "You're not talking to any of my friends," he complained to a reporter recently.

"All right," the reporter said. "Who are your friends?" The pause was long enough to be embarrassing. Finally, Davis said, "George Ross. Why don't you talk to him?"

Ross is sports editor of the *Oakland Tribune*. He likes Al Davis, believes he's a football genius and that he's responsible for bringing big-time sports to the city that was counted as a mere doppelganger to the real city across the bay, San Francisco.

Among the legion of people Davis could not put on his list of friends are some of his players. "My ambition is to tell Al Davis, 'Sorry, I can't afford to play for you,' " says Ben Davidson. At least one Davis-Davidson contretemps has broken into print. It had to do with a commercial Davidson filmed largely for the benefit of the AFL Players Association. When Davis discovered that the Raider emblem was visible on Davidson's helmet in the spot, he demanded and received a large fee. As an upshot of this ploy, there were no visible team emblems in the AFL All-Star Game. "Instead of getting good public relations for the teams," Davidson says, "we were individual football players out for themselves."

Then there's Tom Keating, the defensive tackle with the leprechaun face. Keating injured his Achilles tendon in the 1967 title game with Houston. In the All-Star Game that followed, he snapped it altogether and was out for the 1968 season. "Davis said he was under no obligation to pay me for the season, but he would give me half," Keating says. "Later on, he said two-thirds. I told him if he wanted to release me he could, but if he didn't I wanted full pay. Not only that, but nobody had paid my hospital bill. I was even getting dunned for a TV set I'd rented there. My credit rating was going all to hell. They were threatening to take my wife and sell her into white slavery. The whole thing.

"Davis' point was that he felt the league was responsible for paying me, and I said he should pay and then get it back from the league. I had to threaten to sue. Eventually, I got the money from the league, and I don't know how much of it he paid."

This was the case that led Elinor Kaine to elect Davis Super Rat.

"I don't really dislike the guy," Keating says. "He's hard to like sometimes but, well, it's like he's talking to you, telling you a lie and you know it, but you want to believe it. He's like the movie mogul in *The Bad and the Beautiful.* Kirk Douglas played the part. This guy really used people. But in the end, when he's down and out, those very people are willing to like him again."

Despite Davis' apparent penury in the business of football, he often shows great personal generosity. It's said that the bash he threw for his son's Bar Mitzvah was one of the most lavish in the history of Oakland. Keating, who counts himself as something of a gourmet, was one of the 500 invited guests, and with beluga caviar in one hand, Piper Heidsieck in the other, he was heard to remark, "Kill me now, this is the way I want to die."

There is no fun in Davis, though, when it comes to football. Football is not an entertainment to him, it's a "vicious battle." Which is why, when other people make out an itinerary for their players, it might read "2 p.m. Game Time," Davis' itineraries read "2 p.m. WE GO TO WAR!"

He can't help it if he means it.

THE LONGHORNS SILENCE THOSE "SOOOOOOIE" PIGS

By Mickey Herskowitz

From The Houston Post

And now at last we know what Mr. Nixon means by the silent majority. It refers to those Arkansas fans who filed out of Razorback Stadium in the gloom of a Saturday afternoon, whose cheers froze in the misty December air, who watched with a growing disbelief and then died a little as mighty Texas, No. 1 Texas, won what may well have been the game of the century, 15–14.

So it had been billed, and so the teams did their utmost to see that the deed would equal the promise. You knew in your heart, and in your stomach, that the 100th year of college football would end this way, the season and the century compressed into the last two minutes and 20 yards.

Nearly destroyed by their mistakes, acting as though they had never played in front of a Republican President before, the Longhorns found themselves down by 14 points as they turned in to the final quarter.

Still, they could not have picked a better time to discover themselves. Quarterback James Street, cool as a Boy Scout leading a little old lady through an intersection, broke free for 42 yards and the first touchdown, then kept for the two-point conversion that would later be the margin of glory.

Street passed for 44 yards to Randy Peschel to set up the winning score purchased by Jim Bertelsen from close in.

The 15th point, Happy Feller's place-kick, will be remembered as the one that counted, but in truth it was the easiest of them all.

The victory wasn't secure until the clock showed a minute and 13 seconds to play, when Tom Campbell of Texas tumbled to earth with the football in his arms, 21 yards from the Texas goal line.

Arkansas had been moving toward it with a taut fury, shrinking the field and racing the clock on Bill Montgomery's passes.

Montgomery had been throwing all day to Chuck Dicus, the quick and explosive split end who caught everything but the President's helicopter. On that last measured drive Montgomery threw away from Dicus, who was now being held hostage by the Texas secondary.

He was looking for flanker John Rees on what turned out to be the last Arkansas play of the game. Campbell went up with him and wrestled the ball away.

So Texas, haunted by four fumbles and two pass interceptions, unable to cross the Arkansas 30-yard line for 45 minutes, shaken by a swarming Razorback defense, rallied to win it all.

It was a one-game bundle including the Southwest Conference title, an unbeaten season, a possible national championship and a ticket to the Cotton Bowl. Texas will begin college football's second hundred years by meeting Notre Dame, in another dream game, on New Year's Day.

It was a remarkable, storied comeback under any conditions, but especially so when one considers the number of Texas errors and the quality of the team that received them. Arkansas, unbeaten in nine games, ranked No. 2 in all the land, is no hamburger sandwich.

The Longhorns fumbled the ball away on the second play of the game, then got warmed up and fumbled it on the second half kickoff. You don't make boo-boos like that and win. Just ask Darrell Royal. Ask Frank Broyles. Never mind what the scoreboard says.

The head-to-head battle between the nation's first two teams was played in a somewhat bizarre setting, before a crowd of 44,000, including President Nixon, the evangelist Billy Graham, Senator Fulbright and lesser politicians. The crowd did not include a few dozen antiwar demonstrators who stood, quiet and reproachful, on a grassy hill overlooking the stadium, holding signs addressed to the President. The largest read: "Give peace a chance."

On the field, Arkansas and Texas ignored the plea and waged mayhem. They hit each other with the sort of force that produces whiplash. Steve Worster limped off, and Carl White, the fine Texas tackle, had to be helped to the bench. The Porkers lost defensive end Rick Kersey, and Montgomery was dazed at least once.

Another sign, not very subtle, carried the legend: "50,000 dead . . . wooo pig sooey." Inside the stadium a more hawkish banner appeared on a wire fence behind the Arkansas bench: "Victory in Vietnam."

You conclude that as a platform for protest, whatever the cause, a football game is a rather silly choice. In a downtown window, one sign promised "We'll win the game for you, Mr. President, if you'll win the war for us."

Presumably, Mr. Nixon said, "No deals."

Still, this was a national showcase, attracting a television audience of 50 million, the season coming down to one last gunfight.

The helicopter carrying the President and his party didn't arrive, landing softly on the practice field to the south of the stadium, until the teams were lined up for the kickoff. "The President better hurry," said one press-box humorist, "or he'll miss the Texas first team."

The reference was to the ease with which the Longhorns had disposed of their other opponents, letting the scrubs mop up.

But not this day. On the second play of the game Ted Koy burst through the Arkansas line, only to discover that he had forgotten the ball. Bobby Field claimed it for Arkansas at the Texas 22.

On third down, setting a pattern of big long yardage plays, Montgomery passed for 20 yards to John Rees, who spilled out of bounds at the two.

Tailback Bill Burnett needed two cracks to get the touchdown, hurdling over tackle from the one as the crowd exploded. Bill McClard's kick made it 7–0, with a minute and 27 seconds gone.

Texas fought back on the ground, as it was expected to do, but Arkansas had momentum and a play that couldn't seem to miss, Montgomery to Dicus. At the finish it had clicked nine times for 146 yards and one touchdown, and another called back.

Most of the yardage resulted from a pattern that saw Dicus cut in front of the Texas deep backs and slant over the middle. The Hogs had a groovy thing going.

Meanwhile, Texas worked hard and honestly and nothing happened. The Steers controlled the ball for 10 plays and again for 14 in the first half, and yet never crossed the Arkansas 30.

Terry Stewart's pass interception stopped them once, and later the Hogs held after Texas had driven 51 yards to the 31.

Time and again the Arkansas line, led by Cliff Powell and Dick Bumpas, tunneled through to pressure Street and challenge the bullish Texas backs.

It was going Arkansas' way. Three times on one advance Montgomery made long yardage on third down, and once he fumbled forward for an eight-yard gain, a hallelujah bounce.

A pass to Dicus that covered 26 yards would have given the Hogs another touchdown in the first quarter, and might have caused a stampede, but a penalty wiped it out. On the next play Bill Atessis and Dave Arledge chased Montgomery and buried him for a 24-yard loss. At that point, Arkansas faced third down and needed 49. Montgomery is a cool customer, but not many teams have a play designed for those third-and-50 situations.

The longest Texas rush had been for eight yards, and the Horns went to the dressing room behind for the first time this year at the half, 7–0. (They had been tied by Oklahoma.)

Darrell Royal had feared that it would be like this, with Arkansas in flames. "Do you know what it's like," he had said before the game, "to play those people with their eyes drawed up like BB's?"

The second half began with Arkansas kicking off twice out of bounds, and McClard finally teeing it up from his own 30.

When the kickoff finally fell in fair territory Cotton Speyrer returned it 30 yards for Texas, and then fumbled at his own 37. Paul Blevins recovered for Arkansas. Those observing the Texas bench wondered why Darrell Royal had not yet fainted.

The Hogs went nowhere with that gift, but shortly thereafter they were blessed again. Street passed for 18 yards to Speyrer, who was hit hard, the ball squirting loose and bouncing crazily around midfield.

A joyful Terry Stewart came up with it for Arkansas. A few feet away Speyrer sat more or less in the lap of Bobby Wuensch, his teammate. They looked at each other, and got up slowly.

The Razorbacks needed five plays to travel the 53 yards that made it 14–0. Montgomery kept for 18, then passed to Dicus down the middle, angling to his right, swiveling away from Tom Campbell for 29 yards and the score.

Nine minutes were left in the third quarter, and four plays later Arkansas had the ball back on an interception by Dennis Berner.

So now the game seemed as suspenseful as Captain Bob's Saturday morning kiddie show.

On that hill overlooking the stadium the demonstrators leaned their signs against a building, said to hell with it and left, looking for someplace warm.

It was time for Texas to test its poise and courage. They went 80 yards to heat up the action, to remind the crowd who they were and why they had come here.

Along the way Worster was hurt but Texas never stopped coming. On the first play of the fourth quarter a pass rush flushed Street out of the pocket. He emerged from a nest of Arkansas players and fled 42 yards to score.

Texas went for two right now, dealing with that decision first and avoiding more agony later. On the counteroption Street dived across, and it was 14–8. Texas was breathing again.

Except for that defensive lapse, Arkansas had played an errorless game to this point. Now they were to make them all in the fourth quarter, which is clearly the worst time.

Montgomery was moving them on his passes to Dicus for 20 and then for 27 and to Rees for 14. He drove the crowd mad, dancing around, waiting, waiting, as time passed and people grew older.

Sometimes he waited too long. From the seven—easy field goal range, if it had come to that—he had Dicus open in the corner. But Danny Lester cut in front of him and intercepted for Texas.

The Horns hammered out to the Arkansas 38 before Koy fumbled a high pitchout, and Gordon McNulty fell on it for the Hogs.

But Billy the Kid waited too long on third down, and Arledge dumped him for an eight-yard loss and Arkansas had to punt. The clock showed six minutes.

Here came the drive that ended the first 100 years. Texas took it in with a flourish, a gamble and a long pass.

It turned up fourth and three at the Texas 43, with 4:47 left, and the Longhorns had to go for it. Street sent Randy Peschel deep down the left sideline, and the senior end went up between Berner and Jerry Moore and plucked it down.

The play covered 44 yards, and Texas was at the Arkansas 13. Ted Koy on a hand-off burst for 11 and a first and goal at the two. There was no stopping them now. Jim Bertelsen, the sophomore from Wisconsin, burrowed through guard for the touchdown, and Happy Feller converted.

For the first time, after 56 minutes and two seconds, Texas led, 15–14.

The Razorbacks made their last charge and Tom Campbell cut them off at the 21, and when the clock ran out Texas was still undefeated, still No. 1.

On a freezing, ugly day Texas and Arkansas had produced another classic, the 16th time since 1939 that the game had been resolved in the fourth quarter.

It had gone according to party lines, Texas blast against Arkansas slash. When the Longhorns move on the ground they seem to get their entire student body into the play. The best of the student bodies this day was Worster, who finished with 94 yards on 25 carries. Burnett led Arkansas with 18 for 82.

Montgomery attempted 22 passes and connected on 14 for 205 yards. The pass is not a Texas weapon, as you may have heard, and Street risked only 10, completing six.

It seems woefully inadequate to say that Arkansas, now 9-and-1 and bound for a Sugar Bowl date with Ole Miss, lost with honor. At the finish Royal and Broyles met near midfield, and one of Frank's two daughters, hugging his sides, seemed to be crying.

Darrell reached down and put an arm around her neck and pulled her to him, consoling the little girl who lives in the home of the losing coach.

Alas, there was no one to hug and console the thousands of Arkansas fans who filed slowly, stiffly, unhappily out of the exits and toward the muddy parking lots.

About 15 minutes later, after visiting the locker room, Mr. Nixon climbed into his helicopter and whirred off into the distance. He had seen a helluva football game. And he had seen the Texas first team all day.

Texas had scored 15 points in 15 minutes against the second best team in the country and fought from behind to win what may be its second national title in six years.

As the Reverend Mr. Graham no doubt would point out, there is a message in here someplace about faith, hope and perseverance, and a good defense.

HE WHIPPED THE ESTABLISHMENT

By Si Burick

From The Dayton Daily News

The Little Old Champion has put the lie once again to the adage that they never come back. At 60, Paul Brown has scored the greatest victory of his career as an infighter.

The bald man with the pink complexion has brought another adversary, the strongest he ever faced, to his knees. He beat Art Modell. He whipped Pete Rozelle. He conquered the whole damn National Football League. He whipped The Establishment.

What Paul did on his day of glory was to strong-arm the Cleveland Browns, the team he organized in 1946, then directed and coached through 1962 before he was summarily dismissed out of the NFL and into the American Football League.

More than that, he forced Modell, the man who canned him and a scrapper of renown himself, to put the realigned Browns into the same four-club division that includes the Cincinnati Bengals. The Bengals are, of course, the new team, which Brown founded a little over a year ago and began coaching last July.

To say that this is the ultimate in revenge for Brown is putting it mildly. Once the switch of the Cleveland club to the AFL was achieved, it became perfectly logical to put the Browns in the same division with Cincinnati, but this merely tops the abject defeat suffered by Modell.

This is enough to put an ulcer on top of the ulcer that already has put Art in a hospital. Not even the $3 million he is expected to get for moving will pay off for that kind of physical and mental torture. It should be remembered that Modell not only operated the Browns, but also was president of the National League. Not many giants of sport have had to eat quite as much crow as this.

The Cleveland transfer means that starting in 1970 there will be two annual games, home and home, between the Browns and Bengals.

These are confrontations-to-come that are most pleasant to contemplate for those who adore the kind of violence in competition that may end on the field but starts in the front office. This is the stuff of which family feuds among the hill people were created.

It is a far better deal than Modell, who isn't quite the meanest man in the world, gave Brown earlier by agreeing to play a 1969 exhibition in Cincinnati. That was just tossing Paul a bone. Now Brown gets a chance at the whole roast.

The realignment which at least numerically equalizes the two football leagues at 13 teams apiece, now that Baltimore and Pittsburgh are also joining Cleveland in the AFL, must be scored as a Paul Brown achievement. The deal that puts the Colts and the New York Jets, who were adversaries in the last Super Bowl game, in the same division is also a master's stroke. The Jets pulled the shocker of early 1969 by beating the heavily favored Colts, thus taking the word parity out of politics and putting it logically into the councils of pro football.

When you get down to the nitty-gritty of the football world, Brown has made a habit of winning his important battles eventually. He founded the Browns in 1946, when they played in an upstart league known as the All-American conference. The NFL Establishment hated the new organization, which stretched from coast to coast, and competed for the signatures of boys fresh out of college by offering impossible bonuses.

Brown won five straight championships in his league and put pro football over in Cleveland, where it never had been successful in previous National League days, spectator-wise. (The old Rams had to move out to Los Angeles.)

The NFL smartly looked around and invited the three best franchises in the rival league to become full-fledged members. The AAC was destroyed, but Brown now was where he always wanted to be.

The old-timers in the NFL decided to give Paul a lesson in a manner he would never forget by booking the Browns against the defending champions, the Philadelphia Eagles, in their first game. Brown prepared well. He devised the five-man defensive line that so confounded the Eagles' blockers that their offense went to pot. Brown won the game, 35–7. And the Browns won the NFL title in their first year. Paul never was a man to be bothered by the odds.

Success came for a number of years. Then Modell bought the club. As an owner, he demanded to know more of what Paul was doing than any of Brown's previous bosses. Their relationship reached an impasse. One day, Brown was hatcheted out of his job.

So, he sat around in misery, drawing around $80,000 a year for not . . . repeat NOT . . . coaching the Cleveland Browns. Modell, honoring Brown's long contract, which had years to run, put him on the payroll as a consultant. Art did not ask for consultations, and Paul did not volunteer.

Eventually, Brown wearied of what could have been the tranquillity of the rich retirement. Yearning for another football team, he put together the syndicate that acquired for nearly $10 million the expansion franchise the AFL put in Cincinnati. Solidifying his honest intentions, he put in a bundle of his own cash. And the Bengals were born.

Modell, a onetime TV producer, wise to the importance of labels, was not about to give up his club's tag as the "Browns" even though they were named after the founder, who had become his archenemy.

Paul was back for only a year when he attended a league realignment meeting in March. There were 16 NFL teams, 10 AFL. The rival leagues had "merged" before the 1966 season. The agreement was to finalize the merger through realignment by 1970.

Most of the AFL boys were so pleased by the Super Bowl "parity" deal, they were willing to let matters stand. It was rigged for things to stay as they were, which tickled the rich NFL brothers no end. It also cheered Commissioner Rozelle, no matter how fair he wanted to be, because he, too, was NFL-oriented. This *fait accompli* pleased all but P. B.

Paul Brown got his hackles up. What was going on, anyway? He had it on paper. He went into the AFL, and took his partners along on the basis of honest reevaluation and, by 1970, an assured realignment. What the hell kind of a merger was this, if everything was status quo?

His kowtowing colleagues, listening to Paul's logic, had second thoughts. Adjournment was called for. So they met again in New York last week. Brown, this time with strong backing, conceded nothing.

Something and somebody had to give among the smug gentlemen of the National Football League. And capitulation came from, of all people, Modell, to give Brown, as I have said, the greatest comeback success story in sports history.

GALE SAYERS: THE HARD ROAD BACK

By Al Silverman

From Sport

Gale Sayers lay on his bed in a motel room in Washington, D.C., a day before the Chicago Bears' first exhibition game of the 1969 season. He was wearing white jockey undershorts and glistened like a bronze god. A friend, Henny Young, had come in the room and noted immediately that Sayers' skin was a deeper brown than usual. "You got a tan!" Young exclaimed. "Where'd you get that tan? You been sittin' in the sun?" Sayers laughed, a flashing, self-assured laugh, showing his white teeth and sharing his secret with no one.

The bronze body was hard and lean and the five-inch scar that ran along the inside of his right leg, thighbone to knee bone, knee bone to leg bone, that jagged badge of fellowship among professional football players, was not noticeable. But it was there and it filled the room with its presence; unspoken questions, urgent questions, were in the air.

The knee had been cut into last November 10 and cartilage removed and ligaments sewn up and now the finest runner in professional football the last four years—until November 10, 1968—was about to play in his first game since the injury.

Finally, a question was asked, not to Sayers but, warming up, to Sayers' roommate, Brian Piccolo, who lay on his own bed, the whiteness of his skin a startling contrast to Gale's bronze look.

"There's one big difference in Gale now," Piccolo said. "He runs all right until the knee starts to wobble." He laughed and Gale laughed and the visitors in the room laughed and, suddenly, the air was lighter.

Piccolo played fullback at Wake Forest. He was born in Massachusetts but raised, he said, in Fort Lauderdale, Florida.

"By way of He-Hung-High, Mississippi," said Sayers.

Pick grinned. "Don't get me started, Massa Sayers," he said. But he was started. The two had become roommates two years ago in Birmingham, Alabama, before an exhibition game, when the Bears decided hastily to room men according to position.

"Of all the places to spring it on us," said Piccolo. "I came up to the room and saw Gale and said, 'What are you doing here?' But it's been okay. We talk about everything, whatever goes on."

"Mostly race relationships," said Sayers.

"We're okay," said Piccolo, ignoring Sayers, "as long as he doesn't use the bathroom."

Someone asked Sayers, "Who would you want as a roommate if you had a choice?" He replied, "If you're asking me, what white Italian fullback from Wake Forest, I'd say Pick."

Some people find it difficult to understand the black humor, the needling that goes on between Sayers and Piccolo. The two keep it up even on the field. When Ross Montgomery, a rookie running back from Texas Christian, first heard it, he was astonished. Sayers and Piccolo use it therapeutically, as a way of easing into each man's world, a world that has been vastly separate for so long. The needling helps take the strangeness from each man's world, and it lessens tensions.

Sayers said, "Pick, show him the letter you just got." The letter had come from Chicago, from a man who had actually signed his name. It began:

"I read where you stay together with Sayers. I am a white man! Most of the people I know don't want anything to do with them. I just don't understand you. Most Italians I have met say that they stink—and they really do."

Piccolo interrupted. "Well, of course that's true. You can't get away from that."

Sayers roared, shaking his head. "I don't like your racist attitude," he said.

The rest of the letter described how the Bears smelled, how they had no quarterback, no receivers, no offensive line. And it ended: "Sayers will fold up like an accordion when he gets hit."

That was one question Sayers hoped to settle right away in the game with the Redskins. But he was disappointed to learn, earlier in the week, that he would not start, that he would be used only to run back kickoffs and punts.

Jim Dooley, a tall man with curly hair, who wears horn-rimmed glasses and looks more like a scoutmaster than the head coach of the

Bears, explained why Sayers would not be starting. "He's fine," Dooley said. "I know he wanted to start this game. I told him, 'Gale, look, we got an inexperienced line. Two of our regulars are out. They make a mistake—boom.' When he scrimmaged last week someone made a mistake and Butkus hit him. He understood afterward."

Perhaps he understood, but he was not happy. "They're babying me," he said. "I know they are."

All along, Sayers had refused to baby himself. He would not use crutches when his leg was in a cast. Right after the cast was removed, he began to lift weights on the leg. He started jogging in early February. He was examined on February 27, and Dr. Theodore Fox, who had performed the operation, told Sayers, "If there were a game this Sunday, you'd be able to play."

Dr. Fox believes in Sayers. He once defined the special quality that made Sayers the finest runner in football. "Factor X," he called it. "This stands for drive and motivation," he said. "Factor X elevates a player one plateau. It makes a star out of an average player and a superstar out of a star." Dr. Fox said that his operation on Sayers' knee would contribute 60 percent to Sayers' recovery and "Gale's strong desire to return—Factor X—will add the other 40 percent."

There could be no doubt about that desire. "I worked hard to get up there," Sayers had said midpoint in his recuperation period, "and I'm going to work twice as hard to stay up there." At that time, an article in a Chicago newspaper suggested that running backs with knee injuries rarely come back to top form and that Sayers might have to spend the rest of his career as a flanker or at some other position. The article infuriated Gale. "I saved it," he said, "because when I do come back as a runner, I'm gonna show it to him." And then, as if to underscore his determination, he drew out the words—"I . . . Will . . . Be . . . Back."

When rookie camp opened in Rensselaer, Indiana, in mid-July, Sayers was there. His first day in camp, he insisted on taking part in the scrimmage. On one play he started running to his right. Willie Holman, the Bears' huge and mean defensive left end, came across and blind-sided Sayers, crashing him to the ground. Others piled on. Sayers got up by himself. He continued to play. Finally, the scrimmage was over. He had carried the ball a half-dozen times, gaining six yards through the middle once, five another time. But no one said a word to him. Sayers felt he was being ignored by the coach, the trainer, the Bears' doctor. But that was the game plan. Trainer Ed Rozy says, "The instructions on him were don't even mention it. Make him forget it."

In desperation Sayers went up to Ed McCaskey, who is the Bears' treasurer, a son-in-law of George Halas and a confidant of Sayers.

"How'd I look?" Sayers asked.

"You're all right," McCaskey said, and turned away.

When the veterans came in to camp, Gale was used sparingly. The younger backs, Mike Hull, Ralph Kurek and Montgomery, did most of the hitting. Dooley was going easy with Sayers, but also with veterans Piccolo and Ronnie Bull, who had a record of preseason injuries. But the lack of contact drills worried Gale because of his timing. "With Piccolo or Bull in there," he said, "the timing is different. The guards can be a little slower. But with me in there they've got to go full speed. I'm much quicker, so they have to set up their blocks fast. When I'm in there, I'm running up their backs."

But he did scrimmage a bit. In the Saturday scrimmage before the Redskins' game, he went up the middle. Someone grabbed him by the legs and Dick Butkus rammed him in the chest. Ed Stone, who covers the Bears for *Chicago Today,* was there and says that Sayers seemed to show his old moves. "I talked to Johnny Morris, who's on TV now," Stone says, "and he said that on a sweep it looked like Gale might have the slightest hitch. But," Stone said, "I can't see anything. It looks like it's all there."

On the morning of August 2, at breakfast, Sayers and Piccolo talked about Vince Lombardi and Washington and playing the first exhibition game of the season. Both men were dressed casually, in T-shirts and shorts. A waitress came over to Sayers. "Can I ask you your name?" she said to him. Pick mumbled loud enough for all to hear, "They all look alike."

Piccolo said he thought he would like to play a little bit for Lombardi before his career was over.

"I can arrange that," Sayers said.

"Would you? I'm tired of playing in your shadow. I want to be a legend in my own time."

The game was less than 12 hours away and they talked about what it meant to them. "You can't treat it as any game," said Sayers. "Do that and you have a short season. Every game is important, and you always like to start off with a win after all that training."

"But it's not like life or death," said Piccolo. "Lombardi and Washington is not the same as Lombardi and Green Bay. Certainly, you want to beat Vince, but it's not the same as beating him with a team that's in your division."

"I know Lombardi's going to be up," Sayers said. "The Redskins are going to be up." His thoughts suddenly became disconnected. "I hate to lose," he said. Then, as if the real meaning of the game had just come to him, he said, "I just want to show people I'm ready."

That was it—to show people that he was ready. It was a secret he had carried around for eight months, and even he did not know the answer. He had jogged, played handball, basketball and touch football. He had run full speed, he had made his patented Sayers cuts, he had been hit in camp and, through it all, the knee had held up. Now there was one more test, contact in battle against another team. He was 26 years old with four glorious and rewarding years behind him and now he must know about the future.

While Sayers attended a midmorning team meeting, I talked with the Bears' trainer, Ed Rozy. He is a grizzled Walter Brennan type who has been with the Bears for 22 years. "I'd say Gale's 99 percent now," Rozy said. "The big thing to overcome is the mental attitude, the subconscious feelings—is it or isn't it? See, he's got to believe it, it's got to be proven to him. Better than that, he's got to prove it to himself. That's why he had to go right out that first day in camp and scrimmage and try to get it over with."

Rozy talked with admiration about Sayers' dedication. At Rensselaer, Sayers would come down to the basement at 8 A.M. each day. He would take a whirlpool bath for 10 minutes to loosen up the knee, then go into the weight room and lift 60 pounds on the knee, lift those 60 pounds 50 times. Morning and night he would be down there lifting. "That's the mark of a champion." Rozy said. "The guy never quit on himself."

Rozy talked abstractedly about the injury. "It was a beautiful shot," he said on the film clip and still photo of the injury. "It shows Gale planting his foot with pressure applied to the outside of the leg. A beautiful shot," Rozy repeated, as if he were admiring a Picasso painting.

Sayers himself saw little beauty in the shot. One night last March he brought home the Bears' 1968 highlight film to show some friends, including his teammates George Seals and Frank Cornish. When the film came to the injury—the first time Sayers had seen it—Seals hollered, in jest, "Get up! Get up!" And a chill, almost like an electric shock, went through Sayers' body. After the guests had gone, he told his wife, Linda, "I'm never gonna look at that film again as long as I live." A couple of days later when he had to show the film to a group, he left the room just before the injury sequence. Eventually, he got over it, said to himself, the hell with it, and stayed and watched.

It was, no doubt, the most traumatic moment of his life. The Bears were at home and, in the second quarter, held a comfortable 24–6 lead over the 49ers in the ninth game of the season. Sayers had gained 32 yards in 10 carries. That gave him 856 yards rushing for the season so far, well ahead of all the NFL runners; he seemed on his way to the best year of his career, perhaps a record-breaking year.

In the huddle, quarterback Virgil Carter called for a toss to Sayers. Gale broke left, hoping to go outside the defense behind the blockings of tackle Randy Jackson. The 49ers' right linebacker, Harold Hays, began to string along the line, keeping his hands on Jackson in order to control him and prevent Sayers from breaking to the outside. Right cornerback Kermit Alexander, who also had the responsibility of turning the play inside, was trying to strip his blocker. Hays was controlling Jackson and defensive tackle Kevin Hardy was barreling down the line toward Sayers. So Gale knew he couldn't go wide and he tried to slip inside the blocker, as he often does.

At the instant he planted his foot, Alexander hit him with a low, rolling block. The cleats of Sayers' right shoe were anchored in the turf, preventing give, and the knee took the full shock of the blow.

Sayers knew immediately that the knee was gone. He thinks he turned to Alexander, who was standing over him, and said, "It's gone." He remembers motioning to the bench to come and get him and putting his arms around a couple of the Bear players. Then he passed out.

He came to as he reached the sidelines. Dr. Fox was there. "It's gone, Doc," Sayers said.

Dr. Fox checked the knee. "It's okay," he said, and started to walk away.

"Come back here!" Sayers screamed. "Tell it to me straight."

Dr. Fox looked at Sayers for a moment, then said, "Yes, you have torn ligaments in your knee."

At that moment, Sayers felt an overwhelming sense of loss, also of self-pity. He asked himself, why me, why did it have to be me? And he began to cry.

He was operated on late that afternoon. The quicker the surgeon can get in there, the better job he can do. "You wait 24 hours after one of those things," Dr. Fox said, "and the injury is like a bag of mush. It really would be like trying to stitch together two bags of cornmeal mush."

In medical slang, Sayers' injury is called "The Terrible Triad of O'Donoghue." This describes the tears of the three ligaments in the knee and is named after Dr. Don H. O'Donoghue of the University of Oklahoma, the dean of football physicians. It is a common operation now. The estimate is that there are 50,000 football victims each year, 50,000 who require knee surgery.

The operation took three hours and when Sayers came out of it he remembers the doctor saying, everything's okay, and Sayers not believing him. "You wouldn't lie to me? You wouldn't lie to me?" he kept repeating. Linda Sayers was there and she says that Gale actually got up and started screaming to Dr. Fox: "YOU WOULDN'T LIE TO ME?"

He is much more emotional than has been generally understood. He is much deeper, too. In his first couple of years with the Bears he was very shy, a little frightened, unsure of himself off the field and wary, very wary, of strangers. He began to change about two years ago. Symbolically, he stopped cutting his hair short for football. He wears a natural now and someone wrote him a letter blaming his knee injury on his "long" hair. He became a stockbroker for Paine, Webber, Jackson and Curtis in the Chicago office. He worked on his public speaking. He began to respond to people, and to the world around him. Recently, Ed McCaskey has helped make a reader of Sayers. McCaskey gave Sayers *The Autobiography of Malcolm X* and Sayers devoured it in three days. In quick succession he read a novel, *Siege,* Eldridge Cleaver's *Soul on Ice* and the classic Ralph Ellison novel *Invisible Man.* All are on black themes and all seemed meaningful to Sayers. "Something," he says, "keeps you going into books and you don't want to put them down." He seemed to relate most to Malcolm X. "He was a drug addict for so many years and got out of it," Sayers said. "I believe he could do anything he wanted."

He admires people like that, people who can overcome. He is that way himself. In his rookie year, he would vomit before every game. Finally, he decided he had to stop, that he was using up too much nervous energy. "I would go out of the dressing room," he said, "tired, beat." So he started talking to other players, thinking of other things and he disciplined himself to stop vomiting.

Now the discipline, the fight, concerns the knee. He rested in his Washington motel room an hour before the team dinner, which would be followed by the ankle taping and then the bus ride to Robert F. Kennedy Stadium and a football game. The television set was on. The Baltimore Orioles were playing the Oakland Athletics and Sayers watched idly. And as he watched, the question was slipped to him:

"Do you think about the knee?"

"I think about it," he said, "I never stop thinking about it. When I'm in my room listening to records, I think about it. Every day a thought about it goes through my mind. I know it's fine, but I think about it."

He has considered seriously about going to a hypnotist. "I remember Don Newcombe went to one about his fear of flying. If I knew of a hypnotist in Chicago, I would probably go to one." But then he said he was not sure that he was the type to be hypnotized.

His mind was a jumble of emotion. He thought of an old teammate, Andy Livingston, who had hurt a knee against the Packers a couple of years ago and was never the same again. But he also thought of the old Bear halfback, Willie Galimore, who had survived two knee operations and come back fine (only to die in an automobile crash); and of Tommy Mason, who has had six knee operations and still plays. Gale blamed the failures on human weaknesses. "They didn't work at it," he said. "I worked at it." He groped for words. Finally, words came. "I consider this my game. A damn injury like that is not going to keep me out of it."

Looking at Sayers in the Bear dressing room deep beneath RFK Stadium, the strong statement he had made a few hours earlier seemed remote and irrelevant. He sat slumped in front of his locker. It was five minutes to seven and he would have to go out on the field for pregame drill in 15 minutes. He was wearing his cleats, his white game pants with the orange piping down the side, and a white T-shirt. He sat on a folding chair in front of his locker. He was bent over. His head was bowed, his eyes were closed. He was leaning on his elbows, holding his head in his hands, his two thumbs resting between his eyes. He sat there quiet as stone, as if in a trance. He was unapproachable.

George Seals, the 265-pound offensive guard, the man Sayers had ridden behind for so many of his long-gainers, was dressing in a corner. A close friend of Sayers, he was asked whether he felt any extra pressure to protect Sayers because of the knee. Seals shook his head. "To me," he said, "that would be conceding something. Football is a very emotional game. When you step out onto that field, you cannot concede a thing. Gale certainly wouldn't want it that way."

Seals, who had his own knee operation last March and was still far from being 100 percent, was with Sayers when the cast was removed from Sayers' leg. He was astonished to see that there was very little atrophy in the leg. "He's not human," Seals said. "After he got that cast off, he'd go out in the afternoon, morning, every night, doing things constantly. Many athletes come back from knee injuries lacking quite a bit. I feel if Sayers comes back, he'll be the one that comes back all the way."

And still Sayers sat there, bent over, trancelike, almost in the fetal position. Bennie McRae, the Bears' veteran defensive back, came over, leaned down and whispered to Sayers: "Are you ready man?" Sayers nodded. "You all right? You're gonna be all right," McRae said soothingly. "You're ready. I know you're ready." He put an arm on Sayers' shoulder. "Hang loose." Sayers nodded again. McRae drifted away and Sayers remained cast in stone.

I was thinking various things. I was thinking about the knee . . . how it happened, could it happen again, how would it hold up . . . hoping I could make it through the game. That's the mental torture of football and I think this is going to afflict me as long as I play this game.

Finally, it was 7:10 and the players started out. Backfield coach Ed Cody came close to Sayers and said, "About a minute, Gale."

Sayers shook himself, rose, slipped on his white jersey with the big navy blue numerals, 40, picked up his helmet and clattered out of the room.

As you come through the runway leading up to the field, a distorted sound hits you, an eerie sound, like a piece of heavy machinery sucking out air. It is only when you get through the runway and hit the dugout that you finally recognize the sound—it is the roar of the crowd.

It was a stifling night. The temperature was in the 80's, there was no breeze stirring and the humidity menaced the soul. The weather forecast was for scattered thunder showers, but the clouds in that Washington twilight looked benevolent.

Sayers was throwing left-handed with Ronnie Bull, he and Bull trotting up and down the field exchanging passes. Then the Washington Redskin players poured out of their dugout and milled around the entrance. Sam Huff was leading them. He stood there, waiting for them all to come out before leading the charge across the field. "Everyone up?" he asked. Vince Lombardi, wearing a short-sleeved shirt, black tie, black pants and the look of a bus driver, grew impatient with Huff. "Okay," Lombardi barked, "let's go, let's take 'em." There were joy and exhilaration in his voice as he ran out on the field with his men. Clearly, he was glad to be back in the game.

Sayers, taking part in a passing drill, caught a short pass and ran by Lombardi. The Redskin coach stopped him. They shook hands. "I'm very glad to see that you've overcome your injury," Lombardi said. Sayers mumbled his thanks.

Sayers remembered meeting Lombardi in Commissioner Pete Rozelle's office in New York last spring, the spring of his recuperation, the spring of his anxieties. Lombardi said to Sayers, "How do you feel, son? I hope to see you out there this fall." And Sayers said, "You'll see me August 2." And so he had.

Now it was 7:30 and two Bear players started the kicking drill. The punts came out of the sky like fireworks, except that the boom was heard first, then the ball was seen soaring in the air. Sayers caught the first punt and ran it back 15 yards, crouched, darting, making the moves that had thrilled people for the last four years. He caught another punt, then a third, and a fourth. Then he was in another pass drill. He went down and out, toward the Redskin side of the field, taking a long pass over his shoulder. Two skinny Redskin kids, No. 5 and No. 3, the field-goal kickers, were together when he went by. They looked at Sayers, then turned to say something to each other, gossiping like a couple of old maids at a soda fountain.

Finally, the drill was over and the Bears returned to the dressing room to put on their shoulder pads and wait for the start.

It had been raining for five minutes when the teams lined up for the kickoff, a hard, slanting rain with thunder and lightning and a rising wind. The field, especially the skin part, the Washington Senators' infield, was already filling up with puddles.

The Bears were the receiving team. Gale Sayers was deep, at his five-yard line, with Ross Montgomery stationed just in front of him. Just as the kicker moved forward, Sayers hollered to Montgomery to deploy right. Sayers, who captains the kick and punt return team, always tells the other deep back where to go. The idea is for Sayers to cover three-quarters of the field, to make sure that he gets the football.

He got the football. He took it easily on his six-yard line and started straight up the middle. One man broke through the wedge and came on to challenge Sayers. "I feel I can always beat any man one-on-one," Sayers has said, "and two-on-one I can beat 75 percent of the time." Sayers gave the one man his inside move, a head and shoulder fake, and the man was out of it and Sayers was flashing to the right, toward the sidelines.

"The thing that makes Gale different," Brian Piccolo had said earlier, "is the way he's able to put a move on somebody and not lose a step. He gives a guy a little fake and he's full speed. I give a guy a move like that and it takes me 15 yards to get in stride."

Sayers was in full stride now, streaking down the sidelines. Two Washington defensive backs angled in on him around the Redskin 40. One lunged at him and Sayers just pushed him away with his left arm. The other threw himself at Sayers, jostling him momentarily. But Sayers kept his feet, regained control and sped triumphantly into the end zone. There was a purity, a shining purity to that run, that contrasted in a strange and rather beautiful way with the indecent weather and the spongy field. The first time he had carried the ball in combat since his knee injury, which was the worst kind of a knee injury you can have, he had broken one. It was as if all the questions had been answered, all the doubts resolved about the condition of Gale Sayers. It was an illusion, of course; it was much too early to form a judgment on Sayers' recovery. But the illusion was heightened by the clap of thunder that accompanied Sayers' last steps into the end zone.

One illusion was, however, quickly dispelled. It was not a touchdown after all. The referee ruled that Sayers had stepped out of bounds on the Redskin 25. Sayers said later that he could not see the sideline markers because they had been obscured by the rain. But it was still a 69-yard run and surely it held some meaning for Gale Sayers, for the Chicago Bears—and maybe for those 50,000 players who fall victim to a knee injury every year.

And that was all there was to the game, really. Later, the Bear coaches had to throw out the films of the game because nothing could be seen. After the Sayers' run the rain intensified and the entire first half was played in a blinding cloudburst that ruined the field and left the players dispirited. The Redskins won, 13–7. Sayers came out on the field 12 times, but carried the ball only once more. Dick Butkus took a short kickoff and lateraled to Sayers who piled 17 yards up the middle before he was pulled down in the glop.

The next morning Sayers was eating breakfast at 7:15. He had hardly slept that night. He says it usually takes him a day and a half to unwind after a game. He ordered ham and eggs but ate sparingly.

He listened while a friend read accounts of the game from the Washington morning newspapers. Sayers, it seemed, had almost gotten equal play with the Redskins. One story began this way: "It took the sellout crowd of 45,988 at RFK Stadium last night only a matter of seconds to see for themselves that Gale Sayers is as good as ever . . ."

He grinned when he heard that. He thought it was true and now he felt more assured because he had passed the first test. After months of hard work, months filled with doubt and pain and the mental torture that only a knee victim can understand, he had passed his first test. He knew it was only a beginning, but it was a good beginning.

BEATEN AT THEIR OWN GAME

By Kaye Kessler

From the Columbus Citizen-Journal

You've probably had a hundred days like it—you know, bounce out of bed, look at your big, beautiful No. 1 self in the mirror and the glass cracks. Your dog bites you, car keys fall in the disposal, your kid blind-sides you, coffee's rancid and you electrocute yourself trying to get the toast to pop up. You're up all right, but not emotionally. So you drive your car into a crater right there in the middle of Third Street. Yep, there's egg all over your face.

So Ohio State's almost almighty Buckeyes had one blow up on them!

For them, at least, it was a first. There they were last Saturday in sunny Ann Arbor, Michigan, looking across the line on that elegant Tartan carpet and they saw themselves. Then they were beaten at their own game.

Go tell it to Southern California's Johnny McKay—the Buckeyes are coming to the Rose Bowl again this January. Only they'll be wearing the maize and blue of Michigan and playing an awful lot like OSU.

But don't try to sell it to Henry Hill. Henry is the "walk-on" junior middle guard for Michigan that waylaid OSU on its way to immortality. And Henry was pretty indignant when it was suggested Michigan bashed OSU out of a boatload of prestige and impressive streaks with the Buckeyes' own game.

"That's our game, not theirs," the 5-11, 210-pound junior bellowed.

It was, indeed, Michigan's game from any angle you care to slice it as the 15-point underdogs doubled up the Buckeyes 24–12 and thus settled an awful lot of hish-hash in one fell swoop.

The most stunning upset of the season assured one and all that the Big Ten will not be sending an also-ran "cheese champ" to the Rose Bowl; it answered that gnawing question being bandied about whether OSU is the greatest ever, and it proved that tired old bromide again about these "given" Saturdays.

What it also may have proved is that the inspiration of the Rose Bowl incentive is bigger than outright titles and No. 1.

There were as many reasons for the big "TILT" the Buckeyes registered in this showdown game with the Wolves as there were people in the big bowl—and it was overflowing with college football's all-time biggest crowd of 103,588.

Michigan merely played what first-year leader Bo Schembechler called "our greatest game" at the same time the Buckeyes put their worst on display. Everything that went right for the Buckeyes all season—the good bounces, helpful calls, opponents' fumbles and interceptions—went awry for them just as they were about to become one of this century's rare back-to-back national champs.

"There wasn't anything off forcing a fire game. We're quicker inside than any team OSU faced.

"So what's Kern do on the very first play of the game, ha, he runs for 25 yards," Bo laughed.

Kern did not go far thereafter. In his next 11 carries he got just 28 yards. Rex, whose celebrated and chronic sore shoulder was abnormally painful before the game, hit his first five passes in the drives leading to a 12–7 OSU lead. But then he managed to find a Buckeye only one more time on his next 12 pitches and four times others fell into Wolverine hands.

Woody Hayes, the silver-haired dean whose dream was shattered along with some of his composure, admitted in a terse post-game conference that the "offense was miserable the second half."

It was that. Except for the furiously determined Otis, whose 144 yards pushed his single season total to an OSU record 1027 and career mark to a school record 2542, the Bucks could generate no fire.

Except for crafty Mike Sensibaugh's 18-yard pass to Zelina on a fake fourth-period punting situation, there also was little imagination to it. The Bucks—behind and with rotten field position—fell into the fatal footsteps of some of their victims trying to play catch-up. The wingbacks carried only twice the entire game, the tailbacks only six times.

While OSU's offense slowly came unglued, its dynamic defense was blown apart quickly, unexpectedly.

Don Moorhead, a 6-foot-3, 200-pound junior quarterback, did the real damage. He worked against OSU's closed side all afternoon per instruction, then pecked them to death over the middle with passes mostly to tough tight end Jim Mandich. The old Kern-White routine only more so.

This combo worked for the first two scores and Frank Titas' placements were all the damage needed. What really breathed fiery life into the Wolves was OSU's decision to go for a two-pointer after Michigan jumped offsides when White kicked a good placement after the second Buck TD, a decision flukey, friend, about this decision that snapped college football's longest win string at 22, deprived the Bucks of a Big Ten record 18th straight league win and put a machete to their cherished No. 1 ranking.

It's just that Michigan was on a crusade last Saturday and the Buckeyes tried to take one more game in stride. And emotion won out.

"Our kids were so emotionally high before the game I just knew they couldn't lose," said Schembechler. "Furthermore, I didn't want to go to the Rose Bowl as a runner-up and neither did the kids. I wouldn't have said that, but those people out there wanted a winner. Well, by gum, they've got one . . . we'll play Southern Cal or UCLA and I'll tell you one thing, they won't be any better than Ohio State."

The destruction of No. 1 was a two-way stretch, however, Michigan applying the pressure and the Buckeyes succumbing to it. The Wolverines were inspired to tremendous heights but the Buckeyes were emotionally and, unfortunately, offensively bankrupt.

The game started about as even the dreamiest Wolve fan could imagine. Neither team moved the first series, then OSU struck swiftly, thanks to Larry Zelina's 35-yard punt return to Michigan's 16.

Senior fullback Jim Otis, who was the only Buck to measure up offensively, got the TD on a one-yard dive after a Rex Kern to Jan White pass picked up 14. But the placement by Stan White missed.

Then all hell broke loose. Michigan scored the next four times it had the ball, putting OSU behind for the first time since the Rose Bowl on a 45-yard march capped by fullback Garvie Craw's three-yard burst.

The Bucks went 73 in 11 plays, Kern hitting White on a 22-yard scoring pitch the first play of the second period to recapture the lead. But OSU then succeeded in going the final 44:52 of this game without scoring and that's some feat for a team that was second in the nation and had gone scoreless in only three quarters the eight previous games.

All 103,588 of those fans sat there in stunned disbelief, apprehensively waiting for the Buckeye bomb to explode. Little did they know the fuse was soaking wet.

Surely Rex would come riding to the rescue as he always does, ripping around end with 43 Buckeyes running interference. Or he'd quick flip to Leo Hayden. Maybe even a halfback pass, huh?

So Jan White hurt an ankle badly in the second quarter and was done for the day. That's where Buckeye depth wins out. Dick Kuhn is even better than Jan. You say Rex's shoulder is killing him? Shucks, that's the cue for Ron Maciejowski to do his tricks.

But what's this? The Bucks are gambling for a yard on fourth down at their own 42 starting the fourth quarter, and Wolverine tackle Pete Newell smears Rex for a two-yard loss? It's gotta be fiction. That's OSU you're messing with there, Michigan.

What was Michigan's secret?

"Our No. 1 plan was to keep Kern from running the football," said Bo. "We knew Otis would get his yards [144 in 28] but we wanted to stop Kern."

Putting the lid on OSU's coffin was senior defensive halfback Barry Pierson—who intercepted three passes—returning a punt 60 yards to set up Moorhead's touchdown making it 21–12.

Nailing it down was Frank Titas' 26-yard field goal after a Buckeye try from 53 yards fizzled and it mattered not that Titas went for an NCAA record missing four field goal attempts the scoreless last half.

One of the more than 21,000 Ohioans who made the 185-mile trip from Columbus sat stunned before starting the 185,000-mile trek home. "It's really a dream, isn't it?" he asked. "I'm going to wake up pretty soon and then they'll start the game."

A woman with a scarlet and gray pompom emerged from a rest room and said, "It just shows they're human, but they sure picked a helluva time to prove it. And beaten at their own game, yet."

Try telling that to Henry Hill and his Big Ten co-champion Rose Bowl-bound Wolverine buddies. They're going places.

For the 8–1 co-champion Buckeyes, they've got only Monday night's appreciation banquet in Ohio Union—and next year to look forward to—as they start picking up the No. 1 pieces.

THE AWFUL ANACHRONISM

By Jim Hawkins

From The Baltimore Sun

The Army-Navy game, dear reader, is a joke.

An awful anachronism.

As out of touch with the times as a plodding brontosaurus.

Big-time college football has passed the service academies by.

All the ancient and honorable classic confrontation needs now is an all-out endorsement from Spiro T. Agnew.

Saturday, for the 72nd time since 1890, the ballyhooed but boring battle will be reenacted near the banks of the Schuylkill River, in the city W. C. Fields loved, Philadelphia.

And, for the 72nd time since 1890, all America will stop to watch. To even suggest subtly that Army-Navy is anything less than Armageddon is to be branded forever a fellow-traveling communist conspirator.

By mid-morning, the lines will be drawn. The "Beat Army" flag-wavers on one side of the sprawling stands in John F. Kennedy Stadium and the "Beat Navy" banners on the other.

Only Philadelphia would tolerate such a place. One look at the gaping white elephant and you understand why the WPA failed.

There isn't a good seat in the joint. The bleachers are all backless and well sprinkled with splinters—and at least 60 percent seem to be out of sight in the end zone. Pigeon droppings from the days of Doc Blanchard and the "Team Named Desire" still cover the steps and hang from the rafters.

The attendance will once again be announced as 102,000. It's always 102,000, even though there are only 98,000 spaces to sit in and a lot of the tickets are never used. How would it sound to have less than 102,000 in the crowd? Somebody might get the idea somebody didn't care.

Particularly this year. One has to wonder why anyone in his right mind would waste $8.50 to watch two teams with a combined total of four wins flail away for a while.

Even the New Mobilization Committee to End the War in Vietnam has decided to abstain from even a token demonstration at the game, stating, "It's not worth the effort of demonstrating against."

But tens of thousands of fans with their full flasks and flowers—and 40 or so million more at home with their peanuts and beer—will bear witness just the same, fighting the miles of traffic jams and the impossible parking maze just to say they saw it.

After all, Army-Navy is a national institution. The social event of the Eastern college season. The two academies could send their 150-pound plebe teams for an afternoon of two-handed touch, and the attendance would still be 102,000.

The caliber of competition has nothing to do with interest or attendance. Army-Navy is just the place to be Saturday, like the Kentucky Derby, or the Masters, or the World Series. The Pied Piper didn't have any more pull.

The city fathers in the City of Brotherly Love estimate 60,000 people will converge on Philly this weekend, specifically to see Army against Navy. And they'll spend about $1.5 million that the city ordinarily never would have seen.

It's the time for all those corny quotes from the opposing coaches, like "they put their pants on one leg at a time," and "the second season starts Saturday," and "throw out the record books for this one."

Gosh.

The brigade of midshipmen, well scrubbed and decked out in their sailor suits, and the cadence-conscious corps of cadets will, of course, be there, filling in in their time-honored 7,500-man formations that take half the morning and fill the whole field. Ordinarily, anytime you put that many young people together, all you can smell is the marijuana burning.

Unfortunately Saturday, at 1:20 P.M., the football game must start.

Then the social set can start thinking about leaving early to beat the traffic.

Because something might start to smell after all.

GAMBLERS ARE IN THE PRO-FOOTBALL HUDDLE

By Bill Surface

From Argosy

Gale Sayers, the Chicago Bears' leading halfback, winced as he tried to step down on his aching, heavily taped leg. He grimaced so much that his worried-looking coaches knew that he would not play and the Bears would be unable to realistically compete against the Cleveland Browns in their game six days later. Instead of concentrating their defense to stop Sayers' running, the Browns' defensemen could simply anticipate what the Bears had to do: pass. Their only logical alternative, a member of the Bears decided, was to hopefully surprise the unprepared Browns with passes after they had practiced all week on containing Sayers.

From the outset, the plan received unprecedented secrecy. First, the Bears' management omitted Sayers' name from the list of injured players that every pro-football team is required to send to the National Football League office by each Tuesday so that all meaningful injuries can be simultaneously announced in order to prevent gamblers from secretly capitalizing on them. Then, the Bears' practices were so tightly guarded and the players so cautious that none of the hometown reporters covering the team, tipsters for the Browns, or the former FBI agents hired by the NFL to ferret out suspicious information, learned about Sayers' condition until minutes before the kickoff.

The injury, to be sure, had not been concealed from big-time gamblers. So much money was suddenly bet on the Browns while they were favored to win by only six points that major bookmakers in Chicago and Louisville put the game in what they call "the circle" by declining all further bets until they also found the reason for the large volume. After apparently learning about Sayers' injury, records seized in raids indicate, major bookmakers quickly laid off their bets on the Bears in Cleveland and Youngstown, Ohio, New York, New Orleans, Miami, Las Vegas and Nassau before revising their line to make the Browns 8-point favorites. The Browns, by winning 24 to 0, beat the original point spread by a comfortable 18 points.

One fact about the incident is obvious: although Pete Rozelle, the pro-football commissioner, reported that he failed to establish any connection between the Bears and gamblers after questioning Sayers and George Halas, the Bears' owner, the betting "edge" could hardly have changed unless someone who knew about Sayers' condition leaked it to the gamblers. More important, this type of apparent relationship is far from isolated. As early as 1967, *Argosy* revealed that gamblers were making such a determined effort to penetrate the inner workings of pro football that they could eventually destroy the sport. Instead of being subsequently abated by pro-football's anti-gambling unit, bookmakers and gamblers not only are continuing to gain ground; they are, in the parlance of the game, also making a surprising number of "first downs."

The first downs have occurred in such strategic places that the current season began on the embarrassing note of Joe Namath, the heralded quarterback of the world-champion New York Jets, being unable to report to his team's training camp without facing suspension from football because he had not complied with an order to: 1) end his alleged "associations [with undesirables] problem"; 2) sell his reported 50 percent interest in the Bachelors III bar that, he was told, has been a reported meeting place for both petty and major bookmakers, layoff men, odds makers, narcotics dealers, hired gunmen and some of the Mafia's highest-ranking members. Many of the men's calls from the four pay phones on the wall of Bachelors III, not unexpectedly, were said to have been to other bookmakers or to claim "inside stuff" on forthcoming football games.

Such indiscreet men don't necessarily obtain the "inside stuff" at places where they telephone. But professional gamblers have developed techniques in most if not all cities where pro-football teams are located, to help anticipate the outcome of a game without risking outright bribery and the resultant imprisonment for themselves and lifetime banishment from the game for players. Specifically, some gamblers find it more profitable to know in advance that an undefeated team favored to beat a mediocre opponent by 17½ points is dangerously overconfident than to have fixed the game by paying a fullback to deliberately fumble in a crucial play. Chances are, in pro-football's age of specialization and speed, that the fullback would be replaced by a competent substitute and negate the "lock."

It is equally widespread for gamblers to have prior knowledge of innumerable seldom-discussed situations that, they insist, "keep you on the right side of the points." Has a team, for example, shown in practice that it is plainly "up" for a game or is it "down" because of dejection, demoralization or dissension? Is there unreported bitterness between players and coaches, or racial strife in which a black is unlikely to block for a white player in a certain situation or vice versa? Is a flanker, listed as having an "injured hand," fully recovered? Or has a key blocker's ankle been injected with Novocain and is it unlikely to withstand a full game? Is a quarterback upset by problems concerning money, a wife, girl friend, Internal Revenue Service or (as occurred just before the 1969 Super Bowl) an irate hoodlum's direct threat to "get you"? Such intelligence, constantly updated until game time, sometimes even includes items about a carousing player who either has a hangover or fears he contracted syphilis the previous night.

Insidious gamblers, in some cities, have almost instant access to the answers to these types of questions. Sometimes, using ex-football players as intermediaries, gamblers simply befriend rookies on pro teams and, by the time the men become starters, tend to be considered good friends. Such acquaintances are conveniently developed among players who live in the favor-seeking world of college football that often enable them to buy 69 cents' worth of toothpaste and leave the pharmacy with $10 worth of toilet articles. Though now professional athletes, some players still look for the deal. Obligingly, the seemingly respectable friend can get the player cheap rates on an apartment or might even pay a proportionately higher share of the rent and use the apartment while the player returns to his home during the off-season. The friend is an introduction to saloons where the player can put reasonable amounts on a "tab" that is never collected and, on many occasions, can meet friendly women.

Few "good deals," it seems, are too trivial to be rejected by some high-salaried players. At least two members of a team in the American Football League were accused of regularly stopping at a dairy and fruit store, allegedly owned by the Mafioso gamblers, while a player in the National Football League rode so often in a known gambler's Cadillac that he was compelled to take at least two lie-detector tests on whether or not he had fixed games.

Once such men become trusted acquaintances, they are not hesitant to move into places where they can obtain last-minute information on a team and, as the game progresses, know about injuries that may never be reported. A plain-looking bettor and a business partner of a Detroit Lion even rode the team bus to one game and, during most Lions' games, held ice packs on injured players. The bettor and his friends remained on the bench, despite warnings by police, until the Lions' management was fined $4,000 by the NFL because "unauthorized persons . . . were permitted to have sideline passes and sit on the Lions' bench during games."

Fortunately, many frightened players terminate such friendships when they are warned that associating with "undesirables" could cause their suspension.

Many more players, it appears, escape warnings about associating with probable gamblers simply because betting on pro football has outgrown the sport's oft-praised security unit. Rozelle has, to be sure, had the fortitude to demand that Namath end his alleged associations with "undesirables" and to suspend two outstanding players in 1963. As a result, a sort of legend has arisen that the "NFL's Security Unit of twenty-six ex-FBI agents" keeps players under such close surveillance as to make pro football the most heavily policed sport in history.

Actually, the NFL Security Unit consists of two qualified full-time employees—Jack Donahy, a member of the FBI for sixteen years, and Bernie Jackson, an attorney and former policeman—who 1) visit each team's training camp to caution players about betting or providing information that would assist gamblers and 2) attempt to trace ominous but unfounded rumors that games are fixed. As need arises, the security unit employs former FBI agents working as private detectives in areas where pro-football teams are located. Such men try to find any variance in the opening odds of games on Monday and the closing line on the following Sunday. Or, if asked, the detectives stop in bars patronized by players. But, judging from the players whom the commissioner has publicly reprimanded, only obvious indiscretions surface. The fact that one part-time detective in a city can't easily determine if all players on a team are associating with "undesirables" was vividly illustrated when Big Daddy Lipscomb, the Baltimore Colts' outstanding lineman, suddenly died from an overdose of heroin.

The inability of investigators to determine if some players are associating with gamblers is further compounded. They usually cannot identify gamblers unless such men have been arrested or convicted for bookmaking or are Mafioso, and few if any such acquaintances have police records. Many bettors—and informants—are former players piqued at being prematurely released by a team or are neatly groomed executives of companies employing football players during the off-season at undeservedly high salaries.

Other gamblers have numerous techniques of obtaining information without befriending players. For one thing, gamblers simply watch the movements of players, as possibly occurred two years ago when Joe Namath rode from his apartment to the Jets' practice field to disclose that a thumb was too stiff for him to work out. Whereupon the Jets' publicity director telephoned newspapers. Bookmakers, according to one source, had already disseminated the information. For another thing, gamblers can sit in certain bars and wait for football players. Just as Mafioso assertedly operate in Bachelors III, gamblers appear in many of the approximately 100 bars and bowling alleys reported owned or operated by football players.

Some bars make Namath's bar look like a lunch counter. It is rumored that bettors can sit in one such joint near New Orleans' Bourbon Street, for example, and periodically see a Mafia bookmaker standing at the bar. People who were in a bowling alley near Chicago that was owned by an end periodically saw undesirables and brawls, but perhaps none more violent than the one that left a former guard for the University of Illinois dead with a bullet through the brain and a fullback for the Bears with lacerations in the skull. Or men can sit in a quieter bar on Chicago's North Side, where many of the swinging Bears and Cubs hang out, and watch or joke with football players as they drink and who usually leave with women who admit a preference for sleeping with huge football players. A sophisticated bettor must wonder if such women, regardless of where they are found, are paid by bookmakers to slip players drugs that could affect their performance in games.

Some players disobey the league's anti-gambling guidelines about visiting bars because, they argue, the question of gambling on pro football goes beyond players and their activities. It reaches, or has reached, so deeply into pro-football's ownership and management levels that, by comparison, its scope would scandalize baseball. For example, there was such widespread concern last summer following the disclosure that Charles Finley, owner of the Oakland Athletics, and William Bartholomay, president of the Atlanta Braves, purchased stock in three Las Vegas casinos that they were persuaded to voluntarily sell it. Yet the late Bert Bell became commissioner of the National Football League despite his salty reputation as a close friend of bookies, on the contention that his knowledge would enable him to detect any suspicious fluctuations in the odds of NFL games. (Accordingly, one of Bell's first decisions as commissioner was to suspend two members of the New York Giants for failing to report a bribe offer.) Moreover, Bell helped award a new franchise to Carroll Rosenbloom, a summer neighbor and wheeler dealer, even though Bell assertedly had to caution Rosenbloom about betting before and after he became owner of the Baltimore Colts.

After Joe Namath tearfully announced his "retirement," he claimed that Rosenbloom bet a large sum on the 1969 Super Bowl (in which Namath's team upset the heavily favored Colts by nine points).

There is no question, moreover, about the source of the money used to purchase several pro-football teams. Phil J. Iselin, the Jets' president, is also president and board chairman of Monmouth Park racetrack. Attorney Edward Bennett Williams was given control of the Washington Redskins, although he had made his fame and fortune as a criminal attorney by representing clients that ranged from gamblers to Frank Costello, once called the prime minister of the underworld. The New York Giants were founded by a former legal bookmaker and are now operated by his sons. Stories persist that Arthur Rooney started the Pittsburgh Steelers with $200,000 he won at Saratoga Race Course.

While there is no evidence that any owner of NFL or AFL teams has done anything illegal, it is apparent that some other owners gamble so precariously with money and mortgages, per se, as to conceivably become vulnerable to loan sharks or gamblers.

In essence, it has never seemed more imperative for players to be divorced from disreputable characters and gamblers. Rozelle has bluntly summarized the long-standing consequences: "A player betting on his own team could be taking the first step toward something more dangerous—the possibility that a series of losing bets would place him in a position to be blackmailed by unscrupulous gamblers."

But even so-called "inside stuff" on football games, significantly, has never been more valuable or potentially dangerous. Pro football has become such an intensively bet sport that, according to records confiscated by the Internal Revenue Service, bookmakers' clients include a millionaire in California and Nevada who bets between $100,000 and $150,000 on the sport each week and another fourteen businessmen who frequently bet $100,000 on pro football. Such bookies also have given individual credit ratings of $10,000 to 420 other gamblers with an affinity for pro football and $2,000 credit ratings to an additional 3,100 bettors. In all, these gamblers and the men who bet $20 with a bookie or five dollars on parlay cards sold in bars or offices now wager an estimated $145,000,000 on pro football each weekend and, in turn, foster a disturbing development.

The volume of bets is so large that many of the 62,000 bookies in the United States now divert enough of their bets to national layoff men for them to hold or reject huge amounts on any game without arousing enough suspicion to alter the game's point spread. Typically, a bookie on Long Island pleaded with two layoff men, in the transcript of a wiretapped conversation that I read, to "handle just part of this one" or promise "that I can count on you for five or ten [thousand] of this bet."

As *Argosy* warned two years ago, syndicated layoff men now control so many bets on football that the possibilities of their attempting to manipulate a game's outcome or margin of victory cannot be disregarded.

Most players probably would not act irrationally if they were offered a $10,000 bribe. Nobody knows what would happen if $1,000,000 were offered. Disturbingly, such a sum is now available.

"THERE'S THE MENTAL THING"

By David Kleinberg

From the San Francisco Chronicle

It was in the mid-60's that Mission High School—in the core of San Francisco's Chicano ghetto—last won a football game. Jim Palmer, a man of both intensity and patience, took over the coaching job in 1967, inheriting an eight-game losing streak from his predecessor.

Palmer, a black man who rarely knew defeat as a tackle during four championship years at San Francisco State, is still looking for his first victory. It's now 32 losses in a row, and next year he'll have a few players back, plus a sophomore team that lost its last game this season by the score of 82–6.

Palmer is hip to the people's needs. His quarterback has hair down past his shoulders. Some of his black men's Afros are so large they can hardly get their helmets on. But still there's the mental thing.

"The whole school's morale is tied up with football," Palmer said. "It's hard to get the kids up week after week. We usually play a pretty good half, then whammo. Things go wrong and the kids let down. It's not their conditioning. It's psychological. I know it's a mental thing."

At the start of the season, you might have looked at the schedule and realized that Game No. 7 would be a day for human drama—a bowl for losers, Charlie Brown vs. Charlie Brown, Charlie Brown vs. archvillain Charlie Brown.

Galileo had not win in six games, had won (excluding a game with Mission) only one of its previous 14 games. Mission had one win in six years, but knew Galileo, the city's usual perennial outcast, would have had a similar accounting except that a good back enrolled there in 1962—O. J. Simpson.

The mental thing. "This is it, men. This is the last chance to win," Palmer told his starters at the 40-yard line, calm deliberate words, positive words.

"You CAN do it. You beat the hell out of them in the first quarter and they'll quit. I promise it. Now we're going to kick off, and I want you to go down there and make them fumble. And if they don't fumble, you're going to hold them. And as soon as we get the ball we're going to take it in. Okay? Now [voice now rising to the occasion] who's going to win this . . . game?"

And Mission, in all earnest, replied, "Mission!" Why not? Mission spirit was high. They had roared, "Beat Gal" as they came out of the tunnel.

Only 150 Mission fans? Doesn't matter. Gal has 24, by body count. More seagulls in section L-LL by the 15-yard line than fans? 59,826 empty seats at Kezar?

Longest losing streak in the city's history? Doesn't count. Victory today. A halfback who had gained only one yard in 28 carries coming into today? Doesn't matter. Victory today. What do you want? All sins purged. When do you want it? Now.

On the field, now full with enthusiasm, after the coaches fire, convinced this might be the day of penance, Mission kicked off. Gal's Milton James took the kick on the 21 and promptly raced down the sidelines 79 yards to a touchdown. Mission was behind, 8–0, after 14 seconds.

Despair but not defeat. There's time left: in fact, a whole game minus 14 seconds.

Mission spirit, which had outlasted many touchdowns, could outlast this one. All they needed was the ball. They got it and quickly moved for a first down. The fans shouted, "First and ten, do it again," and on the bench was the strange spectacle of football players clapping and yelling the yell in rhythm with the stands.

Then it happened: Randy Tanksley, a tiny, black halfback, found light over the right tackle, instead of the usual gopher hole, and was off down the sidelines, the Mission bench running 51 yards with him.

They jumped on the sidelines. "That's my brother," a black kept repeating over and over. "Power to the People," a Chicano yelled. Joy was tempered to reality when Mission missed the conversion attempt to trail, 8–6, but in the second quarter, Mission spasmodically jerked an encore.

End Fealorai Vaita was alone on a deep pattern. Quarterback Mario Soriano wondered why defensive linemen hadn't dragged him down as he lofted a perfect pass. Vaita made the catch on the 20 and went in.

For the first time since the Flood, Mission had scored on its first two sequences. Mission led, 12–8. Oh, the delusion on the bench (and in the heart of the coach).

Galileo scored to retake the lead, 14–12, but Mission miraculously retook the lead, 20–14, when, following a short kick, Soriano threw 31 yards. Then, if needing further momentum, Mission held Gal on the Mission one as the gun signifying the end of the half saved a Gal score.

In the dressing room, Palmer pleaded for a stronger pass rush in the second half, pleaded that his team stop making mistakes, pleaded the things that all coaches plead at the half. We've got to hit. We've got to rush the quarterback. "I'm telling you like it is," Palmer intoned.

Like it was: Besides 20–14 on the board (Mission had scored 12 points all year), it was Mission 169–78 in intermission statistics, and fans had come to the tunnel to urge Mission into the third quarter.

There it was—the cheese on the table, the open door, come in and win. It was static in the opening minutes. It was you-kick, we-kick football. Then the clock stopped.

Mission punter Steve Jenks got a high pass from center, dropped the ball and was grabbed on his own 20. He was swung around and then did the most incomprehensible thing. He kicked the ball out of his own end zone for a safety, and Mission's lead dropped ominously to four points, 20–16.

The 24 Galileo fans went wild. The seagulls in L-LL, perhaps sensing a cold wind, began to scatter. Four plays after the safety, Gal scored again to lead, 22–20. Could Mission come back? It did in the first half.

"How could you?" Palmer strained to his offensive end. "I send you in with the play and you forget it."

Another Mission end dropped a pass. "I've never seen anything like it," a Mission assistant coach yelled. Never seen anything like it? Yes, he had last week, and the week before, and the week before. For 30 games before.

Another gun. Another quarter. Another Gal score: 28–20.

"Don't give up, guys," a Mission sub yelled from the bench. "We can still do it." The mood has changed.

Indeed, time was running out. Gal scored again: 34–20, and it was conclusively over. Palmer knew it and walked symbolically down the sidelines to be by himself. Linemen buried their heads in their hands. Soriano wept on the sidelines. "I don't believe it," he told himself.

With seven seconds left in the game, Gal scored its 30th point of the half to close it 44–20 and 149–14 in second-half yards. "If they start a fight," the Gal kickoff man hollered to the other 10, "turn and run."

The fight, for Mission, was gone. It even took a "God damn it, at least run off the field" to get them through the tunnel.

Palmer, grim and dejected, said to anyone who would listen, "They did it again. They played one good half and then went to sleep."

In the tunnel, a photographer tried to give his condolences to back Mike Bell. Bell had knocked the cameraman down accidentally in the first quarter and had apologized at the half.

"I guess it can't get much worse than this," the photographer offered in empathy.

And Bell replied with a half smile, "Have you ever been a black man in New Orleans?"

"TOO WEAK AN ETHIC FOR ME TO FOLLOW"

By Ray Didinger

From the Philadelphia Bulletin

The drill is called one-on-one. One ball carrier and one tackler, no one else in the whole world.

There are no draws. The man with the ball either stays on his feet or the tackler knocks him down.

One man must succeed and one must fail. The drill is designed that way. It is meant to be lonely.

One day last season at Swarthmore College, a coach handed the ball to 195-pound freshman Chris Leinberger.

Leinberger looked at his tackler, a friend who probably couldn't have stopped the muscular linebacker with two sets of brass knuckles.

But Leinberger was a freshman fighting for a starting position on the Garnet varsity. He wanted to make an impression so he put his head down and trampled his friend just like he knew he would.

However, instead of being the beginning of a great career at Swarthmore, it turned out to be the beginning of the end. That short 10-yard run made Leinberger take another look at this game he was playing.

And the more he looked at it, the fun seemed to evaporate.

"I began to think about the sport itself and what it takes to succeed," he said. "You can't be a nice guy, you can't give your opponent a break.

"There I came up against a friend and I ran over him because the football ethic said I should. It is too weak an ethic for me to follow when it means I have to step on people I care for."

So Leinberger has announced his retirement from football at the end of the current season. That means his brief collegiate career will be over November 22 after the traditional game between Swarthmore and Haverford.

Nobody called a press conference to announce Leinberger's decision. One of the things he likes about the Middle Atlantic Conference's College Division is that you can come and go in absolute privacy.

"I don't think my departure is going to excite many people," he smiled. "Last year we were the worst team (1–7) in the smallest conference in the country."

But Leinberger was an exception. Coach Lew Elverson admits the former Central League all-star center from Upper Darby High "is all football player."

Somebody even told Chris he was named to the All-ECAC team for his defensive play last season against Franklin & Marshall.

"Maybe I was, I don't know," Leinberger said nonchalantly. "I didn't bother to look it up. It doesn't make much difference now."

During that frosh year, he also competed for the varsity as a heavyweight on the wrestling team, a diver on the swimming team, and a pole vaulter on the track team. Even at Swarthmore some people got excited about his athletic ability.

Leinberger might have set some records at the little Quaker school if he had not become so involved with his Christian philosophy which now consumes most of his time and all of his thoughts.

"I'm in charge of the Swarthmore Young Life, a group which goes to high school kids and presents the teachings of Jesus Christ," he said. "We believe we should go out and love people the way He said we should. I'm trying to spend time where the kids go so I can get to know them and their hangups.

"From some kids I get a positive response immediately, but others are very suspicious. I think that tells something about our society. These students can't believe someone is willing to give them something for nothing even if it is only his own time."

Leinberger would be going to his weekly Young Life meeting in about 90 minutes, but that afternoon he was lying on the trainer's table with his left wrist throbbing. He had injured it last week against Dickinson—another typical losing Swarthmore opener.

Chris had scored the Garnet's only touchdown, a 28-yard run with an intercepted pass.

"I was glad I had scored, people pounding me in the back, but you can't let that go to your head," he said. "It's just a game, no different than a two-hand touch game in the street except we wear fancy jersies on Saturday. Some people just like to blow things out of proportion."

Leinberger still has the deep feelings of resentment toward football. They've been gnawing at him since that one-on-one drill last season, but he is still playing.

"Well, last year, I was a freshman and I enjoyed the ego-building, frankly," he said. "I told myself this was good for me because it released all my frustrations, but I know that's a simple rationalization. I either ignored my feelings or masked them.

"Then this year I came back by force of habit and then I left after the first week of practice. My mind was totally blown, it was all over when I realized I had come back to this again. But I talked to the coach and I felt compelled to fulfill the commitment I had made to him for this one season."

Leinberger sees no similar commitment next year.

"I believe I'll never play again," he said firmly. "If this season ended today and the next one started tomorrow, I'd leave tonight and never look back."

Chris is not sure if his disdain for the sport has had any effect on his play this year. He knows it does not help his sleeping.

"I couldn't sleep the night before the Dickinson game," he said. "All the thoughts went through my mind again, I remembered that to be the best I would have to treat people as inhumanely as possible. That wasn't what Christ taught.

"During the game, I guess I didn't play poorly but I know I've played better. I'm not sure if my thinking had anything to do with it," Leinberger said.

The 6-foot-1 sophomore spent his summer living and working in a Southwest Philadelphia black ghetto, which might account for his apathetic attitude toward games.

"I didn't even want to come back to school when I knew it meant leaving the community," Leinberger said. "I felt like I was copping out and running away from real life and returning to my convenient fantasy world here in college.

"I was born and raised upper-middle class and I've finally learned that this suburbia concept is just an illusion, something people run to when they cop out on what's really happening."

Leinberger slid off the trainer's table and put on a blue shirt with a "Work for Peace" button with a dove and the October 15 date of the Vietnam war moratorium pinned to his pocket.

Practice was over and the team was coming back to the locker room. "Will you be okay for the next game, Chris?" one said. Leinberger nodded.

"The guys on the team all know how I feel, the coach told them and I've talked to them about it," he said. "They seem to respect my opinions.

"Life is basically a very absurd thing, the more philosophy I read and study the more I am convinced," Chris explained. "But I think we must all find our own ways of giving it meaning. I must find mine."

And Leinberger knows he won't find his on 100 yards of grass on a Saturday afternoon.

Basketball

THE SPECIAL LEVEL OF LEW ALCINDOR

By Smith Barrier

From Greensboro (N.C.) Daily News

Reprinted by permission.

UCLA plays basketball on a special level, up there a couple miles above everybody else, and that's where Lew Alcindor operates.

The big guy was at his 7-foot-2 best in the 1969 NCAA national championship event, and when he unloosened the nets as his personal property, it was the third straight time for him and the UCLA Bruins to capture the most prized honor in collegiate basketball.

UCLA in the process beat a quick, alert Purdue team 92–72, and Alcindor himself made the triumph possible with his own operation on the level above the crowd. He swept the backboards as if he owned them, and he got 37 points, most of which he got by shooting the ball down into the basket.

If Purdue had had a hot hand with its own shooting, as it did in the semi-final win over North Carolina, it might have stayed even with Alcindor despite his towering advantages, but it did not. Rick Mount made his first two shots, then shot blanks for the next 14 attempts. That was Purdue's disintegration.

Alcindor did make several mistakes. He missed five shots of the 20 he tried, which seemed a shame, and he only wrapped up 20 of the rebounds. Naturally, that was far more than anybody else, but Big Lew did allow a few to get away from him.

It was Alcindor's game from the beginning, and 18,669 basketball fans applauded even though they might have been yelling for the underdogs.

Alcindor also took a hand, which appears to reach into the heavens, in the defensive maneuvers which shut out Purdue's great outside shooter, Mount, and his backcourt mate, Bill Keller, both of whom ruined North Carolina two nights ago.

Kenny Heitz drew the assignment on Mount, the job of keeping a hand in his face. Mount got his first two and then ran cold. From the time the score was 11–6, UCLA, Mount tried every possible angle, and nothing fell for him. Coach George King finally took him out, and Mount at that time had hit two of 15 attempts. The score was also 26–14 with eight minutes left.

But occasionally Big Lew moved outside a few steps (even his steps are giant-size) and stuck his hand in Mount's face, and thus further complicated Purdue's scoring problems. But despite Purdue's 23.5 shooting percentage it only trailed 42–31 at half time.

Maybe the Boilers, the Big Ten champions, did a little better the second half, but the Bruins never allowed them to build hopes too high. Mount had three of 18 the first half, Keller four for 13, and this had to improve. Mount did add 20 (for total 28) but Keller didn't scratch. One shot at their basket, and the Bruin forwards were able to lob the ball into Alcindor's level—he just dropped the ball down through the nets.

About the best competition was the infighting at UCLA's end of the floor, Alcindor versus Frank Kauffman, then Alcindor versus Jerry Johnson. The defense was shoving and pushing and leaning all over Big Lew, and he defended himself quite well, too.

But it ended almost as expected, UCLA with its third straight title, its fifth in the last six years. No team and no coach had ever achieved either. For Coach John Wooden it had been a great Alcindor era—one which he calls "an era of considerable efficiency."

And when it was over, Lew Alcindor got his folding chair and placed it under the goal. Methodically he unfastened each cord from the rim, just as methodically as he had operated in that same area for the 40 minutes previous.

Then he walked to the Purdue bench and shook hands with the Boilers, and the crowd applauded, and somehow Lew Alcindor moved up another level.

HIGH-SCORING CATASTROPHE

By Al Stump

From True

On the wide lips of Red Auerbach curved a smile of contempt. Auerbach knew what he knew. The Boston Celtics, for whom he is ex-coach turned general manager, were playing the Los Angeles Lakers last April, and although the Lakers, led by their incomparable captain, Elgin Baylor, held a 12-point, third-period lead in pro basketball's championship series, still the confident Auerbach smiled.

Most Celtics fans were not so relaxed, however.

"Red," said one of them, leaning down from his box seat and pleading for comfort, "I'm worried."

"Getcha goddam hands off me," replied Auerbach, equably. "What's to worry about? These L.A. goofballs are positively guaranteed to screw up and lose it."

Soon afterward Auerbach's words came true. Once more the Lakers found a way to beat themselves and prove again that they're the most self-destructive, dizzily frustrated team in National Basketball Association history.

This time the tale of woe began with Willem Hendrik (Butch) van Breda Kolff, leader of the West Coast aggregation.

Willem Hendrik is a large, shaggy, loose-lipped 46-year-old who is known as "Bigmouth Bill" and "Doghouse Dutch" and is the wildest actor and most-penalized coach in the league. In the Celtics' game he already had one technical foul for cursing the referee. A second foul would mean he would be bounced from the arena. To guard against such a loss, Lakers' owner Jack Kent Cooke assigned two subs to sit alongside the fiery coach and place strangleholds on him whenever he leaped off the bench to protest a decision. Van Breda Kolff, however, is a 200-pounder. Every time he shot up, he took his guards right with him.

But as his team went ahead, van Breda Kolff quieted down and behaved himself. Then suddenly he let out a roar.

In a struggle for the ball, Baylor was knocked to the floor by Boston's John Havlicek. The Lakers' trainer, Frank O'Neill, fearing Baylor had been hurt, danced around the bench excitedly. Concerned that O'Neill might run onto the court, take a punch at Havlicek and draw a technical penalty, van Breda Kolff threw off his guards and leaped upon O'Neill to restrain him.

O'Neill hadn't seen the coach coming from behind and thought he was being attacked by vile Bostonians. He began to kick, punch and yell.

Seven-foot-tall sub center Mel Counts jumped in to break it up. The three men thrashed around in a comic embrace. Somebody's foot sent the water bucket clanging. Counts slipped and hit the floor with a crash. Fans screamed.

"Technical foul on you, van Breda Kolff, for fighting on the sideline!" ruled the referee. "You're outta the game."

Surrounded by his Celtics, his smile become a grin, Red Auerbach reached for his traditional victory cigar. "See?" he said. "Even when they try to help each other, they screw up." Without leadership, with no one to inspire them, the Lakers folded and lost by eight points, a defeat which eventually cost them the NBA title.

It was an old, old story with this organization. Defeat is hard for them to take because the Lakers, when not in a state of total confusion, are capable of sensational performance. Shortly before the play-offs, for instance, they went into Boston Garden and crunched the champion Celtics, 144–104.

Five times since 1962, as Western Division champs, the Lakers have fought their way into the finals against Boston. In these showdowns they've beaten Bill Russell & Co. by such scores as 119–99, 126–105, 123–115 and 119–105. They won 12 of these play-off matches so impressively that champagne was put on ice in preparation for the victory celebration. But the big, key games always have gone to Boston—for a total of 19 victories and five pro titles. "If I was a Laker," says Sam Jones, a veteran Celtic, "I'd take the pipe. Twice they've forced us to the full seven play-off games, had the thing won and then missed some cinch shot that woulda made them the champs and rich."

Celtic coach Bill Russell more eruditely remarks, "They're masochistic. They're the Suffering Jesuses of pro basketball. These guys were just born to blow it all in the last 10 seconds."

In 1963, the Lakers prepared for the play-offs grimly. They called a special practice session. They went into the gym healthy—and staggered out ruined. Their 6-foot-10 ace, Gene Wiley, broke his hands. Superguard Jerry West pulled a hamstring muscle. Star center Jim Krebs fractured a finger on his shooting hand. The club owner at the time, a trucking fleet operator named Bob Short, put his head down on his desk and cried.

Short, after losing $200,000 or more, sold the team in 1965. But nothing about them changed under their new management. Once the Lakers' Mr. Hot Rod Hundley had the ball with three seconds left in the seventh play-off game with Boston. The score was tied in overtime.

"This time there was no way on earth we could lose," relates Hot Rod. "I'm a great passer and Frank Selvy is wide open under their basket. Three seconds left, and Frank's got the easiest dunk shot of all time. I fire him a perfect pass—but damn if it doesn't hit him on the thumb. The ball spins around in his hands and crawls up his arms and he misses the dunker! Boston grabs the ball, heaves a long one, hits and we lose by two points."

Did the Lakers get raving drunk after that?

"Yeah. We're a drinking club in defeat like the world never saw," says Hot Rod, presently a Laker publicist. "This coach we got now, van Breda Kolff, is the former beer drinking champion of the U. S. Marine Corps and he expects us to keep up with him, win or lose."

It is one of the Lakers' many charms that they don't con anyone into thinking they practice sobriety. Van Breda Kolff boasts that he was flunked out of Princeton University (where he later coached) for various misfeasances, including drinking, and once got thrown into a Marine guardhouse for hitting a sentry over the head with a pair of laced-together field boots, while stoned out of his head. "I like a nice, loose team" says Butch. "If the boys don't have some booze when they're dehydrated after a game, I worry about 'em. That doesn't mean they can show up for a game crocked. We draw the line on that. But after a game is different."

Van Breda Kolff's bed checks are notoriously unique in the game.

"They start around 2 o'clock in the morning because he's lonely and wants somebody to talk to," says Elgin Baylor with a sigh. "There's a bang on the hotel-room door and you climb outta bed and there's the coach with a drink in his hand, saying, 'This is a bed check! Is everybody asleep?'

"How the hell can you sleep? What he wants is to be invited in to rehash ball games over another beer, but we tell him, 'Oh, no, you don't. You're not getting in here. If you do, we'll be up all night.' "

The bibulous, night-walking, fun-loving Butch, the only coach whose athletes have to call a curfew on him, also has the richest Pier Six vocabulary in basketball and the largest hate for the whistle tooters: last season he led the NBA in technical fouls with 30, at the cost of $25 each. For being quoted as saying that modern pro players are rotten passers and so poor in fundamentals that they often bore him, he drew a $250 fine. After that, van Breda Kolff swore he'd control himself, but recently in Boston, his horror town, he exploded when it seemed to him Referee Mendy Rudolph failed to see the slightly built Jerry West of the Lakers being viciously shoved around by 6-foot-7, 220-pound Bailey Howell of the Celtics.

Butch rushed the length of the bench. He kept going past the stands and out the Garden door into the street, where he narrowly missed being hit by a car. He was too hysterical to know what he was doing. Reversing course, he reappeared through the door and sprinted back to his seat. There he was met by a patiently waiting Rudolph.

Rudolph had one index finger perpendicular to the other, forming the "T" sign. "Technical," he droned. "Twenty-five bucks."

Although VBK earns around $30,000 per season, his players often take up collections to pay his fines. Other times they match the fines, paying into a fund to go for a season's-end team blowout at some action-filled place. If the fund seems to be falling short of what will be needed for Fun Week, van Breda Kolff assesses his men $2, $5 and $10 fines for such offenses as not attending church, spilling drinks in public, not wearing a tie and being late for airplane takeoffs. He contributes the money to the fund.

Last April, Fun Week was held in Las Vegas. Wives were not invited. As well as those attending can recall, the fun lasted five or six days. "This season with Butch again leading the league in fines and with Wilt Chamberlain added to our roster," says a squad member, "we have bigger plans. Wilt is always late for planes. He gets out to the airport when he feels like it and if he misses the Laker flight, he charters his own plane.

"Honest to gawd, we've looked out the plane window and seen Wilt flying alongside in a Bonanza, waving at us."

With a Chamberlain contributing strongly to the fund, this year's party is scheduled for Rio de Janeiro. And the Lakers aren't kidding.

Wilton "Big Dipper" Chamberlain's arrival on the scene this season adds a new fillip to the ball club's already bizarre character. A man of majestic mien, cantankerous disposition and independent wealth, Chamberlain has never gotten along with owners and rarely with his coaches.

The Dipper was acquired last summer by Jack Kent Cooke, who earlier had bought the L.A. franchise from Bob Short for the all-time record price of $5,175,000. Cooke is a dynamic hustler with a foghorn voice who has poured more money—some $30 million—into pro sports than anyone in recent history. An ex-Canadian of 56 and a self-made multimillionaire, Cooke determined to end the Lakers' humiliating series of losses in the NBA title round by writing the largest basketball contract of all time—somewhere around $1 million—to lure the 7-foot-2 Chamberlain from the Philadelphia 76ers. This makes the Lakers the first hoop team to own three superstars simultaneously.

"I've built the greatest tribute man ever paid to athlete's foot!" trumpets Cooke, speaking of the $16 million plant in which his team performs its rites. "Now I've put the greatest cast ever assembled into it."

Veterans Baylor and West (who in nine years have scored 41,001 points between them for the Lakers) earn around $100,000 annually. With Wilt prorated at about $175,000 a year on a long-term deal, Cooke's payroll breaks all records.

Can Chamberlain live peacefully with an owner who can buy and sell him many times over? Many doubt it. For the proud Dipper, perhaps the richest living athlete, had a bigger bank acount than the last two men who "owned" him—Franklin Mieuli, president of the San Francisco Warriors, and Irv Kosloff, of the 76ers. Wilt could tell them to go to hell in any dispute. "Which he did. Oh, how he did," relates Kosloff.

Everyone agrees Jack Kent Cooke is a different sort. For example, in early 1968 Chamberlain joined Richard Nixon's campaign tour as a high-level aide. Nixon brought up the subject of Cooke and said, "He must be a fantastic person. I've heard so much about him that he sounds like a legend." The then Presidential candidate wanted to know what Chamberlain's impression of Jack Kent Cooke was.

Well might Nixon have inquired. In 1933 Cooke was a 21-year-old, door-to-door salesman of encyclopedias in the dreary back provinces of eastern Canada. He was earning $30 a week.

Cooke and his wife sometimes went hungry. Within 10 years a series of shrewd, almost miraculous business deals gave him a Dun & Bradstreet rating of several million dollars. Today his worth is calculated in eight figures.

Remarked Nixon to Chamberlain, "In 1960 the Congress passed a special act, Private Law 86-468, which granted Cooke immediate American citizenship. It was remarkable. The Congress waived the required five-year waiting rule—one of the few times in history this has been done."

"Yes, sir, he's a cool cat, all right," replied the Big Dipper moodily. "Cooke owns a house that's got more rooms in it than a hotel and owns 50 pair of shoes at $75 each. He's loaded with antique art and old masters, too. The only thing where I thought I had an edge on him is that my custom-built Bentley Continental [which cost Wilt $27,000] is air-conditioned and Cooke's isn't."

But Wilt then related that when he paid a visit to Cooke at his pink villa in Bel Air, next door to Jerry Lewis' mansion, he suffered a shock. Glancing out a window, he saw two more custom Bentleys in the driveway, along with a Silver Phantom Rolls-Royce.

The sight took even Wilt's breath away. "And then the butler came in and moved an ashtray away from my elbow, so I wouldn't knock it over. You know why? Because even the damned ashtrays in Cooke's house are made of gold and they cost $167 each!"

There is no way the Big Dipper can lord it over a man of such substance, and anytime Wilt feels he is No. 2 he's in psychological trouble. That fact became evident this past November when the Lakers, picked by most experts to win the NBA title, went on a losing streak. New York, Detroit and Philadelphia each defeated them by margins of up to 10 points. Coach van Breda Kolff took Chamberlain aside. With a cigar jutting from his mouth, he put it bluntly:

"You're no help playing in close to the basket in the low post. I know that's where you like to play, but with this team you can forget it. You clog up the middle too much and prevent Baylor and West from driving in for quick-break shots underneath the net. The two guys guarding you just switch off and block out Elgin and Jerry. Get it?"

"Yeah. What do you have in mind?" said Chamberlain.

"Why, I want you out further, in the high post, 15 feet away from the basket, what else?" barked the coach.

Chamberlain, glowering, said he'd give it a try.

He did, but a few road games later he reverted to parking under the cords and again jammed up the Laker attack. A feud was in the making between van Breda Kolff and Chamberlain; another with Baylor and West lined up against Wilt. The other two superstars declared they wouldn't tolerate Chamberlain's piling up personal glory by grabbing rebounds at the expense of their scoring totals. Van Breda Kolff phoned Cooke from Boston, seeking a way out.

JKC gave VBK instructions while seated in his office at The Forum, a sports structure unlike anything in the world and one which Los Angeles city fathers had bet never would be erected. Two years before, Cooke had engaged in a battle with the city over rental and other factors at the civic-owned Sports Arena, the Lakers' home court. Cooke threatened to pull out and erect his own gym unless his requests were met. Mayor Sam Yorty's representatives were highly amused. "It'd cost him $10 or $12 million he hasn't got. He's bluffing."

Nine days later Cooke bought 29.5 suburban acres and before long Yorty, red of face, was flying in by helicopter to dedicate "Taj Mahal West," as some people call the $16 million monster arena. Seating 17,000, the Forum towers on 80 columns like a huge slab of ice cream. It features $500,000 worth of art, a $125,000 scoreboard, mobile bars rolling down richly carpeted corridors, gaudy colors, mini-skirted usherettes and an executive suite more ornate than that at IBM.

Handsome and ruddy, Cooke snatches up one of three phones while seated at a genuine Chippendale desk the size of a Reno crap table. His thronelike chair is an antique Bedemeyer. He is, in fact, surrounded by antiques worth far more than the rights to Lew Alcindor. His phone bill runs $10,000 a month.

"Perplexity is the progenitor of defeat!" roared Cooke to van Breda Kolff on the occasion of the Boston call. Cooke likes polysyllabic words and rarely misuses them. "I want a swift resolution of this problem—not from you, but from the players themselves."

If the Lakers didn't find an answer, Cooke said, he was prepared to bench all three superstars, go with his reserves and to hell with the won-lost columns.

Captain Baylor at once called a squad meeting at which all problems were put on the table. Chamberlain was invited to explain himself. Charges flew back and forth. Over it all hung the menace of Cooke, an owner who would trade a man to Saskatchewan tomorrow if it pleased him.

Emerging from the meeting, the Big Dipper appeared thoroughly chastened. He went out that night against the Celtics, in the Lakers' jinx city, did just as he had been instructed to do and helped win a stunning 93–92 upset victory. With Cooke exhorting them via regular messages, the team went on to take a wide early-season lead in the Western Division of the NBA.

"I abhor failure and won't tolerate individualism acting negatively upon total squad effort," said Cooke to this writer, in his Forum quarters. Then he interrupted himself to ask, "Would you care for a libation?"

On a nearby worm-pocked Chippendale sideboard which once belonged to an English duke is arrayed the most complete collection of liquor offered in any arena, including Houston's Astrodome. Attendants costumed as Roman spear bearers hurry in to mix drinks at Cooke's summons.

A plaque hung at one Forum gate tells how unique and mammoth Jack Kent Cooke is in sport and commerce. The holdings listed on the plaque all have been acquired since 1960, when he burst upon the U.S. scene from Canada, almost unknown in American sports.

Division One of Cooke's holdings comprises California Sports Inc., which includes the Lakers, the Los Angeles Kings of the National Hockey League, the Wolves of the North American Soccer League, the Springfield Kings of the American Hockey League and the Forum. Division Two covers Pro Football, Inc. through which JKC owns 25 percent of the Washington Redskins, with an option to buy more. Division Three embraces cable television: such Cooke interests as American Cablevision Co., Trans-America Microwave, Inc., Southwest Cablevision and American Cable Electronics. One of the first to realize a fortune can be made by bringing TV to fringe areas not receiving standard transmissions, Cooke has some $50 million involved in the innovation.

"Communications is how I made my fortune," he says. "I was starving to death selling encyclopedias. So I switched to buying up diseased, almost bankrupt little provincial radio stations. I juiced them up with a good programing, sold them at a big profit and parlayed the money into larger stations." Within a decade Cooke operated a chain of major broadcasting units as well as a string of Canadian national magazines. He began collecting sports franchises as though they were stamps "just to relieve the tedium and because I love to win."

Of the incredible angles about Cooke, the most startling may be that before he paid $5.1-plus million for the Lakers, he'd seen only two or three pro basketball games and knew nothing about the sport. "It's a challenge," he says blithely, "to start with a handicap."

A touchy bunch, the Lakers engage in many fights with opponents, often with bizarre results. One Laker substitute, Johnny Block, had his nose broken while on the bench. Standing up for a better look at a brawl that had broken out on the court, Block was hit by a New York Knickerbocker's fist and knocked into the third row of seats.

Drawls Jerry West, the quiet backcourt ace and the most normal member of the team (if you take in stride his record of having had his nose broken no fewer than seven times): "There's never been a club like this one, I guess. Our guy, Ray Felix, who's 6-foot-11, got into a fight one night with Walter Dukes, who's just as tall. They couldn't hit each other at all but they wound up knocking down the referee with their long arms. The next day we noticed that a horse named Fighting Felix was running at Hollywood Park. We rushed over and got bets down. Fighting Felix came in and paid $20.40."

Hot Rod Hundley was removed from the lineup and appointed to the Lakers' publicity staff after he took to reading comic books and playing with a Yo-Yo while on the bench.

At present, with no end to him in sight, Jack Kent Cooke's most valuable property is another individualist, Elgin Gay Baylor, who is perhaps the finest cager ever to step onto a court. At 34, Baylor is a physical phenomenon who has been written up in the *Journal of the American Medical Association.* He runs on legs that have undergone surgery four times. On each occasion doctors said he was finished, but he came back. Baylor also has a backbone nature didn't bother to finish—what doctors call a "pseudo-spine," four inches shorter than normal. Yet the older Baylor grows, the better he gets. His 3,010 points scored in play-offs are the most in NBA history; his lifetime average of 28.1 points per-league-game is second only to Chamberlain's 36.0.

The sleepy-eyed Baylor, called "Motormouth" by his teammates because he is a compulsive talker, adds touches to the Lakers you don't find anywhere else. A few years ago a bad slump hit the team. Baylor responded by introducing a dog into the training drills. An aggressive German shepherd named Bozo, he was trained by Baylor to play defensive guard. Bozo was stationed under the basket and ordered not to let anyone get around him. He took the order literally.

In one-on-one situations, Bozo often would steal the ball with a swipe of his paw or a thrust of his nose. "But when we'd beat him and get around him," says one Laker, "he'd get sore and try to tear your leg off. Gawd, what a dog!"

Red Auerbach of Boston, upon hearing of the experiment, said, "I always knew that's where the Los Angeles franchise would go."

Despite their tribulations and their ability to thwart themselves, the Lakers are one of the top drawing cards in the business and may be on the verge of realizing all their ambitions. Under Cooke they're in far better shape than they were under Bob Short. Once during the Short era, the box office was robbed by thieves who crept in at night and took $1,600 in cash. The burglars left untouched some $20,000 worth of tickets for an upcoming game. "We didn't take them," explained one thief, after his capture, "because you can't sell tickets to see those bums in this town. In fact, you can't even give them away."

But now, if Wilt Chamberlain remains tractable, which doesn't seem entirely likely, and Baylor's back doesn't collapse, the Lakers may indeed down the Eastern champions and become kings of the hardwood. Butch van Breda Kolff says this is inevitable because of an outstanding virtue of the organization. "We're dead honest with each other," he says. "We have the greatest talents in the world, but when the boys mess things up, we let them know about it, loud and clear."

This philosophy, too, is something to marvel at.

A genius such as Baylor, for instance, never would be treated as anything else by any other team, even after a bad night. However, in Seattle not long ago, he made a wild last-minute pass which cost Los Angeles the game. Coattails flying, van Breda Kolff chased Baylor down a tunnel and into the dressing room, shouting at the top of his lungs: "Ten years an All-Pro! Ten years and you make a pass no stupid rookie would make! Ten years All-Pro? It should be 10 years a dum-dum! That's what you are—a dum-dum!"

Friends led Baylor away before he clobbered the coach. Later they suggested to Butch that he should amend his remarks before they were published. "Okay," said VBK, still steaming. "I was wrong. Baylors been All-Pro only nine times. Change it to nine years a star and a dum-dum."

Still later, the Laker family went out together and had beer—a lot of it. They got back to the hotel hours after all sensible ball teams were sound asleep. And Butch and Motormouth, Big Dipper, Zeke from Cabin Creek and the rest were singing a ballad composed by none other than Jack Kent Cooke, Esquire, who plays the saxophone and the clarinet and composes songs in his spare time.

Told that the boys had blown the Seattle game and then had a locker-room battle followed by a beer bust, the multimillionaire smiled benignly. "Now that," he said, "is what I regard as and would term a winning spirit."

THE WORLD'S TALLEST CHEMIST

By Al Levine

From The Miami News

Bob Guy knew David Kisker was going to be a challenge. It's impossible for them to see eye-to-eye. Guy, the University of Miami's new freshman basketball coach, is 5-foot-8. Kisker, Guy's center, is seven feet tall.

"Psychologically," Guy said, "the little guys hate bigger guys. You know, generals are always pictured as short. I holler and scream at him because he's got me one up already with his size. If I lost control of him he'd have me on three strikes: size, strength and he'd put me down mentally, too."

But they are not only poles apart in stature. Kisker's introduction to college basketball was a series of misunderstandings.

When the coaches suggested that the basketball players work on their own the first part of October, Kisker's reply was "practice officially starts October 15." When Guy scheduled a morning practice during the Thanksgiving break, David Kisker failed to show up—just like the night before, when his bed was empty for the midnight curfew.

"I went to the airport to pick up a friend and I told the curfew monitor," Dave said. "I thought he'd understand. And my roommate swears he tried to wake me up the next morning but I don't remember a thing."

So while Miami's freshman basketball team was playing its first two games, Kisker was on suspension and running off the penalty for missing curfew—which is 25 laps around a quarter-mile track, a six and one-quarter mile jog.

As a warm-up, Kisker ran 14 laps one day and 20 the next, with a manager keeping him company. "I don't work too hard on my own," Dave said. "There's always something better to do."

Kisker's something better is chemistry. He's just as happy in a laboratory as he is in a gymnasium. This makes Kisker a unique coaching problem. This seven-footer hears a different drummer.

"My ambition," said Kisker, "is a doctorate degree, maybe go into research for a company like Dow or Monsanto."

"He doesn't realize what he has," said Bob Guy. "His size is money in the bank. If I were seven feet tall I'd sleep with a basketball. But no," Bob laughed, "he wants to be the world's tallest chemist."

"People," said Kisker, "think that just because a guy is seven feet tall that he must want to play pro basketball. If a pro team can put up with a portable laboratory in the back of the dressing room, I'll be interested.

"I realize I can't play this game more than 10 years. Okay, I'll be 21 when I graduate. After 10 years of pro ball I'll be 31, with a B.S. degree in chemistry. By then chemical science will have come so far that with what I knew my B.S. degree will mean so little. Trying to go back to school would be impossible and there's not a whole lot you can do with a B.S. degree."

For Kisker, it's a matter of putting things into perspective and Dave's perspective may be difficult for someone from the school of basketball to understand. "There are a lot of gray areas in athletics," said his coach.

Kisker is probably the tallest package of brains to enroll at Miami. While averaging 18 points and 15 rebounds last year for Central High in St. Joseph, Missouri, Dave graduated seventh in a class of 486.

At Miami, his 16 hours of classes include organic chemistry, German, English, history and calculus. Next semester it gets rougher—12 hours of lab.

Dave grew rapidly during his junior high school years, from 5-foot-11 at the beginning of the eighth grade to 6-foot-7 by the end of the ninth. Right now, he is "a little less than seven feet, depending on the shoes I wear."

But he didn't grow quite as quickly, athletically. "I didn't play organized basketball until the ninth grade," Kisker said. "That's comparatively late. Some guys on our team have been playing since the second grade."

The catching up has been difficult. "Coordination," Dave said, "has always been a problem because I grew so fast. You take my coordination problem in high school and double and triple it and you have an idea of what it is now. I can't do things now that I couldn't do then.

"I was always the tallest guy on the court. Last year I played against a lot of good players but none over 6-foot-5. Consequently, I have all kinds of problems against somebody close to my own size."

Kisker is smart enough to be his own worst critic. He has the potential to be a good one, the coaches believe.

"'When he gets a rebound in practice," said Guy, "and a guy grabs for the ball, his natural reaction is to move to the side. Pretty soon, he'll move so far that he'll be walking with the ball. I said, 'David, just give the man an elbow and he'll give you some room.' He said, 'Coach, you don't want me to elbow my teammate.'

"But he's learning. He's quick, has a pretty good set of hands and he's a smart kid." He's also out of the doghouse with 37 points in his last two games, including 21 in last night's 91–88 overtime loss to Miami-Dade Junior College South.

"He's got high school habits," said Ron Godfrey, the varsity coach. "He reaches a lot instead of jumping. But he's like a diamond in the rough."

Perhaps only Dave Kisker knows how rough this diamond really is. "I don't have the things Alcindor has," he said.

"I was sitting out the second half of our game at Brevard Junior College last week when someone in the crowd yelled 'Put in the jolly green giant.' I knew they wanted me to go in there so their big man could make me look sick."

Golf

A SERGEANT OUTSHOOTS THE GENERAL

By Jesse Outlar

From The Atlanta Constitution

While the Army followed the General a Sergeant won the 69th National Open.

When Arnold Palmer barely missed an eagle at the thirteenth hole, the Army spread the word that the General was making his charge. But this wasn't the year for stars and Sgt. Orville Cleve Moody outshot the field with a two-over-par 72 and took the back-door Open via a total of 281.

Sergeant Moody is one of the longest longshots ever to hit the million dollar Open jackpot. For the second straight year the golf elite was shocked by a first-time winner from Texas.

Lee Trevino, a former Marine corporal, won the Open last year, and Sergeant Moody gave the enlisted men another boost Sunday afternoon. Moody isn't too familiar with some of his fellow pros, but he says he used to beat Trevino by 30 strokes in service tournaments.

When the 35-year-old Moody tapped in a 14-inch putt and averted a four-way play-off, the Commander in Chief was on the line to the Sergeant. Unaccustomed as he is to congratulating Texans, President Richard Nixon phoned from the White House.

The President observed that it isn't often a former sergeant with 14 years in service wins the Open.

"I told him this was the first time," drawled the moon-faced Moody when he met the press. "I was in such a daze I don't know exactly what all he said. I know he told me he feels it's a good thing that the elite didn't win it. It's good to see the middle class do something . . ."

On the Champions course the champions had a woeful week.

Palmer, who finished with a 284, was the lone superstar to survive. Pre-tourney favorite Gary Player logged a horrifying 295; Billy Casper skied to 293 and Jack Nicklaus scored 289 despite a second round 67.

Out of the original field of 150, not a single one of the world's greatest golfers finished below par on the long, flat layout. So it was a fitting ending that a former sergeant who had never won a tournament, a man who joined the tour at age 34, should win it.

Moody will baffle golf scientists across the land. He defies all their theories. He doesn't believe in practicing? He's never taken a golf lesson in his life, and he putts cross-handed.

"I just don't believe in practicing . . . never did," explained Moody, who packs 200 pounds on a stocky 5-foot-10 frame. "Before this tournament I took a week off. When something gets wrong with my game, I can usually correct it by hitting less than a sack of balls."

"Naw, I never did take a lesson. My father was a greenskeeper so I got a chance to play a lot. But I never took a lesson. When somebody offers me advice I listen; I'm diplomatic about it, but I never intend to take a lesson."

In the PGA fraternity that's sheer heresy. A man who doesn't practice or listen to the golf professors wins the coveted Open.

Needless to note, the $30,000 check was the biggest payday of Moody's life. He pointed out that 14 months ago he was receiving $508 a month from the Army after his insurance was deducted.

His closest approach to the winner's circle since he joined the tour in December of 1967 was the Greensboro Open this year in which he lost the play-off to Gene Littler.

Alas, in a commercialized era, the new Open champion hasn't endorsed a single product.

"That's right," said Moody, "I have not put my name on a single thing . . . clubs, balls . . . or nothing. But I'm fixing to start. How much you figure a club endorsement will be worth now?" said Moody to his new agent, Bunky Woy, who helped pal Trevino parlay the title into "more than a million bucks."

"Maybe 50 or 100 thousand, huh? I had a chance to sign last week, but I'd have got $5,000. So I'm pretty lucky."

The new Open Champion allowed that he isn't playing his best golf now. He thinks he reached his peak when he was winning the Korea Open and other Army titles.

"If I hadn't made it on the tour, I would have probably reenlisted," said Moody. "I like the Army. If they ask me to help recruit or visit the troops in Vietnam, I'll be happy to go.

"Why didn't I turn pro earlier?" Moody restated a question.

"Well, that's simple. I didn't have the money. When I found my sponsors, I turned pro, went to the PGA School in 1967. My sponsors are from Kileen, Texas. I was born in Chickasha, Oklahoma, and I play out of Yukon, Oklahoma, but I live in Kileen."

Moody introduced Tom Carlile and Leonard Cohen. Blackie Blackburn is the other sponsor. They staked Moody to $350 weekly for expenses for a year, and receive half his golf earnings. It has proven a sound investment, because Moody now has collected almost $70,000 this year, and he expects to reap a million.

Moody was a natural for the unlikely Open, because there is nothing ordinary about any phase of his junket from Chickasha to the Open crown.

As a youngster in Oklahoma, he received a football scholarship to the university with the understanding that he'd play golf instead of football. He resided at Norman a mere six weeks, however, and enlisted in the Army after a quarrel with his sweetheart. He spent 14 years in the Army, married a German bride, divorced her, then married a colonel's daughter.

He started out in the Army as a rifle instructor, but he then switched to special services and spent most of his Army career operating Army golf courses and a bowling alley and other recreational facilities.

Moody wanted to turn pro, but he had no backers.

"A lot of people say they'll back you, but they don't put up. So that's why I had to wait until I found the sponsors."

Somebody wanted to know when Moody last won any tournament and where?

"The National Open at Champions Sunday," he drawled. "I guess one of those service tournaments at Fort Hood was the last one before today."

While Moody talked he received an invitation to the British Open, and his sponsors say he'll accept.

Orville Cleve Moody is going a lot of places from now on. He held the fort that day when the General and others fired and fell back at Champions Country Club.

PURGATORY, WITH 18 HOLES

By Furman Bisher

From The Atlanta Journal

I want to be there the day that Tommy Bolt hits a 270-yard tee shot and winds up behind a sailboat.

Still on the golf course, understand. And on dry land. But behind a sailboat—in a sandtrap—about 180 yards from the green.

Tape his monologue and they could use it for a soliloquy in *Oh! Calcutta!*

Or wait until he hits one of the traps with a palm tree growing in the middle, directly in his line to the green.

But if you're waiting for the kind of explosion that doesn't require a club, wait until he hits one of the U-shaped greens and finds himself with no direct putting route to the pin.

I don't know how the PGA is about the use of wedges on greens, but it's either a wedge shot or you putt for position, then you putt for the cup.

You want to see a green turn blue, wait until Tommy pronounces his benediction over one of these.

Oh yes, there's more than one. There are several on which you're advised to get your approach on the side of the pin, or it's a one-shot detour.

There are par three holes which command you to hit the shot from tee to green, or you hit until you run out of balls. In some cases, you don't dare retrieve your misses, unless you're on good terms with alligators.

There's a 600-yard hole on which the fairway is so narrow it's like trying to play a shot through a wind sock.

The finishing hole—now there's a dream. It's 430 yards along the side of Calibogue Cay, which pokes its watery fingers into the fairway at irregular intervals. This is like playing into a wind tunnel at the wrong end on the average day at Hilton Head.

It is designed to be played in four strokes. Actually, there is only one way to get there when the wind is presiding. You call a cab.

Then there are the holes with bunkers of wall-to-wall centipede grass. I don't know how good you are at hitting golf balls out of centipede grass, which is like hitting out of coiled wire, but there are places on the course where you can be within 10 feet of the green and not have a shot.

There are fairways with trees in the middle, limbs that jut out over the fairway and are draped with Spanish moss hanging there like an eerie snare, and greens about the size of a contact lens. The name of the course is Harbourtown, third in a series produced by Sea Pines Plantation, but the last word in outdoor torture chambers.

About the only thing normal at Harbourtown is the number of holes. It has 18.

The only hazard missing, alive or inanimate, is the dinosaur. The man who built the course simply wasn't able to find one. Alive.

Naturally, the designer is suspected of being Dr. Frankenstein. Or at best, Mr. Hyde, when he was on the soup.

In reality, the designer is a reformed insurance salesman with a round forehead and a round nose and a round face. Generally a rather average type with a wry disposition.

His name is Pete Dye, and he seems to have originated in the Midwest. He suddenly abandoned a rather secure nest in the insurance world 10 years ago to take up golf course designing, explaining to his employer at the time, "I'd rather go broke this way than nuts the other way."

Pete has over 20 courses on his record, but none will get him the attention—ranging from curses to praise to awe—of Harbourtown. In addition to the excruciating aspects of the course, another reason for its notoriety is that Harbourtown is the first course on which Jack Nicklaus has participated as a designer.

This has developed into a source of some irritation to Pete. He took Jack on as a consultant. "When I read it in the papers, it usually comes out that I'm his assistant or I turn on the sprinkler system or something."

In his own diabolical way, Pete has extracted his revenge. The first shot that Nicklaus hit on the new course traveled deep into the woods.

When he was known as "Fat Jack," there would hardly have been enough room for Nicklaus on some of the fairways. "You can't shoot a .22 rifle down some of them," he said.

This is the prime fruition of Dye's philosophy of course designing. "Golf wasn't meant to be a fair game," it reads. This is the ultimate achievement in unfair play.

It isn't likely to become a favorite of tourists, but it is so different, so dramatically unusual, that it is likely to become one of the most talked about golf courses in the world.

There is a lot of the old Scottish aspect to the courses that Dye designs. He builds to the land, where it suits his devilish attitude, but he will improvise by ear as he moves along. The sailboat, located in the middle of a trap about 100 yards long on the 16th hole, is a hellish illustration.

When Dye says rough, he means rough. When you are in trouble here, you may be in need of last rites. There are holes that rightly should be par 16 for some resort players, but this isn't the purpose of Harbourtown.

The course will be put to use first in late November, when Sea Pines and Delta Air Lines interlock in a $100,000 PGA tournament called the Heritage Classic. All the horrors are being withheld to the public until then, at which time they will be unlocked and let loose as a sporting form of Pandora's box.

Charles Price, director of golf and a historian of vast stature, made this appeal to get Sam Snead involved in the Heritage Classic—he said, "Sam, there isn't a green on which you'll have a putt of more than 25 feet." He didn't go ahead to explain that it might be around a corner.

Bill Dyer, director of the Heritage Classic and its originator, suggests that it may become the first PGA tournament ever called off on account of lost players.

Incidentally, what is the penalty for a lost player?

FRANK BEARD IS DULL . . .

By Nick Seitz

From Golf Digest

The nice thing about images, to use the term as Madison Avenue does, is that they make life so much easier in a fast-paced society. For example, one saves much painful mental labor by thinking of hippies only as young people who need baths and haircuts. There is a neat pigeonhole for everyone, right?

On the Professional Golfers' Association tour, Doug Sanders is pigeonholed as the guy with the garish clothes, Lee Trevino as the funny ole boy from Texas, and Arnold Palmer as the bold charger. And Frank Beard, the leading money winner of 1969 ($167,000 through the Alcan Championship), Frank Beard is dull. The newspapers say so, the fans say so, and Beard says so, and that is his one-word label.

"He's always telling me how uninteresting he is," says Dick Schaap, the Manhattan-based sports writer, who in the past year has collaborated on best-selling books with pro football heroes Jerry Kramer and Joe Namath and is presently using the same diary treatment with golf's anti-hero Beard. Schaap, his hair fashionably long and his tie fashionably wide, speaks from behind a neat desk in his working apartment on East 56th Street; he lives in an apartment next door. "Actually, Frank is one of the most interesting guys I know. When I set out to pick a golfer for the book, I wanted Trevino, but he was too busy. I met Frank by chance and found him very outspoken, witty and articulate, and I knew I had met my man. He had been on the tour long enough to know everyone, and he seemed the type who would be conscientious about the day-to-day job of keeping a diary."

Talk about conscientious. Kramer, the former Green Bay Packer lineman whose book with Schaap, *Instant Replay,* set a sales record for a sports book, ultimately amassed 100,000 words of unedited, tape-recorded material. Beard has given Schaap 1,000,000 words—and isn't finished yet.

"Almost all of it is readable, too," Schaap says. "I am also doing diaries with an airline pilot, a rabbi, Bill Freehan of the Detroit Tigers, Derek Sanderson of the Boston Bruins, a violinist, a Marine captain in Vietnam, a single career girl and Dave DeBusschere of the New York Knicks, and Frank's and the rabbi's are the most complete."

Schaap believes the book will broaden Beard's image. "He will come off as intelligent and occasionally highly amusing. He is not a joke teller, but he reacts to situations well with dry, almost sarcastic humor. He thinks about a lot of things beyond golf. He knows what's going on in religion and politics and the arts to at least a limited degree. I'll tell you, the book would be a lot less interesting if I were doing it with Arnold Palmer, or even Trevino. You'll enjoy talking to Frank."

The following week this writer approaches Beard on the practice range at the Portland Golf Club in Oregon where the Alcan Golfer of the Year Championship with its $55,000 first prize will be played, and conveys Schaap's regards and requests an interview. "Can you write in a saloon?" Beard wants to know. This is the dull Frank Beard? The answer is affirmative, and an appointment is made for after the pro-am that is about to begin.

Beard is a model pro-am partner, calling his partners "Sir" and helping hunt lost balls and giving instruction tips to the amateurs in his group. His own play is unspectacularly steady, and he has a 67 that will tie for first money. Afterward he is questioned by a Portland newsman. It rains as often as not in Portland, and when the newsman asks Beard if the course looks about as Beard remembers it from previous trips, Beard says, "Yes. It's still under water."

In the locker room he orders a double Chivas Regal on the rocks and joins his pro-am partners for the traditional post-round drink. Then he orders a second double Chivas to go, and, with the golf writer driving, heads downtown in a "courtesy car" furnished by the tournament sponsors.

"Pro-ams are just awful," he says. "I don't mind poor players, but some of them have to make such a production of everything. Next year these guys will come up to me somewhere on tour and say 'You don't remember me, but . . .' and one of these days I'm going to say 'No, I don't.' They're nice people, I suppose, but . . ."

Is Beard enjoying doing the book? "Not any more. I enjoyed it at first. I have to protect so many people, it's discouraging. I could never write the book I want to, not while I'm playing the tour anyway. You have to live with these people. I talk into a tape recorder at least 15 minutes every day. If my wife and three kids are traveling with me, I go into the bathroom where it's quiet. I guess that's probably a commentary on my early toilet training. I think the book will have a lot of bite, though. It should be the best book on the tour, simply because nothing much has been done on the tour.

"It probably would sell better if it were by one of the superstars. Consistency is my game. Eight wins in seven years and no major wins. That's a superstar? In my game, I just eliminate the garbage, that's all. I'll hook hell out of the ball and still be in the fairway. I'm sneaky long. I play a lot—about 30 tournaments a year, as many as the rabbits. I want to make enough money in the next few years so I don't have to worry about it any more. I'm on this bike, pedaling fast. I go up and level off in a nice nonwinning rut. I won Minnesota and Westchester this year, but last year I made over $100,000 and didn't win a tournament. It's profitable for me to play a lot. I could take three weeks off to get an edge for the major tournaments, but I don't know that I can win the U.S. Open, so it's too great a gamble. I'll take my $2,000 and $3,000 every week. I'm blessed that at the age of 30 I've been thrown into a fantastically profitable arena. It's like finding money on the street."

We leave the car at the Benson Hotel where Beard is staying. A native asks Beard what he thinks of the hotel, and he replies, "I think it's the greatest hotel in the world. Really. The rooms and the food and the service are terrific. It's the best. Of course, I don't travel much."

A block away in a corner of a small, darkened saloon, as Beard persists in referring to it, the conversation resumes on a fiscal note. Casually dressed in a red sweater, yellow collared shirt and gray slacks, his straight dark hair half-combed and his blandly handsome face untanned despite months in the sun, the bespectacled Beard goes unnoticed by the collection of traveling salesmen and locals.

"If there's anything I hate worse than hypocrisy," he says, "it's false modesty. Golf to me is a way to make money. I never think that people are cognizant of the fact I'm alive. Sometimes it scares me, but mostly it doesn't bother me. All I care about is making money. I don't think about the limelight. If I had a rich uncle die and leave me a pile of money, you just might never see me again."

Still, Beard is becoming better known; his very dullness lately is almost a point of interest in itself. "Yes, but I couldn't care less," he says. His tone is objective, dispassionate. "A person buys a ticket to a golf tournament and buys four hours of my life. He has no right to bother me at breakfast the next morning. I give him what he pays for, the best golf I can play. On the course I appear dull. I would love to have fun playing golf, but it's impossible for me. To me, a tournament is a job, with a lot of money at stake. If you let it be fun today, 50 or 60 fellows taking it seriously will beat you. Look at Lee Trevino. I'm not saying he's having a bad year, but he could do better if he didn't walk along joking with the galleries.

"People don't realize that when they see me on the golf course, they see me at my most serious. During those four hours I concentrate as hard as I can. Afterward I might be an entirely different person, but they don't see me then. That's fine. I'm not going to change. I've walked around with two other golfers and three caddies most of my life, and I'm used to it."

The Frank Beard that the fans at the Westchester Classic did not see is the Frank Beard who asked Dick Schaap to show him New York City. The night after the third round, Beard attended the nude off-Broadway show, *Oh! Calcutta!* Frank Beard, sports fans! "I went out of curiosity," says Beard, doubtless the only pro golfer to see the show. "I was basically impressed that these people were exploring a new area in theater, but I was disappointed. It was antisexual. It wasn't satire—it was just a money-making scheme. The nudity only served to point up that allurement is still in the pricking of curiosity. The only thing that aroused me was a dance scene in which the performers were clothed. It was far more suggestive than the skin scenes. The content was shallow, but it's making money. I deserved what I got."

Beard also deserved his victory that week in the Westchester Classic, richest event on tour, when he finished 67–67. Beard is as much a charger as Arnold Palmer, believe it or not.

"I don't have the figures to substantiate it, but I'll bet I have shot as many low third and fourth rounds as he has," Beard says. This year Beard has shot 66 three times in the closing round, 67 three times, and 68 three times. It will be recalled that twice in the space of three weeks in 1967 he sank birdie putts on the 72nd green to edge Palmer and win tournaments.

But consistency is his outstanding asset.

"I save more bogeys than I make birdies," he says. "Everybody asks me what the difference is this year. Pathetic as it sounds, the answer is obvious. Nothing has changed, but I'm a little more experienced. After seven years, if you can eliminate a half stroke to a stroke per tournament, it can amount to $60,000 a year. I've done that. I'm putting the same—not quite as well as before actually. Mechanically, my sand game has improved. I'm still a bad sand player, but maybe instead of knocking one in seven close to the hole from sand, I'm knocking one in six close—and there's that shot a tournament I want to pick up. I'm using an old wedge that Dick Hart, a club pro in Chicago, gave me. He also gave me a lesson at the Western Open this year. I think it was largely psychological, but it worked. I started choking down on my wedge and chopping at the ball more.

"Technically, I'm not up to the standard of maybe 100 other guys I've seen out here—75 of whom have left the tour. Which proves the point I have always stressed, that this game is 99 percent psychological once you acquire a basic grasp of technique. I joined the tour and saw that a lot of guys who didn't hit it worth a damn were making a lot of dough. I realized right away that if I could just play my own game and not worry about how arty I looked, I could make good money. Look at Bobby Locke. He beat hell out of everybody with a big ole hook and his putter."

It is early in the week, and Beard enjoys his Chivas. The waitress returns at regular intervals with fresh drinks, and Beard—the dull golfer—is caught up in the spirit of the evening and he unwittingly regales several tables of men and women who have abandoned their own conversations to listen to him, fascinated. The mention of Hogan alters the course of the interview.

"You know how cold and single-minded Ben is supposed to be," Beard says. "I played in an exhibition with him once in Fort Wayne, and I never saw anything like it. A few of us sat around until 2:30 in the morning listening to Ben tell stories. He got so carried away recalling his great moments in golf that all of us nearly cried. You have to have great emotion to be a great champion. Hogan suppressed his emotions to succeed. Ted Williams is the same way. He's one of the most warm, sentimental people I've ever been around. So is Vince Lombardi. But they stifle their emotions.

"That kind of sacrifice isn't worth it to me. I value my friends and family and intimate moments. I'm lucky in that respect, I think. I won't say that being an immortal doesn't appeal to me. I want it. But I don't desire it. My dad was a club professional in Dallas and later ran a hardware store in Louisville, and he made a good living, but not a great one. When you come from not much to a lot, the way I have in such a short time, you don't care that much about going higher. I don't anyway. So what if you win the Masters? I want that, but I don't desire it. My immediate concern is with making money. I don't think Arnold Palmer ever thought about making money. He was obsessed with the idea of being the best. And yet he and I come from about the same type backgrounds.

"There are no incense fires burning in me. I've never had any trouble with my temper. It has always been fairly easy for me to concentrate. I've always been pretty confident. I didn't work on it, it just came, from being patient more than anything else. Patience is the byword of this game. You have to have patience to build your confidence. I remember finding Gary Player on the practice green one time, with about 50 balls beside him, and he was hitting one-foot putts. Now that's not a long putt. Of course he was making every one of them. 'Gary,' I said, 'what in hell are you doing?' He is a serious man and I knew he had a good reason for hitting one-foot putts by the hour. 'Frank,' he said, 'I've checked with people I trust and they think my stroke is excellent. But I'm not making enough putts. The only thing I can think of is that my confidence has slipped a bit, so I'm working on my confidence.' He was watching the ball go into the hole, and his subconscious was registering success. You can build confidence, you see, but it takes patience."

This writer remembers Dick Schaap saying that Beard does not consider himself an athelete, and raises this subject.

"We're not athletes in any strict sense of the word," Beard says, his neutral accent reflecting none of his Southern upbringing. "I define an athlete as a man who is first of all in good physical condition. A golfer's legs are in shape, and he has a little wind, but basically he has no muscles. We're entertainers. But not essentially." He hesitates, stirring his drink thoughtfully. "I don't know for sure what an athlete is, but an athlete doesn't have a paunch." (Beard is thickset, with virtually no neck and a growing waistline.)

Beard notices one of the touring caddies alone at the bar and invites him over for a drink. Beard is often quietly considerate.

Several U.S. Ryder Cup players partook of the hospitality of a Washington, D.C., golf club en route to England, and Beard alone wrote the club a note of appreciation. He and the caddy soon are immersed in a congenial debate over the value of tour caddies.

At 11 P.M., Beard eats a steak and then takes the elevator to his room.

During the first round of the Alcan, as he was fashioning another solid score (he would finish third), moving around the course completely without ceremony in the manner that has led reporters to liken him to a pharmacist, a grocer and a floorwalker, Beard was being discussed by Dan Sikes, who like Beard went to the University of Florida and is another of the half-dozen or so acute observers of the tour from within.

"I like his action better than anybody's," Sikes is saying. "His temperament is just about ideal. He doesn't emote for the fans, but he's a very interesting person off the course, much more so than other players you might think would be better company. Frank may never be a superstar in the sense of a public attraction, but how can people know what he's like by watching him on a golf course?

"I can assure you that Frank won't phony up to please the galleries, because he's too honest, and maybe he's just a little bitter. He doesn't go out of his way to help newspaper reporters sometimes."

Does Sikes see Beard's insistently commercial outlook on the game as a defense mechanism, a guard against possible failure to win major tournaments and greatness status? "We all have our defense mechanisms," he replies.

Beard's open admiration of Hogan suggests that Beard is more enamored of immortality than he admits. And nothing else about his often engaging personality supports the seeming crassness of his philosophy of golf as essentially a money-producing enterprise, although a near-fatal attack of encephalitis in 1964 (Beard was given the last rites of the Catholic Church), the death of his close friend Tony Lema in an airplane crash (Lema introduced Beard and Beard's wife Pat), and his father's bout with cancer of the throat (the family which includes former Kentucky basketball All-America Ralph Beard is extremely close) have conspired to instill in Beard an almost compulsive desire to insure the future financial security of his wife and children as soon as possible.

There is the strong possibility that his book with Schaap and the accompanying television appearances and other widespread promotional exposure will give the public an insight into Frank

Beard that it has not previously gained. Probably Beard will make no effort to sell himself beyond what it takes to sell books. He has resigned himself to living with his image as a dull golfer. He will always keep a dark corner of himself hidden; one senses that something bothers Frank Beard that no one else is privy to. But isn't it high time to find a new pigeonhole for Frank Beard, who never really deserved the old one—even if he won't assist in the quest?

NOT WITH POWER, BUT WITH POISE

By Art Spander

From the San Francisco Chronicle

It was an afternoon of haze and hazards, an afternoon when the rolling acreage of Augusta National Golf Club frustrated the plans —and perfection—of her aggressors.

But George Archer still was able to retain his composure and a magnificent touch with his putter.

Thus, Archer, the lad from Gilroy, California, the large-nosed kid they said would never make it on the pro tour, yesterday won the Masters Tournament.

He did it not with power, but with poise. He bogeyed but rebounded. He birdied but didn't change. And he never stopped scrambling, coming from the depths of sand traps and the heights of mounds to get his pars.

He shot only an even par 72 on the cool April afternoon, but it still was good for a four-round total of 281, seven under par. That was a stroke ahead of three others—George Knudson, Tom Weiskopf and Billy Casper.

Then he slipped into the green blazer of Augusta National, emblematic of victory in the tournament—one of the so-called big four of golf—and was handed the $20,000 check for first prize.

"I did what I thought I could do on this course," said Archer, first Californian ever to win the Masters in its 33 years.

"I attacked when I thought I could, and other times I played safe. I was thinking positively, and believed it."

The 29-year-old Archer needed his optimism—and all of his talent—late in the day as he strode down the 15th fairway.

His chances for the victory seemed to drop deeper than the ball he hit into the pond that fronts the 15th green. He had tried for a birdie—going for the green in two—and seemed certain to end in a bogey.

But Archer wedged to within 12 feet of the cup and then dropped the putt for a par. It kept him within one stroke of the lead, then held by Charles Coody. Several minutes later Archer was ahead.

"I had hit a good shot," said Archer, who won the San Francisco City Championship in 1963—but was told he'd never make it as a pro because he wasn't long enough off the tee.

"When I saw it splash in the water, I was very surprised. I knew I was a stroke behind, and I saw Charles Coody make a birdie when I was standing at the top of the hill.

"It was a gamble, but I had to take it. I was really downhearted—but I knew I had to keep trying. I didn't figure to make the putt, but I aimed the break just inside a spike mark."

Asked if he was prepared to make a charge, Archer smiled: "Whenever someone says that, I can tell them I left my credit card at home and I'm going to pay cash.

Now Archer has earned $57,000 while winning his second tournament of the year—George took first in the rain and strain of this year's Bing Crosby.

"When I used to caddy at Peninsula Golf Club in San Mateo," said George, "I used to talk about playing in the Crosby. But winning the Masters? I might as well have dreamed of taking a trip to the moon."

He'll never make it with Project Apollo.

"I made a lot of key putts during the tournament," said Archer, at 6-foot-6 tallest of the alpaca-sweatered gypsies who play the game. "I made them when I had to make them—the big pars, or a birdie."

That isn't surprising. Archer, who was coached on his short game by the late Bud Ward at Peninsula, is considered one of the two or three top putters on the tour.

Of course, so is Casper, and he held the lead entering the final day.

Adopting an extremely conservative style, Casper tiptoed to a one-stroke lead after three rounds.

Palmer and Nicklaus used to pick up their drivers and smash birdies up Augusta's verdant throat. Casper laid off and laid up, refused to go for the par-5 greens, and bogeyed only two holes in three days.

So as the massive crowd surged through the gates yesterday—a crowd that included practically everyone except George Archer's wife, Donna, who had gone home to Gilroy—the leader boards read thusly: Casper eight under par, Archer seven, Mill Barber six, Weiskopf five, Coody five and Knudson four.

Before the leaders had played the first nine, Don January was in with the day's best round, a six-under-66 that eventually moved him into a tie for sixth with Coody at 283.

Casper started out trying again to play his game, but it was obvious these are radical times. Even going for the center of the greens, he soared to a four-over par 40. When he bogeyed the 10th hole, Casper apparently was finished.

Archer took the lead, then lost it. But at the end of nine, George had gone ahead by three strokes. Then he bogeyed 10 and on came Weiskopf and Coody, the latter eagling the par-5, 475-yard 13th.

Coody, winner of only one tournament, the 1964 Dallas Open, seemed an unlikely Masters winner. He was. After taking the lead at 15, he bogeyed 16, 17 and 18. Coody momentarily "felt greater pressure than I've ever known" and bogeyed 17.

That left Archer walking up the 18th fairway, smiling and acknowledging the roars of the gallery. He had to wait for Casper's birdie try, but it failed.

"I thought I could win before I teed off," Casper said. "But life is like that. You learn a great deal of humility. And I was fortunate I was able to play in the tournament."

Not as fortunate, of course, as Archer.

"I owe this all to General Selvage," said Archer. "He encouraged me and sponsored me. And we live at this ranch in Gilroy. I used to work down there, cleaning troughs and painting fences."

And, undoubtedly, working on his putting.

A PROFITABLE BAG

By Marty Ralbovsky

From Newspaper Enterprise Association

On the morning of the third round of the Cleveland Open, a slender man in shirt and slacks of matching powder blue leaned against the back end of a maroon Mustang near the entrance to the locker room at Aurora Country Club and chain-smoked mentholated cigarettes.

He said he had been waiting there for three hours, and to prove it he pointed to 14 crushed butts near his feet.

"I gotta find me a bag today," he said, identifying himself as T. B. Foy ("No first name, just initials") from Houston. "My man [Rod Funseth] picked up [withdrew] yesterday and now I gotta do some prospectin'. No way I'm gonna make money here unless I find one. I'll just wait here till somebody comes along . . ."

Twenty feet behind him, under an oak tree near the 18th hole, seven men clustered around a transistor radio, eating hot dogs and sipping Cokes and watching sun-tanned girls wiggle by in two-piece peek-a-boos. One of them was Angie Argea, 39, from Las Vegas. Running his hand through thick graying hair, he said he was "damn good and mad" over the prospect of being idle during the week of the British Open.

"I lose my bag that week," he said. "No sense going all the way over to Annie's [St. Anne's Country Club] because those Limey guys are doing the same thing we are. They're hustling for a buck and they know what they're doing. They're beating us at our own game. I'll take that week off, or maybe I'll drive some cab in Vegas, and wait till my bag comes home." His bag, incidentally, belongs to Jack Nicklaus.

Foy and Argea are professional caddies, two of about 45 who

travel the PGA tour at the players' expense to perform a variety of subservient duties, the least important of which is carrying monogrammed golf bags. ("Any dummy can carry a bag," says Argea, "but a real caddy knows how to read a green, club a player, spot pins. No pro wants some punk kid following him around all day making goo-goo eyes at him like he's some kind of God. Hero worshipers they can do without.")

The status of professional caddies was enhanced considerably this year when the PGA sanctioned their presence at tournaments for the first time. Now, any pro who figures to cash with any degree of consistency has his own caddy and bankrolls him along the stops in return for his exclusive services. On the average, the caddies say, they net $11,000 for a full tour.

"It all depends on who you've got," says Foy. "Last year Billy Casper's boy earned himself $23,000. He's lucky. He's got a winner who's a good player. My man Funseth ain't won a tournament in three years, but still he don't pay bad. He picked up here after two rounds and still gave me $100.

"The pros gotta pay five percent of their winnings to a caddy, and sometimes more, in order to keep him. The local kids get about three percent, maybe less. Ain't no picnic traveling from city to city stretching nickels and dimes and the pros know it. If they got a good boy they pay him well. But there are still some cheapskates. It's up to us to land the guys who pay the best."

Traveling the pro circuit, the caddies say, is a grueling experience. They travel mostly by car, in groups of four, sharing expenses and motel rooms. When they arrive at a tournament, usually on a Monday, their first job is to walk the course with pad and pencil, transcribing the physical layout of each hole. Their arrivals, however, are greeted with something less than enthusiasm at most of the tournament courses.

"The local clubs hate us," says Gardner Dickinson's caddy, a portly man who said he preferred anonymity. "They figure the local kids should be caddying for Palmer and Nicklaus and Casper and making all the loot. What a joke. When we come into town they start looking around for rule books which say we can't work. But the pros don't want to hear any of that stuff and they sign us in right away.

"You know what happened at one tournament this year? The committee held a contest for the local caddies. The kid who sold the most tickets would get to caddy for Palmer. That was first prize. So some kid went out and sold a whole mess of tickets and was all jollied up about caddying for Palmer. When Palmer got there he took one look at the kid and said, 'You guys serious?' The kid wound up caddying for some rabbit.

"They call us gypsies. Right here at this tournament the kids were lined up Monday waiting to sign up for Palmer and Nicklaus and the big boys. When we got here the committee was mad as hell. One guy said, 'Look at those poor kids. You gypsies broke their hearts.' What a laugh. The pros are happy they got us and not those kids. Those kids can put a guy right out of a tournament."

Julius Boros' caddy, slender, 40-ish and a veteran of 15 years on the pro tour, says the kids, besides being inexperienced, sometimes do peculiar things.

"Billy Casper got burned good last year," he said. "They gave him some rich kid whose father was president of the club. Casper won the tournament and asked the kid how much he wanted. The kid said he didn't want money, he wanted a set of Billy Casper Golf Clubs. So Casper got on the phone and called his people and within two hours they had a set of $600 clubs for the kid.

"But the kid didn't want them. He said he wanted a set of Billy Casper clubs. So Casper got back on the phone and called his people again. But they didn't have any autographed clubs in stock. When Casper went back and told the kid, he had a helluva time because the kid started making a scene. Finally, to calm the kid down, Casper gave him his word that a set of clubs would be delivered in a week.

"You know, Casper was happier about getting rid of that kid than he was about winning the damn tournament."

Whenever the value of professional caddies is questioned, the caddies themselves bring up, as the strongest point in their favor, an incident that occurred during the 1967 U.S. Open at Baltusrol, New Jersey. During the first three days of that tournament, a young hopeful named Rives McBee hired—and subsequently fired—seven different caddies.

"I was so fed up with those kids," he says, "I just couldn't take it any more. They didn't know anything. So, for the final round, I hired some sports writer to carry my bag. He wasn't much of a caddy either, but it didn't matter much because I was out of it by then anyway. But at least he knew the difference between a three-iron and a three-wood."

There have been numerous instances when inexperienced caddies have hindered pros during a tournament, and sometimes even cost them strokes. During a tournament last year, one pro was assessed a two-stroke penalty when his eager caddy stepped into a bunker and removed some debris before the shot was made. Another time, a caddy actually started raking sand in a bunker before his player even made his shot. That move, too, cost the player two strokes.

"A good caddy," says Lee Trevino, "is worth good money. I paid my man 10 grand last year and I figure he made at least that much for me. He knows what he's doing and I never have to worry about him. He knows my game, too, and when he spots me doing something wrong he tells me and he's almost always right. I have no complaints about making a 10 grand investment in a guy who's going to help me make 10 times that much."

"If you're playing for fun," says George Archer, "it doesn't matter who's caddying. But when there's money—big money—riding on every shot I want somebody around who knows what's going on. A pro caddy does a lot of little things for you, too, a lot of detailed stuff a golfer doesn't have time to worry about. I just gave my guy two shag bags, for instance, to bring with him to the Whitemarsh in Philadelphia.

"I won't be needing them in England because they use the small balls over there. But when I get back to the States and get to Philly, I know he'll be there and so will the bags."

Working for Trevino or Archer or any other pro, for that matter, requires, the caddies say, rising at the crack of dawn. Every morning during a tournament they get to the course around seven o'clock and walk it to check the new pin placements.

"Every day the pins are placed in a different spot on the green," says Foy. "Sometimes they're 15 or 20 feet deeper, or shorter, than the day before.

"That means a change of irons for approach shots to the green. A golfer may have used a five-iron to get to the green one day, but the next day he'll have to use a three-iron for the same shot because of the new pin spot. We can walk 18 greens in a half hour, spotting pins, because we know how to cut a course."

Despite their closeness on the course, the pros and caddies rarely associate off it. "We know what time our player tees off," says Archer's caddy, a man named Cricket, "and we're there. When the round is over, they go their way and we go ours. Sometimes, though, when a player wins a tournament he throws a bash and invites us along. We go, of course."

There are, the caddies say, still several tournaments—the Masters, U.S. Open and Thunderbird Classic, among them—in which they are not allowed to work. During those weeks, they hook up with the women's tour—"the girls don't pay as much, but they're a lot more fun"—or else they head for their next working stop and wait for the rest of the tour to catch up with them.

"There's only one thing that worries us," says one of the caddies, "and that's the tax people. I know one guy, and I ain't mentioning any names, who hasn't filed income taxes in years and he's made a bundle. Last year they called in one of the pros and wanted to know how much he's been paying his caddy. When he told them they said, 'How come you're paying him that much?' And the pro said, 'Because that's the way we do things.'

"Lucky for us they don't call us in . . ."

Boxing

QUARRY'S MISTAKE

By Roy McHugh

From The Pittsburgh Press

Joe Frazier did not come out smokin'. Jerry Quarry did. It was Quarry's mistake.

Like the little boy who played with matches, he knows better now. He was peering dimly through a bloodshot left eye—his bloodshot right eye had closed after the fashion of a clam shell—when Dr. A. Harry Kleiman, at the end of the seventh round in Madison Square Garden last night, exercised his authority as ringside physician and said to Referee Arthur Mercante, "Let's call the whole thing off."

Thus, by a technical knockout, Joe Frazier retained the heavyweight championship of the six American states and various foreign nations that recognize neither Jimmy Ellis nor the unemployed Cassius Clay as heavyweight champion.

And after seven rounds with Quarry, Frazier was still full of fight. His glance fell on Ellis in one of the $100 seats, Ellis a pastel vision in summery shades of blue. "You're next," Frazier shouted. "You're no champ."

Ellis, his dignity affronted, jumped to his feet, shaking an index finger at Frazier. Briskly, Frazier started to climb through the ropes, but not so briskly that his manager, Yank Durham, wasn't able to pull him back. The stage managing would have done credit to Clay.

Quarry, meanwhile, circled the ring despairingly, his long chin burrowed into his chest. Later, he was to say, "I wanted to go out like a man." Dr. Harry Kleiman had infringed on his right to catch punches for eight more rounds or perhaps to hear the neatly conclusive count of 10.

From the second round on, Quarry had taken a beating.

He had failed to set the trap that Frazier was supposed to walk into. Frazier's way of fighting is to overwhelm his opponent, to advance in a straight line on his short, thick legs and to let the punches fly. It was a style made to order for the counterpunching Quarry, boxing's wise men all said.

But Quarry, it seems, has renounced counterpunching.

In his native California, the public and the press call it stalling. At the weigh-in yesterday, Quarry came dressed in shocking pink—shocking pink velvet robe and shocking pink velvet tights. "This is something to look pretty," he said. "Tonight I'll go out in these trunks and fight like a savage animal. I'm going to try to get it over with in the first 20 seconds if I can. Like he said, he's gonna be smokin'. Well, I'm gonna be burnin', and if I land the right punch it could happen."

Quarry's intentions were good. At the bell for the first round, he met Frazier more than halfway. He threw the first punch. Instead of waiting to counter, he led. He landed punches, but never the right one. He was toe to toe with Frazier, head to head, shoulder to shoulder. Quarry won the round, but Frazier endured.

In the second round, reluctantly, Quarry began to back up. Frazier has nothing that can properly be called a jab, but he was stabbing his left into Quarry's face. He was slowly establishing dominance.

He controlled the fight from the third through the seventh. He banged away at Quarry with left hooks and short rights. His straight left snapped Quarry's head back. He cut Quarry under the right eye.

Between the third and the fourth rounds, Dr. Kleiman was in Quarry's corner, anxiously appraising the damage.

Quarry counterpunched because he had to, but not effectively, not sharply. Frazier, keeping him on the ropes, persisted. Quarry's puffy, troubled face was twisted in something like a scowl.

At the weigh-in, with Quarry scaling 198½ to Frazier's 203½, Jerry had predicted "one of the better fights in the last 25 years." It wasn't that—it was far too one-sided—but as Quarry said afterward, "I tried. I had too much fighter in there with me."

Jack Quarry, his father and manager, thought so, too. "Joe's the best fighter in the world today," Jack said. "He's better than I thought he was—he changed my mind. He's better than Clay."

And Jerry's mother made it a point to congratulate Frazier, breaking into his postfight press conference.

"See," blurted Frazier, "this wasn't no racial thing. No hard feelings. We were just in there to see who was best."

The black champion risen from Philadelphia's gym wars, unbeaten now in 25 fights, had heard the 16,000 in the Garden greet Quarry with a thunderous roar. He had heard boos intermingled with the cheers for himself.

But Frazier's resentment seemed directed toward Ellis, a black man, too. They share the title, somewhat unequally, and Ellis, in the past, has dodged a showdown. "I'm the champ," Ellis says. "I'm not challengin' nobody. He says he's a bad man, come out smokin'. He says he can't be beat. It's a lie."

If so, Jerry Quarry has not exposed it as such. And for Jack Quarry, the self-styled Okie, a moment of truth had arrived. Jack could not resist looking for someone to blame. He had tried to talk Jerry out of taking the fight to Frazier, he said.

"He wasn't trying to please the crowd, he was trying to please the sports writers," Jack went on bitterly. "You got what you wanted—you wanted blood and you got it."

But deep down Jack knew why Jerry had lost.

"Joe at this stage is a better fighter," he said.

THE UNLIKELY HEAVYWEIGHT CHAMPION

By Shirley Povich

From The Washington Post

Rocky Marciano didn't make it to that birthday party they'd planned for him in that Des Moines steakhouse Sunday night because the end came in a small plane that plunged out of the overcast into an Iowa farm field. It had to be factors beyond his control. Rocky's single-motored heart would never have failed him.

He'd gotten there as heavyweight champion of the world in 1952 through an absolute courage. It was the fount of his success, a flaming valor that was the biggest thing he took into a prize ring. On style, he was as unlikely a heavyweight champion as ever showed in boxing trunks, and in physical stature he appeared too small for the tasks. Yet nobody ever walked out of the ring a winner over Marciano.

Once it was chronicled of him, by a writer who shall be unnamed, "Rocky Marciano can't box a lick, his footwork is what you'd expect from two left feet, he throws his right hand in a clumsy circle and knows nothing of orderly retreat. All he can do is blast the breath from your lungs or knock your head off." It was fairly descriptive.

When, abruptly, in his fourth year as champion, he said he would retire, and made it stick, the full appreciation of the figure of Marciano dawned. He'd had 49 fights, won them all, all but six by knockouts, never was close to being licked as champion, and had moved up among the legends. Dempsey, Louis, Marciano. It began to have a decent ring.

Cassius Clay won his heavyweight title in his 20th fight, but little notice was taken of Rocky Marciano until he'd licked 27 guys, all in a row. It wasn't until his 43rd fight that he got a shot at Joe

Walcott's title. The trouble was that Rocky didn't give a very good impression in the ring. Awfully crude, very short arms, easy to hit, couldn't last long against the first good fighter he met.

They were underrating Marciano all this time. If his moves weren't classic, his ability to take a punch was extraordinary. The source of his energy was much his own secret. The blocky son of a Brockton, Massachusetts, shoemaker was a physical culture fiend. What was good for the body, he wanted. What wasn't, he rejected. No smoking, no drinking, no night life, ever, because he had work to do.

At Grossinger's, where Marciano set up training camp for many fights, he liked to do his early morning roadwork on the hills of the golf course. A young caddy once leaked one of Rocky's routines. "See them 51 steps going up to the next tee? Mr. Marciano goes down them steps every morning on one leg. And then he goes up again, on one leg. It makes him strong, don't you think?"

He hadn't licked a single name fighter except for Roland LaStarza in his first 26 fights, and LaStarza was no great figure. But when they put Marciano in with aging Joe Louis that night in Madison Square Garden, and he knocked out Louis in the eighth round, a special truth was established. In the sixth round, the easy-to-hit Marciano was swatted on the chin by all the right hand that the 37-year-old Louis could muster—and nothing happened. Rocky's absorption powers had been tested and they were enormous.

A year later in Philadelphia, few would guess that the fellow knocked to the seat of his pants in the first round would get up to win Joe Walcott's title. The stylish Walcott hadn't wasted much time with this abysmal crudity in the ring with him, who hadn't bothered to learn the lessons of the gymnasium, and whipped a left hook to Marciano's chin.

Marciano beat the count, beat three rounds of half-blindness caused by the medication flowing from the later cuts by Walcott, and won the title. It happened in the 13th round. Walcott, at 38, was not a victim of the devouring years. He was done in by a curving right-hand punch that was the last of the fight.

In that Walcott fight, Marciano was down for the first time in his life. The second time was in his last fight. That one was against Archie Moore, who also unloaded against him in the first round. It is notable that Walcott and Moore both could throw elegant left hooks. Marciano licked Moore mostly because he could take a punch and was fatigue-proof. Against Archie he needed those two resources.

The two times he was on the floor during his career he was more embarrassed than hurt, Marciano later said. His main concern, he said, was the loyal horde from his Bockton neighborhood who came to all his fights. "They couldn't afford to see me lose," he said. "They couldn't afford those $25 seats. I always knew I would get up."

Those short arms which deprived him of reach were his friends, Marciano often said, not a shortcoming. "I can take a punch, and when I get inside I'm free to hit." Years later when Sonny Liston, as champion, was supposedly the invincible armed fortress of a man, Marciano said he thought he could beat Liston. "But don't print that," he said. Marciano was never the braggart. He was unaware that "the less a man thinks or knows about his virtues the better we like him." But then, of course, Rocky never could find the time to read Emerson.

Wrestling

RACE WAR IS ALIVE AND WELL AT MADISON SQUARE GARDEN

By Jerry Izenberg

From Jock

It was the wrestlers who first showed them how to find the Garden. The nonstop airlift from San Juan was a fact of life by then, holding forth the rich promise of full-time employment. Some of them were simply trading the slumlords of San Juan's La Esmeralda for the slumlords of Harlem's El Barrio, but the money was there and they became the guts of the food service industry. They became the shock troops of the garment center, pushing the clumsy racks of clothes across Seventh and Eighth Avenues.

In some cases they earned four times as much as they could in San Juan or in Ponce or in Santurce. They were not afraid to spend it. "Se habla Espanol" signs blossomed in the pawn shops and the cheap clothing stores and the credit appliance joints.

But it was the wrestlers who found them first. Baseball was too slow, too dull. Football was too alien, its weather too cold. But the wrestling people thought of all those monthly payments on all those televison sets, and any sport which is smart enough to let the good guys win, is smart enough to tell everyone about it.

So along came clean-cut Miguel Perez, darkly handsome and from San Juan. And after the match, there was the double-image close-up of Miguel Perez at the microphone coming to you, amigos, directly from the beautiful Uline Arena in beautiful downtown Washington, and Miguel Perez was speaking in Spanish and he was shouting into the microphone:

"Next week . . . next Friday night . . . we will teach them a lesson at Madison Square Garden on Eighth Avenue and 49th

Street, next to the subway station." All that was missing was "In New York the number to call is . . ." The announcer supplied that.

There was a genuine feeling about what would happen at the Garden the following week. Consider the guy coming out of El Barrio or down from the Bronx or up from Brooklyn.

He could lose in the morning and lose at night, but then there is Miguel Perez, and for a delicious three-hour period in Madison Square Garden he can sit in the balcony and be a positive winner, because the man in the ring, who also speaks Spanish, is going to do it all for him. He will get off the floor and handle the Man, and this is all the Passion Play the balcony set requires.

So the wrestlers showed the way, and when they did, the responsive chord was struck with the boxing people, whose sport has always existed on the emotional principle of ethnic matchmaking. The Puerto Ricans did as much for boxing in this city as boxing did for them. Things had gotten so tough you couldn't even find an Irish fighter in a bar. The Italians and the Jews had moved on to other businesses. The great neighborhood fights—which were in themselves ethnic—were gone. Once when Brooklyn's Al Davis fought Mickey Farber, the pride of the Lower East Side, the cops had to chase the turn-aways off the streets near St. Nick's. They climbed to the roof and watched through the skylight. They had a dandy view until they started leaning against each other, and then the view was even dandier for the guy who came crashing through the skylight and into the ring.

But the ethnic groups which were boxing's lifeblood have found easier ways to make a living. The neighborhoods themselves no longer exist. A couple of years ago, for example, the Garden decided to stage the world's welterweight championship of Queens.

It was a fair fight and a modest financial success, but it revived nothing in terms of the old matchmaking code.

It hardly began to compete with the night Jake LaMotta was the landlord at the Jerome Arena and he matched two neighborhood bullies for the championship of the block. This was neighborhood and it was ethnic—one was of Italian descent and the other of Irish. At the bell, Bully No. 1 walked across the ring, drew back his arm and hit Bully No. 2 smack on his protective cup. As Bully No. 2 sank slowly, the referee prepared to halt the fight. Bully No. 2's fans did not like this approach, and they prepared to enforce their point by breaking off a great many wooden chair legs and starting toward the ring.

It was at that point that LaMotta surveyed the full house, calculated the potential refunds, and shouted to the ref: "The hell with it. Let 'em fight." After a brief respite, the bell rang again. Bully No. 2 walked across the ring, drew back his arm, and etc. . . . etc. . . . etc. . . . It went thus for eight rounds. For eight rounds nobody got hit above the navel. And nobody—but absolutely nobody—asked for a refund.

Well, you simply cannot do those things any more without having somebody form a picket line, just as it is impossible today to promulgate the ethnic myth of a Primo Carnera.

Boxing people in New York remember quite well a man named Leon See, who was Carnera's European manager. Mr. See carried around a small black book which listed the Italian-American populations of every city in the United States. When the mob, which had its hooks into Carnera, booked him to win in Jacksonville, Florida, See protested. "There are only 11 Italian families there," he pointed out. "We will not even draw the fruit flies off the oranges." Mr. See was right. After that, they listened to him.

Primo Carnera was the ethnic box-office creation of a man named Good Time Charlie Freedman. He would kibbutz the card games down at Solly's on the Lower East Side, and he would hover over the cheese cake at Ratner's, and he would tell people how this tribe of giants living in the heart of Central China in a place known only to God and Good Time Charlie could produce a heavyweight champion. All he needed was a little financing.

It was, of course, that kind of world back in the 1920's, so he got his financing. Which brings us to Billy LaHiff's restaurant the night that Bill Duffy got the cable. Good Time Charlie was in London, which as every schoolboy knows, is the most direct route to the heart of China. He had seen a giant of a man. A man who was 6-foot-6 and weighed 260 pounds and who had cleverly managed to beat Young Stribbling by getting himself hit in the groin in the fourth round. He couldn't fight much and he wasn't Chinese, but even Charlie would be the first to admit that nobody is perfect.

"I'm gonna book him all over the country," Duffy said.

"You're lucky," said a man named Willie Gilzenberg, who subsequently promoted two Carnera fights. "Italian is fine. Chinese don't draw two quarters at the gate."

Of course, what followed was the greatest ethnic buildup a fighter ever received. Because of Leon See's black book, a great deal of money was made—none of which Carnera ever saw. Again, in Good Time Charlie's words: "Nobody is perfect."

The thing reached the heights in Newark, of all places, when a man named Cowboy Owens was hired to do a job. It was a very difficult job. Carnera had won two fights without throwing a punch and without getting hit. Cowboy Owens' job was to hit Carnera without killing him and to depart a round later.

To avoid total hysteria, the late Gene Roman, an Italian-American, was hired as referee because he was bilingual. In the first round, Mr. Owens studied Carnera for some time. Carnea studied Mr. Owens for the same amount of time. It was positively fascinating. Finally, Cowboy said "What the hell" and tapped Carnera on the shoulder.

Mr. Carnera dropped his arms and turned his large eyes on Gene Roman. "He hit me," Carnera said.

Mr. Roman thought about that a little bit and then replied in perfect Italian: "Well, hit him back."

Cowboy Owens drowned on schedule in the second round.

Those fights and the crowds who so identified with them are gone. But then came Miguel Perez, and after him a torrent of Puerto Rican kids with fine skills who were willing to get hit on the chin and to hit back in order to beat those ubiquitous credit stores. The talent was there and the bodies were there. What was needed was a hero. Enter Jose Torres.

Torres was out of Playa Ponce. He was then a middleweight. He could punch like hell although his manager, a man named Cus D'Amato, wont to conjure up plots by a mysterious group called "they," threatened to turn him into a Judge Crater in eight-ounce gloves. In the end this cost him.

But in the beginning Torres worked the Puerto Rican Theater up on 138th Street in the Bronx and the Broadway Theater down in Brooklyn, hustling tickets for each subsequent fight. He hit the wedding and wake circuit. He began each day at the barber shops, shaking hands and saying, "Hello. I am Jose Torres, and I am fighting at the St. Nick's this week."

It got results. The Puerto Ricans made St. Nick's their clubhouse and their fraternity. They choked the sidewalks with pedestrian traffic. They paid the specs three bucks for a $1.50 ticket. It was no small financial sacrifice for people whose money is pre-divided among a great many creditors.

Torres was their hero, but he became a pawn in D'Amato's war with boxing's Establishment. His fights became fewer and fewer. Around the neighborhoods they began to call him "coward." Not so much because they believed it, but because they hoped he would go on forever like Miguel Perez, administering the triumphs of good over evil. Torres became a victim of fights which never materialized. The balcony grew impatient. It looked for a new hero.

It had choices. There was Carlos Ortiz, who, after all, was the lightweight champion of the world. But at the time Ortiz had left the Bronx, and the balcony wanted a hero it could touch and see. It had Jose Gonzales, who fought regularly in New York but who lacked Torres' skills. It finally settled on a young kid named Frankie Narvez.

Narvez was a walk-in kind of fighter. Because he moved straight ahead, the balcony believed that as long as he kept going forward he was winning. This was not always the case, particularly when he was catching gloves with his face. The balcony, however, was in no hurry to be convinced. Twice when Narvez lost close decisions, first to Flash Elorde of the Philippines and later to Ismael Laguna of Panama, the balcony offered mild objections.

These objections included the hurling of a fire axe into the ring, a barrage of bottles and an aerial assault with chairs. The night of the Laguna fight, the balcony put music to the words. A half-dozen composers were scrambling around in the darkness of the mezzanine looking for something to throw. The thing they found was the Madison Square Garden organ. But the most exciting was yet to come. On a night in the spring of 1968, Jose Torres, who had recaptured much of the balcony's affections, was back in business, challenging Dick Tiger for the light heavyweight title which he had held briefly. Torres lost. It was a swell fight. It was a pretty good riot, too.

The next morning, management would say that it was just a small flurry . . . a mild irritant. Management was correct in that the building was not dynamited. A writer caught at ringside listened to the whistling bottles shatter around him for a good half hour.

Now the tradition of ethnic matchmaking continues with the Puerto Ricans, but except for the occasions cited, there has been little in the way of mass histrionics. After all, the concept of ethnic matchmaking has always been inherent in a sport whose nuances are as subtle as a falling safe. Consider the recent Joe Frazier-Jerry Quarry match.

"Quarry is going to be the next Irish champion," said Billy Conn, who was in town for the fight.

"Did you know he's a Baptist?" a reported asked Conn.

"The hell you say. I thought you said he's Irish."

"Well, he is."

"We'll see. If he wins, he's Irish. If he loses, he's just another Baptist."

Horse Racing

THE REGAL RED COMET FROM OUT OF THE WEST

By Bob Barnet

From The Muncie Star

Majestic Prince, a regal red comet from out of the West, fought off two bold challengers to win the 95th Kentucky Derby here Saturday before a screaming, sun-drenched audience that included President Richard M. Nixon, first Chief Executive ever to see the race.

The unbeaten chestnut charger from California reached the finish line only a neck in front of the courageous Arts and Letters, with the fast-closing Dike another half-length behind in a wild, whipping finish. Majestic Prince ran the mile and one quarter in 2:01 and four-fifths, somewhat slower than was anticipated.

The Derby victor is owned by Canadian industrialist Frank McMahon and was ridden by Bill Hartack, who won the storied Run for the Roses for the fifth time to equal the record of Eddie Arcaro. Trainer of the winner was Johnny Longden, a veteran of 10 Derby rides who won the Triple Crown on Count Fleet in 1943.

Traffic Mark finished fourth, 10 lengths behind Dike, with Top Knight fifth, Ocean Roar sixth, Fleet Allied seventh, and Rae Jet eighth.

The winner, a 7–5 favorite with a crowd that probably reached a record 125,000, paid $4.80, 3.40, and 2.60 for each two-dollar ticket across the board. Arts and Letters paid $4.20 and 3.00 and Dike $2.80.

The huge audience set a Derby wagering record of $2,625,524 in its effort to sort out a well-matched field. Total mutuel "handle" for the nine-race program was $6,106,346, also a record.

It was a four-horse battle, just as expected, and there were four different leaders. Of the pre-race "Big Four," only Dike never led, but he threatened ominously throughout the race.

Ocean Roar led them past the stands for the first time and clung to the lead until deep in the backstretch, when Manuel Ycaza shook up Top Knight and sent him into the lead as they reached the three-quarter pole.

Braulio Baeza moved abruptly with Arts and Letters as they neared the mile post and the son of Ribot took the lead, with Majestic Prince a half-length behind and Dike only two lengths off the pace in third position.

Then it was Majestic Prince's turn to sweep into the lead and it was he who brought them around the stretch turn.

When they came into the long stretch, Majestic Prince held a lead of a half-length over Arts and Letters and Dike was two lengths away.

Arts and Letters, on the inside, rallied strongly and ranged up alongside Majestic Prince an eighth of a mile from home. But the magnificent chestnut refused to surrender the lead and increased his lead by inches as they neared the wire. Arts and Letters gave ground grudgingly and on the outside Dike came on with a powerful rush. The three of them hurtled under the wire almost shoulder to shoulder.

All three jockeys, Hartack, Baeza, and Jorge Velasquez on Dike, whipped furiously in the pulsing battle through the stretch.

A slow early pace by Ocean Roar probably kept the field from threatening Northern Dancer's track and Derby record of two minutes flat. They were at the quarter in :23 3/5, the half in 38, the three quarters in 1:12 2/5 and the mile in 1:37 3/5 before arriving at the finish line in 2:01 4/5.

The victory was the eighth in a row for the unbeaten Majestic Prince, a towering son of Raise A Native and grandson of Native Dancer, whose only defeat was by Dark Star in the Kentucky Derby of 1953. The 1969 Derby winner was Kentucky-bred at the farm of Leslie Combs II at Lexington. His dame was Gay Hostess by Royal Charger.

Longden said after the race that his main concern had been Arts and Letters, who was only a neck behind Majestic Prince when it was all over. Asked what jockey Bill Hartack had told him after the race, Longden said, "He told me we had a game horse." Hartack declined an invitation to talk with writers in the press box.

Braulio Baeza, who rode Rokeby Stable's Arts and Letters, said of the rousing finish: "It got very close but no bumping. My horse really tried Majestic Prince, three or four times."

Jorge Velasquez, who rode Dike, said ruefully, "The horses in front of me, they never stopped. They never came back to me. At the head of the stretch I thought I was going to win. I hope to catch him in the Belmont."

Top Knight, who faded abruptly after surrendering the lead on the far turn, just got tired, according to Ycaza. "He was laying in a comfortable position," the jockey said. "He just got tired. He ran a good mile. I wish it had been a mile race."

Bobby Stewart, who rode the long-priced Ocean Roar, said his horse tired after six furlongs but said he believes the horse deserves a shot at the Preakness and Belmont.

McMahon saw the race despite the fact that he has been suffering from the flu. He became ill again at an owner's party at the track following the race but recovered quickly and rejoined the party.

And so the story ended, and if the red prince looked in vain for a princess, there could be little doubt that he found the pot of gold. Total purse was $155,700 and the winner's share was $113,200.

Even by California standards, it was a lovely pot of gold.

"BARBARA JO RUBIN IS A GOOD BET"

By Lew King

From the Philadelphia Sunday Bulletin

The field in this race at Wheeling Downs was tilting around the far turn. A couple of horses off the lead, Barbara Jo Rubin, a 19-year-old girl jockey, was riding a live one. The field straightened out for home and Barbara Jo took dead aim on the leader.

The fans who bet her were screaming:

"Come on, baby! You can do it!"

Barbara Jo moved her horse up even with the leader. And then, 70 yards from home, she started to pass. The boy on the fading front-runner couldn't take this thing—this losing to a girl. So he reached out with his whip and gave Miss Rubin a healthy whack on the rump.

That is just one of the many indignities that Barbara Jo Rubin has suffered since she broke into the male world of horse race riding this year.

Jockeys in Florida refused to ride against her at first. When they were forced to compete with her, they shoved her against the rail. They boxed her in. They swore at her.

Some fans who lost money on her mounts threw vulgar remarks at her. Some jockeys, trainers, owners and track officials criticized her riding style.

Through it all Miss Rubin has shown more class than all her critics could muster together.

You could see the class in this slim young lady as she was interviewed at Garden State Park, Thursday, after she had become the first girl to ride a race in New Jersey.

Barbara Jo is intelligent. She's attractive in her little-girl pigtails. And she's got a smile that convinces you she will never turn bitter over the bad experiences she's had.

"I don't want to criticize anybody who has said anything bad about me," she said. "I'd rather ride horses than people. I know I'm not a great jockey. I'm just an apprentice and I'm just learning."

She smiled that smile.

"Please don't get the impression that everybody's mean to me. A lot of people have been nice to me."

She said that jockeys Eddie Belmonte, Angel Cordero, Jr., and Chuck Baltazar have been especially kind.

"They've encouraged me," she said. "They give me tips on handling equipment. They tell me not to copy any other rider. They tell me to pick my own style of riding. They say it will all come to me. They tell me not to get depressed when things go wrong."

Later, Baltazar was told that Barbara Jo spoke highly of him.

"That's nice of her," he said. "Yes, I tried to give her some help. I met her at Pimlico. She used to come around in the morning and we got to know each other.

"I could see she had things to learn. But she was willing to listen. So I gave her some pointers.

"I appreciated help when I was starting out. And if I can help someone else, I'm more than glad to do it."

Baltazar said the most important thing about Miss Rubin is her willingness to listen and learn.

"I really don't know just how far she or any of the other girl riders can go in this business," he said. "But I'll tell you this, Barbara Jo Rubin—right now—can ride better than many apprentice boys I've seen."

Miss Rubin's historic ride at Garden State was aboard Milmay in the first race.

Milmay is a three-year-old filly. She's a chestnut with a white blaze and one white sock. Milmay walked into the saddling area, a brown and white beauty, wearing a yellow blinker hood.

Miss Rubin walked up to her mount. She was wearing the brown and yellow silks of the A. J. Bullock stable. Her pants were white.

When Barbara Jo mounted her filly their colors matched perfectly. It was something special for this special occasion.

Milmay went off at 10–1 in the $5,000 claiming race at six furlongs. Milmay was in Box 9. Twelve horses ran.

Charlie Ulbig, the *Bulletin*'s turfman handicapper, kept his field glasses on Miss Rubin throughout her ride. Here's what Ulbig said as the race was run:

"She broke on top . . . They say she's good at that . . . She can't get over to the rail—too many there . . . She's laying fourth in good position . . . The kid's got good hands . . ."

As the field rounded the turn Milmay was shuffled back to sixth. They straightened out for home. Ulbig continued:

"She's got the rail . . . If the horse has anything she's got an opening on the inside . . . The horse is hanging . . ."

As Milmay finished sixth, like a 10–1 shot should, Ulbig noted:

"She did as good with that thing as any other jockey could do."

Miss Rubin also rode in the ninth race. She finished dead last on a 38–1 shot. That was her 53rd ride. She won 15 of them and finished out of the money only 16 times. A fine record.

Barbara Jo's horses carried 111 pounds in the Garden State races. She weighed 107 that day. She says she'd weigh around 115 if she wasn't riding. So, like most jockeys, she has to watch her diet.

"I eat steak, fish, cottage cheese and a lot of vegetables and fruit," she said. "I drink skim milk and tea. It's not too hard to take. But every once in a while I break down and eat a candy bar or a piece of cake."

There's a certain loneliness to the life of a girl jockey.

This day at Garden State Miss Rubin was kept busy talking to newsmen. But if the day hadn't been a historic one, she'd have spent three hours in a room by herself waiting for the ninth race.

Naturally, she can't join the men in the jockeys' quarters. Garden State provides her with quarters in a private ladies room. There was a big leather couch if she wanted to sleep. And there was a large mirror, a dressing table and a shower.

Barbara Jo was pleased with the setup.

"Sometimes all I get is a large closet," she said. "Sometimes I dress in the first-aid room."

But the inconveniences in a girl jockey's life are worth it to Miss Rubin. She loves horses and she loves riding. She concentrates on what's important to her.

She's not making a fortune. But she's saving money and some day she hopes to buy a ranch and breed thoroughbreds.

How long will she continue riding?

She smiled.

"Until the right guy comes along," she said.

The smile disappeared.

". . . Or until I get hurt," she said.

A jockey can get busted up any time he rides. He could even get killed in the starting gate.

Has Barbara Jo ever been frightened in a race?

"No, I've never been scared," she said. "If you have fear you shouldn't go out there.

"If I ever do get scared, I'll quit. I wouldn't be doing an honest job if I didn't."

You wonder what more her critics expect of her.

CITATION IS STILL A LADIES' MAN

By Ira Berkow

From Newspaper Enterprise Association

The spring is gone now in Citation's legs. He walks with much of his former grace and majesty but, increasingly, with more pain. And he seems to need that little extra oomph provided by the slow, easy swing of his rather sumptuous black tail.

In his paddock, he walks a few yards and stops and lowers his neck and nibbles a fare of grass. His handsome bay coat shines in the warm Kentucky sunlight.

"Ci has got the rheumatism in the legs," said the horse's groom, Hugh Fields, watching and leaning against the white paddock fence at Calumet Farm. "He sets his legs down like a cat with sacks on his feet. That's from an old sayin'—walkin' like a cat with sacks on his feet."

Hugh Fields, a ruddy fellow, tugged his brown cap so it nearly touched his steel-rimmed glasses and he smiled, thinking of Citation. He has been Citation's groom since 1951, when the horse retired from racing after becoming the first thoroughbred to win over $1 million in purses and, in 1948, was the eighth and last Triple Crown winner.

"Ci's 24 years old now," says Hugh Fields. "That's about, oh, 80 years old in human life. He's beginning to break some now—you know, show his age. Got some gray hairs in that black mane and his back is swayed and he's put on 200, 250 pounds since he went into stud. Up to about 1,300 now. He's in top health, though, perfect health I'd call it, 'cept for his legs which been givin' him trouble lately.

"But he's still a ham for posin'. When folks with cameras come 'round, his neck sets up and his ears perk and his back straightens."

For a celebrity of Citation's stature and bankroll, Calumet Farm seems an altogether fitting place to while away the waning days. The cuisine is ripe green (though some say it is tinged with blue). White fences tumble over hills as far as the eye can see. Pink and white dogwood trees are in blossom. Sycamore, pine and oak trees are slipping into green coats. Jonquils and tulips and red sage and blue ageratum are blooming in the sweet springtime. Here and there, colts and fillies frolic.

Yet it is not all a life of leisure for the famous senior citizen. From February to June each year, Citation must perform daily chores, if they may be termed that. Twice a day during that period Citation the stud is asked to "cover" mares.

"I think Ci's enjoying retirement," said Hugh Fields. "He's still a ladies' man, naturally. He's one of the best covering horses in the country. His stud fee's gone down, though. Three years ago it went from $5,000 to $3,500. Some folks think a horse his age won't get a strong foal. But I don't hardly think so.

"His get never did come up to anything equal to himself. He got some useful horses but not sensational, like Silver Spoon and Guadalcanal and Fabius. But you race a horse like the way they raced Ci and they take the stamina outa him.

"But there's no doubt about it that he ain't the greatest horse that ever lived. Would run anywhere any time on any track. You know what Eddie Arcaro said? He said ridin' Ci was like drivin' a Cadillac.

"'Bout once a week now he'll gallop 'round the paddock here, but it ain't easy what with the rheumatism in the legs. He likes to roll around, too. Oh, he sure does. Sometimes he'll get mud and dust caked on him an inch deep and it'll take me an hour to clean it off.

"But there'll come a time soon when Ci will lay down and won't be able to get up. He's in perfect health but he still could die tomorrow. Most horses live only to 18 or 20. 'Course Ci might live to 30, like Man O'War done.

"Bull Lea, that was Ci's daddy, he lived to 29. And a few times a month in those last years he'd lay down and couldn't get up, his legs was so weak. A wrecker would come in with a steel cable and motor and we'd roll Bull Lea onto a girth and hoist him up till he stood and got his senses. Then he'd just walk away.

"Ci still eats good and sleeps good. You can hear him snorin' and groanin' and nickerin' here to Louisville. He's intelligent and level-headed like he used to be. He ain't vicious like some stallions—but he will try to bite you like all stallions if he don't know you. And he'll listen to you if you talk to him right.

"And sometimes, sometimes when some of us are listening on the radio to a race and the people get to hollerin', Ci will raise up his head and stand straight and listen. He still thinks he's at the track, I reckon."

Track and Field

SIX AT TOM BLACK TRACK

By George Leonard

From The Nashville Banner

San Jose State, made famous originally 69 years ago when Willie Heston played halfback there before attaining fame in football at Michigan, won the NCAA Track and Field Championship with only six men in just five events.

How did it happen?

Let's go back to approximately 5:55 P.M. (EDT) last Saturday at Tom Black Track in Knoxville.

This was the three-mile run, next to last event on the three-day show in the 48th annual meet. San Jose was in with 48 points and no entry in this race or in the last event, the mile relay, coming up next.

Kansas, it was known by a few, had 45 points.

"We're gonna win," Neville Myton, a San Jose athlete who didn't compete Saturday, shouted excitedly as the 22-man field in the three-mile run circled the track in the early laps.

"If Jim Ryun [Kansas' Olympic 1500-meter silver medalist] winds up fifth or worse, you've got it," a reporter said.

"Oh, no!" Myton moaned, figuring Ryun was good for a much higher finish than that.

It happened near the last turn on the fourth lap (almost a mile had elapsed). Ryun suddenly left the track and Kansas, favorite for the team title, had lost the meet.

Even then, the San Jose party wouldn't believe the reporter when he said, "That's it. You've got it, the way I figure things."

"What about UCLA?" a San Jose athlete asked. "Can't they win if they take the mile relay?"

"Not a chance—if these figures are right."

"Man, they better be right."

UCLA came in fifth with 39 points, behind Washington State and Oregon State which tied for third and fourth with 40.

Ryun, second in the mile to Villanova's Marty Liquori who set an NCAA record of 3:57.7, was his team's last hope after the "baby whales," Doug Knop and Karl Salb, flopped to fifth and sixth in the discus.

Ryun, world record holder in the mile and 880, quit a race for the third time since he returned from the Olympic Games. Last time was in the Drake Relays when he shocked the crowd in the sprint medley. He said then he was too tired to run. The crowd booed.

The turnout of 8,200 Saturday was stunned, disbelieving.

Ryun made himself scarce to the press afterward. There was no immediate explanation. Finally, Kansas' sports information director Jay Simon said he had talked to the senior distance star.

"Jim said it was so hot, so humid out there to try and run two long races," Simon stated. "As for the mile event, he had no excuse."

Ryun was running last when he dropped out of the three-mile.

Whatever the reason, Kansas, odds-on-choice in the big meet in which 10 NCAA records were set and two tied, was dead.

It wasn't just Ryun's decision that killed the Jayhawks. In the discus, it was figured they would get seven or eight points instead of only three.

If that lost the meet, John Carlos won it.

Completely outspoken, easygoing but a flaming competitor, Carlos feasts on attention and praise. He got all of both he could ask for in Knoxville. And completely deserved everything.

The 6-foot-3, 200-pound sprinter won the 100, 220 and helped San Jose's 440-yard relay team to another first.

Other points came when Ronnie Ray Smith was second in the 100, Lee Evans runner-up in the 440-yard dash (to the world record 44.7 by Curtis Mills of Texas A&M) and John Powell's fourth in the discus.

"You can't underestimate how much that throw by Powell [183–7] meant to us," said San Jose Coach Bud Winter.

"Suppose he takes fifth, instead of fourth—in other words, Kansas gets the fourth instead of us. They get two more points. We get two less. We're beat."

Besides Carlos and Smith, Sam Davis and Kirk Clayton formed the quarter-mile relay quartet.

Six men, including three Olympic medalists, in only five events. That's all it took.

Tennessee seemed a long way from national prominence after scoring 28 points and finishing ninth.

This was Coach Chuck Rohe's greatest team, the finest ever assembled in the Southeastern Conference. Several of his athletes did extremely well, went up to the "big leagues" and competed favorably. Others found it too tough, including some from whom points had been expected.

Two who merit special mention are senior Larry Kelly and junior Hardee McAlhaney of the Vols' mile relay team which finished third in 3:06.5 to UCLA's NCAA record 3:03.4.

Kelly, a disappointment all spring after being heralded by his coach as an Olympic prospect three years ago, had run a miserable heat in the 880 on Thursday. But he went out Saturday with a heroic effort, running the second leg in 46.7.

And McAlhaney, shut out of his heat in the 440 on Thursday, came back with an almost unbelievable 44.7 on the anchor leg.

"It was the greatest race of his life—after a sour spring," Rohe said.

Winter, veteran San Jose coach, was almost beside himself with joy immediately after the meet.

"We came in the back door after a long, long wait," he said. San Jose had been runner-up three times in the past. "Friday night, I didn't see how Kansas could be beaten.

"But every event was so highly contested, it was just a case of who survived. The facilities at Tennessee are just fantastic. This was the best meet and certainly the fastest the NCAA has ever known anywhere, anytime."

CALLING THE OLD SHOTS

By Blackie Sherrod

From the Dallas Times Herald

Every day in every way, there is mounting evidence that many of us were born one hundred years too soon. Don't talk to me about the good old days. The only good thing about the old days is we don't have to go through them again. Like just the other day, we read that a guy predicted pole vaulters would be clearing 20 feet before the turn of the century.

This guy was a vaulting pole manufacturer and goodness knows what synthetic slingshots he has in mind. With the old bamboo poles, a 15-foot jump was considered on a par with a Channel swim or a successful trip over Niagara Falls in a truck casing. Nowadays, if a high school kid can't top 15 feet with one of those new fiber glass catapults, he can't get out of study hall to practice.

You are talking to an old pole vaulter, one who not only failed to forecast the 20-foot vault, but one who predicted that athletes would be vaulting lower and lower until one day the event would disappear from the track calendar, in favor of limbo dancing.

The reason was as simple as pain itself. In fact, that was the reason. Pain.

Back there a century or so, we didn't have a pit stacked six feet high with huge foam rubber blocks to serve as a landing field. You could fall out of the Goodyear blimp on a cushion like that and not raise a blister. What we had was pure old sand. River bottom sand, if you will, with a little sawdust mixed in to keep it from packing. It had, roughly, the resiliency of a cedar plank.

In our particular Central Texas high school, there was only one kid stupid enough to venture into pole vaulting and that was old stupid here. It seemed like a good deal at the time. In a small school you HAD to do something during the track season or the football coach would pout.

And pole vaulting looked like the easiest way out. You were entirely unsupervised. While the rest of the guys were trotting around the track and passing sticks to each other and the coach was yelling this and that, the pole vaulter was over by his solitary. You spent a good portion of the workout time studying the socket where the pole was placed. This looked important; in case the coach glanced in your direction, you didn't exactly want to be stretched out asleep. You could also go over to the chinning bar and study it for a while. Might even chin three or four times if the coach glared hard enough.

As far as actual vaulting, you might try one a day. If the coach questioned this, you could explain you were conserving the pole. This was an ancient bamboo thing with enough friction tape between the joints to patch every bicycle in town. The coach lived in mortal fear it would crack one day and he would have to buy another one. Old stoop here lived in mortal fear it would splinter in the middle of a vault some day and impale him like a shish kebab.

The uncertainty of that pole and the texture of sand in the landing pit were enough to discourage any others. But it was a simple existence. Once a week, you would actually have to enter combat and go through those horrible landing jolts, but then you would have several days to recover.

The graceful vaulter, of course, points his toes sky-high, then curves over the bar and drops into the pit feet first, occasionally bouncing gently on his rump as an afterthought. I never mastered this maneuver. It was such a struggle for old stoop to get over the bar, that grace took a holiday. If, somehow, you could pull and jerk and kick over the blamed thing, then you weren't in any condition to worry about landing. You just dropped earthward in whatever position you happened to be in at the peak, like a book falling on the floor. Sometimes I would hit on this shoulder, or the other one, or frequently on my stomach. I don't remember how high we were vaulting, but falling from something like nine or 10 feet flat on your back in river sand ain't no peanut butter sandwich.

The jolt was usually accompanied by a fearful grunt and sometimes a hoarse scream. It was a beckoning siren for whatever spectators happened to be around. It got to be quite a show.

In those days, the audience milled all over a track meet, standing at the finish line, back of the shot-put circle, around the pits. When things got dull between events and the loud grunts started, one guy would look at another. "Let's go over to the vaulting pit and watch old stoop land."

This took a bit of daring, also, for frequently I missed the pit entirely and fell among the spectators. So it gave them a sense of adventure and participation and sometimes they got to be the one to give the artificial respiration.

It seemed certain at that time, to me anyways, that vaulting would never make 20 feet. It would go down from 10 to nine, then to eight, thereby reducing the pain factor with each drop.

The coach also proved himself a man of vision. He joined the crowd around the pit one afternoon and watched old stoop land sickeningly on his head three straight times. And he confided to a neighbor, if I kept that up, there would certainly be a future for me in sports writing.

Tennis

THE SECOND GRAND SLAM

By Neil Amdur

From The New York Times

Rod Laver achieved the second grand slam of his tennis career yesterday.

With all the competitive trademarks of the true champion, the 31-year-old king of the court overcame Tony Roche, his 24-year-old Australian countryman, 7–9, 6–1, 6–2, 6–2, in the final of the United States Open championship at the West Side Tennis Club in Forest Hills, Queens.

With the $16,000 first prize, the richest singles payoff in the sport, Laver lifted his professional earnings this year to a record $106,000. He also entered the record books as the only player to have achieved two sweeps of the Australian, French, British and American championships, the international events that make up the grand slam.

Don Budge registered the first slam in 1938. Laver completed his initial sweep in 1962, but as an amateur and with such established pros as Richard (Pancho) Gonzales, Ken Rosewall, Lew Hoad and Tony Trabert ineligible for the competition. That situation has been changed with the approval of open tournaments.

"Tenniswise, winning this slam was a lot tougher because of all the good players," the modest, freckle-faced redhead said.

"Pressurewise, I don't think it was any tougher. There's always pressure when you're playing for something over nine months."

Laver and Roche had to wait 1 hour 35 minutes until a rented helicopter could dry the center court, which had been dampened by the morning rain.

"The playing conditions made it very difficult," Laver said. "The ground was very soft, the speeds of the bounce made it tough to return and you were sliding all over."

Before the 10th game of the first set, after having lost his serve at 5–4 on Roche's bankhand passing shot down the middle and three errors off his first volley, Laver made a strategic switch from sneakers to spiked shoes.

"The spikes helped me considerably," he said. "I lost the first set using them, but I felt good and I was able to move better." Roche wore sneakers throughout.

The fine line that separates Laver from Roche, Arthur Ashe, Roy Emerson and others is his ability to concentrate on the big serve or decisive volley at 15–30 or 30–40.

Laver trailed, 30–40, in the opening game of the second set. A service break at this point could have carried Roche to a two-set lead. But three strong first serves saved the game. Laver won the last three service games of the set at love.

The crucial moment in the match, when it seemed to turn dramatically, came in the second game of the third set, after play had been suspended by rain.

Roche had won his serve at love for a 1–0 lead. When the players returned 30 minutes later, the pressure was on Laver. On Sunday he saw the result of the strain of serving first following a delay. At 12–12 in the third set of his match with Ashe, Arthur had to serve the first game. Laver broke him immediately and won the match in the next game.

Roche pushed Laver to deuce twice in that second game. But two more big serves, hopping deep to Roche's backhand, gave Laver the impetus to hold service and then break Roche in the next game, in which he was helped by Tony's netted forehand approach volley and long overhead at deuce.

"Tony didn't seem to be digging in as much," Laver said of the player who had beaten him in five of their previous meetings. "I felt his concentration was off."

Roche, who collected $8,000 as runner-up, could have felt the physical strain of his three-hour, five-set semi-final with John Newcombe on Sunday, particularly after the 30-minute cooling-off period in the third set (he never got beyond 30 on Laver's last six serves).

But when the big money goes on the line, the winning strokes are Laver's. Except for last year's first Open here, when he lost to Cliff Drysdale in the quarter-finals, Laver has won every major tennis money event in the world.

Alastair B. Martin, president of the United States Lawn Tennis Association, called Laver "the greatest player ever," and the 5-foot-9, 155-pounder said "that makes me feel humble and proud and grateful."

Comparing Laver with the stars of other eras—Gonzales, Jack Kramer, Budge and Tilden—might be treasonous in tennis's sacrosanct society, but the Rocket has met every challenge with the discipline and dedication worthy of a place in the hall of heroes.

"Rod showed that he's still the best," said Roche, who is considered Laver's successor. "He's won so much money this year that maybe the money might slow him down."

Laver has three years to go on a five-year, $450,000 contract with the National Tennis League. He keeps whatever amount he makes in prize money above his guarantee.

The pressure began for him last January after he had beaten Emerson, Fred Stolle, Roche and Andres Gimeno en route to the Australian title. In the French and Wimbledon championships, he trailed, two sets to love, twice in the early rounds, but salvaged each match and went on to the crowns despite persistent pains in his left elbow.

In winning here at Forest Hills, the richest tournament in the world with its $137,000 purse, Laver overcame psychological hazards as well as such quality pros as Dennis Ralston, Emerson, Ashe and Roche, his chief tormentor this year. Rain had washed out two complete sessions and delayed the final one day. His tense semi-final match with Ashe had been halted by darkness in the third set and finished the following day.

Meanwhile, in Newport Beach, California, Laver's wife Mary had also been experiencing delays. The couple's first child was three days' overdue and Laver had been calling every morning to make sure everything was all right.

Mrs. Laver reported yesterday by phone before her husband walked onto the stadium court for the final. "I've been telling him everything's fine and to concentrate on his tennis," she said.

If there was a touch of nostalgia to this tournament, it came in the women's doubles final yesterday, in which Françoise Durr and 33-year-old Darlene Hard upset the top-seeded team of Mrs. Margaret Court and Virginia Wade, 0–6, 6–4, 6–4.

The crowd of 3,708 (6,200 tickets had actually been sold) cheered lustily, particularly for Miss Hard, a former national champion who had replaced Miss Durr's regular partner, Mrs. Ann Haydon Jones.

"I guess Frankie [Miss Durr's nickname] cried when she saw my name on the doubles list," said Miss Hard, who is a teaching pro in Los Angeles and lost to Miss Durr in the second round of singles. "But everything worked out great, and a win like this convinces me I should get back to full-time tennis."

One day remains in the tournament to complete the men's doubles. Naturally Laver is still playing for the $3,000 top doubles prize, even though his mind is elsewhere.

"I want to get home as soon as possible," he said, flashing a familiar half-smile. "If you had a baby on the way, wouldn't you?"

Hockey

IT WAS A DEVIL OF A WEEKEND

By Frank Dolson

From The Philadelphia Inquirer

The clock hanging outside the hockey office at Cherry Hill Arena said 6:22. The correct time was 9:20 p.m. That's the kind of year it's been for the Jersey Devils.

They were home for the weekend, back where they achieved their only Eastern Hockey League victory six weeks back where the clocks are slow and the lighting is bad and the heating system is hot and cold.

Since opening night the Devils had gone 20 straight games without winning, their general manager had quit, their veteran winger, Gordie Stratton, had ripped ligaments in his knee, and they were working on their fourth goaltender. Other than that, things were rotten.

To give the Devils their due, they had shown a spark of life shortly after Ross Turnbull took over as general manager. There was a tough one-goal loss at Long Island and tougher one-goal loss at Johnstown and then there was that unforgettable, midweek epic at New Haven.

Surely, Bobby Taylor would never forget it. The 24-year-old goalie had missed the first 19 games of the Devils' winless streak, safely hidden away in Seattle as the backup goalie for the Flyers' minor league team there. Last week, Bud Poile, the Flyers' general manager, called Seattle and asked them to ship Taylor East. The young man couldn't have been happier. "I thought I was coming to Philadelphia," he said.

Packing hurriedly, he left Seattle at midnight Tuesday, and flew all night, including a stopover in Chicago. By noon Wednesday, he was at the Spectrum, ready for a good day's sleep. The news that he had to rush to Cherry Hill and catch the Devils' bus to New Haven came as a jolt. What happened at New Haven came as an even bigger jolt.

Turnbull, showing remarkable good sense for a rookie general manager, didn't make the trip. The brilliance of that move became apparent when his coach, Lou Jankowski, phoned with the final score: New Haven 18, Devils 1. Ross thought it was a bad connection. Jankowski assured him it was simply a bad game. Unbelievably

"I nearly died," Turnbull said. "I mean, how do you lose, 18–1? I'll tell you how. It's easy. You give up. You quit. I've never been associated with a team that lost, 18–1, even in Pee Wee hockey, and I never expect to be associated with one again . . ."

"We didn't quit," Jankowski said. "How could we quit when we never started?"

Poor Bobby Taylor took it hardest of all. Here he was, back in the EHL, where he had played all last season. It was a devil of a mess.

"I didn't know I was coming back to Jersey 'til I got off the plane," he said. "I was a little bitter. Well, not bitter, really, but downhearted. The Flyers pay me well. The people in Jersey and Philadelphia have been great. But it's tough not to know where you're going until you arrive . . ."

The 18 goals compounded Taylor's misery. "I don't think there's a word to describe it," Bobby said. "It was one of those times I wished I wore a mask so nobody could see my face. I suffer every time a goal is scored against me, anyway. But 18 in one game . . . I felt like I had a red target on my chest and they kept shooting at it—and just missing. I was tired and disgusted. I was ready to throw my stick in the stands and say, 'That's it.' I guess pride kept me going."

Turnbull has pride, too. That's what kept him going a decade ago, when the old Philadelphia Ramblers paid him $115 a week to score 40 goals a season. "We can beat any team in this league," the new general manager (and part owner) informed his shell-shocked skaters, and to add a little zing to his words he fined each player who participated in the New Haven massacre $50.

"I told them they could get the $50 back by winning two games this weekend," Ross said Friday night, waiting for the Devils to put their winless streak on the line against the Long Island Ducks.

Amazingly, there was a decent crowd on hand. "We must have 2,000 people here," marveled Turnbull, and if he seemed a trifle apprehensive who could blame him? Only time would tell if the customers had come to cheer the Devils or to stone them.

For the better part of two periods, they cheered. The Devils, hungry for victory—not to mention the $50—took a 4–1 lead. Ross sat in the stands, glanced at the scoreboard and said, "We might have a chance . . ."

It was 4–2 after the second period and Turnbull dashed into the locker room. Another pep talk.

"I told them, 'Whatever you so-and-sos do, don't give up,' " he said. "I told them, 'Skate . . . skate . . . skate.' "

Quickly, the lead jumped to 5–2. Then both clubs took time out for a free-for-all, presumably in honor of league president Tom Lockhart, who was in attendance. More than two dozen players milled around the ice, occasionally taking pokes at each other, and Harold Aranow, the president of the Devils, reached over the railing, grabbed an enemy player by the jersey and yanked—until two Devils pulled him away. "Guess I got carried away," said Aranow later, gingerly flexing his hand. "I think I broke a finger."

Turnbull made no attempt to hide his concern as the battle raged. "Sure, I'm worried," he said. "We have to play 11 more minutes of hockey when they stop fighting. That's what scares me."

His fear was not misplaced. With 6:30 to go, the Devils' lead shrank to 5–3. Less than two minutes later it was 5–4. Now the scoreboard clock showed three minutes left and some of the fans were starting to leave.

"How can they be so sure we've got it won?" Turnbull wondered.

"Maybe they're sure you're going to lose," a friend suggested.

"Maybe you're right," Ross said.

With 40 seconds to go, a Devil had a clean breakaway and hit the post. With 14 seconds left, the home team had a three-man rush with only the goaltender to beat. He made the save. "Three on nobody. I don't believe it," Turnbull said, but something even more unbelievable was happening. The final seconds were ticking off. The fans were chanting, "It's all over. It's all over." The Devils had won.

The following night was more of the same. Another big lead. Another tight victory. General manager Turnbull had a two-game winning streak. The players had their fines refunded.

"I told them I never enjoyed losing money more," Ross said, locking the door of the hockey office Saturday night. The clock hanging outside said eight o'clock, which meant it was at least 11 P.M. The Devils' big weekend was over.

Automobile Racing

BREEDLOVE

By Joe Scalzo

From Car Life Magazine

Look closely at Craig Breedlove, holder of the World Land Speed Record, but lately transformed into a brooding rebel. Breedlove is going his own way—outrageously.

About his long hair, which covers his ears: "I've let my hair grow out. I'll probably let it grow out more before I'm done. I'm wearing it this way and I like it and I really don't care what people think." About his wardrobe, which includes quilted trousers, boots and turtleneck blouses with cuff-link sleeves: "I like 'em."

Day and night he listens to loud rock 'n' roll music. He keeps mostly to himself and does not laugh much. Frequently he sleeps till noon.

Breedlove does what he feels like doing now.

Living this way, he says, helps him forget he has lost everything he had—his business, his savings, his wife—everything. All of it is gone, gone in one year's time, and Breedlove has not yet recovered fully. His face is wan and grim (his friends say he has aged 10 years in the last eight months) and he thinks he has lost "about 30 pounds" through worry.

Four years ago—in late fall of 1965—his jet-powered "Spirit of America" slashed across the Utah desert at 600.6 mph and journalists everywhere ran for their typewriters. Breedlove, who keeps scrapbooks, says that more than 10,000 different stories were printed about his record run. Most of the journalists thought there was something heroic about Breedlove and his all-consuming dream to be the fastest man in the world. And perhaps there was.

The manner in which Breedlove lost all his money was hardly heroic. But it was startling and sudden.

Divorce started it. In mid-1968, his second wife, Lee, left him. Breedlove went to Nevada, received a divorce, and remarried. Then, further muddling things, he had this marriage almost immediately annulled. As of last March, Lee was still suing him for divorce and the expensive, widely publicized case was not yet settled.

At the same time, the tire store in Torrance, California, which Breedlove had bought with his Land Speed Record money, went bankrupt.

Finally, in January of this year, a brutal storm rolled across Southern California, flooding streets and wrecking homes. A wall of water burst through the front door of Breedlove's "Spirit of America" headquarters in Torrance and the water ran four feet high. Wrecked were lathes, milling machines, and several engines and parts that Breedlove was preparing for American Motors. It was a $100,000 loss, and the building was not insured against floods. Not in semi-desert Southern California.

The result is that Craig Breedlove, the fastest man in the world, is broke. Spectacularly broke. He has no money.

His sole means of transportation is a 10-year-old Buick sedan he obtained by trading a friend four tires. The Buick is scarred and dented. It smokes, the windshield leaks, the brakes are weak, and reverse gear has gone out. Breedlove has pasted flower decals on the doors.

For a bed he sleeps on a mattress thrown on the floor of his upstairs office in Torrance. In the morning he wanders into an adjacent room and boils black coffee. He drinks lots of black coffee. (Recently he moved out, complaining, "Staring at the four walls was driving me nuts.")

Mickey Thompson, Breedlove's friend and fellow speed record breaker says, with a shudder, "Craig really has it bad. He has more troubles than one man can use."

Breedlove himself says, "Everything you've ever wanted can happen overnight. You can spend years planning and trying—like I did chasing the World Land Speed Record—and not hit it. And then, for no real reason, you do hit it." He sighs, shakes his head. "And then you lose it."

So he wears his hair long and shaggy, he dresses outrageously, keeps to himself, and swears he doesn't care what people think about him—and all the while he doggedly waits for the bad times to pass. Perhaps as much as $200,000 has slipped through his fingers. He will never see that money again.

The one thing he did not lose, of course, was his World Land

Speed Record. It is 600.6 mph, and right now no one appears capable of breaking it. Art Arfons, the aging Ohio hot-rodder and ex-record holder keeps trying, but keeps crashing. Donald Campbell, the very rich, very brave Englishman, died two years ago in a boat accident. Mickey Thompson is not interested in the record anymore, saying all it takes is "lots of guts." Drag racer Don Garlits is rumored to be getting ready for a record try, but in a questionable rocket-powered vehicle.

Breedlove never had many close friends, and he has fewer now; but his only real intimate was Arfons. Trying for 600 mph in huge, cumbersome four-ton jet-powered cars with flame spurting out the back while hurtling across a lake bed of wet salt is so dangerous that Breedlove and Arfons alone know how dangerous it really is. They, along with a driver named Tom Green, are the only men to have gone so fast. If nothing else, Breedlove and Arfons understand one another.

Outsiders were given some insight into this understanding when Breedlove and Arfons were swapping the record back and forth during 1964. Breedlove would go 500 mph and Arfons would hit 520, and so it went.

One evening Arfons confronted Craig outside a Wendover, Nevada, restaurant and demanded, "What are we going to do? Just keep trying to beat each other until we kill ourselves?" And Craig shrugged his shoulders and answered, "I guess so."

The next day Breedlove's car lost its brakes, parachutes, steering, and careened down the salt out of control at 400 mph. It batted down a telephone pole, leaped an earthen bank and splashed nose first into an 18-foot-deep, water-filled ditch.

Breedlove, who was uninjured, swam to shore, screaming happily, "For my next act I'll set myself on fire!"

This was bravado, nothing more.

At Bonneville, Breedlove always seemed more aware of the dangers than other drivers. Frequently he had nightmares (he could see his car smashing end-over-end at 500 mph). Once he mailed postcards to his five children before going out on the salt, certain he would never see them again.

"To be in the right mental mood to tackle the salt," Breedlove told reporters at the time, "you have to hit an emotional peak. You must really be up for it. But if you don't have desire, you can't do it."

Today Breedlove admits, "Every time I went across the salt I wasn't sure I'd survive the run. I really didn't know. When I'd get the car stopped and climb out this tremendous load would go off my shoulders."

He hit 600 in 1965 and had the record. But he was disappointed. He had built and designed the "Spirit of America" himself and thought she could reach the speed of sound—about 740 mph. But at 600 Breedlove said the car began buffeting fiercely, he could feel the frame flexing and bending, and at one point "Spirit" nearly took off like an airplane.

Stubbornly, Breedlove now claims he would do it all over again if he had to. "The World Land Speed Record," he insists, "has meaning."

Such as?

"Well, it's an international thing. The rich Englishmen used to hold all the records, but now I hold them. I'm patriotic. That's why I named my car the 'Spirit of America.' "

But in the next breath Breedlove wonders aloud if any skill is needed to drive 600 mph. "You have to justify your ego satisfaction, and you have to have the guts to do it. But skill? I don't know about skill." He claims an Indianapolis 500 winner such as A. J. Foyt could adapt to running 600 mph much easier than he, Breedlove, could adapt to Indianapolis and its four corners. "I don't call myself a race driver," says Breedlove. "But I don't like to be thought of as a stunt man, either. It's funny. I've gone faster than anyone else, but I'm not a race driver."

As for another try at the record, Goodyear, Breedlove's primary sponsor, is not particularly eager to try again. Because Breedlove already holds the record, and on their tires, Goodyear apparently sees no need to go back to Bonneville. This may make good business sense, but it leaves Breedlove out on a limb. He wants to go back and try for the speed of sound in a new stressed-skin car he has designed; but he needs a quarter-million dollars to build it.

Breedlove's unswerving determination to become the fastest man in the world has been well documented (among others, *Car Life,* November, 1963). But the highlights of his struggle deserve retelling, if only because they are so incredible.

He was racing cars on Southern California dragstrips when he was 13. By age 17 he was married, and at 20 had three children. Shortly afterward his first wife divorced him. Craig scarcely noticed. He was working as a fireman, making little money and pouring all his spare time into the reading of books about aerodynamics and jet power. Once he had the basics down pat, he went looking for sponsors, big sponsors, and asked for money. He didn't start small.

When he barged into the offices of Shell Oil Company with plans for his jet car under his arm he was ordered out of the building. "They thought I'd kill myself," he chuckles. One prospective sponsor called him a fool to his face, and another accused him of being money-mad, of being willing to sell his life for the publicity he would get.

Goodyear, impressed with the knowledge Breedlove had stored up, approved the idea. They gave him the cash he needed. Shell later agreed to supply the needed jet fuel. Breedlove went to work building his car, 18 hours a day, seven days a week.

"I just seem to have an intuitive feel for this sort of thing," he once said. "If I make up my mind to do something then I try to get all the information I can from the best people."

But Breedlove designed and built the cars himself, including the 600-mph "Spirit of America."

The "Spirit," which will never go onto the salt flats again and now is in a museum, was a fascinating yet savage creation. The big J-79 jet engine developed 15,000 pounds of thrust. It sat inside a tubular frame of chrome molybdenum steel, hidden by aluminum and fiber glass body panels. For suspension, Breedlove used light torsion bars mounted to a tubular beam axle on the front and an independent swinging arm on the rear. The two 50-gallon tanks carried 100 gallons of special jet fuel. Front brakes were 18-inch diameter disks with 3-inch double spots, 4-inch double spots on the rear. "Spirit" also carried a high-speed drag parachute. Breedlove sat belted inside his jet car and operated a steering system that worked—and looked—like the handlebars of a bicycle.

Oddly, it was after he set the record that his troubles seemed to begin. For years Breedlove had chased the dream—and now that he had the dream he felt there was nothing left to chase.

Perhaps that is too pat an explanation, a little too obvious. Nevertheless, after Breedlove owned his precious World Land Speed Record, he admits he ran out of things to do.

To keep busy, he loaded "Spirit of America" onto the back of a truck and toured the country with it, showing it off at car shows. He hired managers to look after his money and affairs. Bored, he indulged in absurd promotional stunts such as setting "the world speed record for 24 hours in a snowmobile." He also raced an outboard boat. It flipped over at 80 mph, threw him out into the water, then landed on top of him. "I was coughing up blood for days," he says, "but I didn't break any bones."

He lived this way through 1966, 1967 and 1968.

His managers, he claims, mismanaged his business affairs and caused him to lose his tire store and most of his money. Then they deserted him. "They didn't let me know how bad things were going until it was too late." (This may be true. But Craig admits he was out of town and traveling so much he was rarely in touch with them.)

Breedlove knew all about jet engines and high speeds and aerodynamics, but he admits, "I'm no businessman. I hired those guys because I couldn't look after everything."

In any case, Breedlove has lost his wife Lee; his tire store; his savings; and the flood wiped out his speed headquarters, where he wanted to build his new Land Speed Record car. "Nothing that can happen now will surprise me," he said one day recently while driving around Los Angeles in his old Buick. "I think I've had everything bad happen that's possible."

He continued: "I was pretty naïve when I first broke the speed record. But there wasn't a whole lot of money involved, like everyone thought. It was a decent living my sponsors paid me for risking my neck. It was a lot more than I ever made working for the fire department. But it wasn't a fortune. Anyway, it's all gone."

He has no sponsors now. No big company appears interested in his services until he rearranges his shattered life. His agreement with American Motors to build a streamliner with a supercharged Javelin engine and attempt to smash the speed record for piston-engine cars is up in the air. Breedlove says he doesn't care. "I used to worry because my sponsors sweated about the way I talked, dressed and lived. I was very conscientious. They didn't want me to portray any kind of image other than the clean-cut all-American boy. That's the commodity they wanted to buy so I sold, I really sold. But it doesn't mean that much to me now. I dress the way I choose. The only person I should be interested in keeping happy is myself."

Saying this, he doesn't sound bitter. But maybe he is disguising it. He still seems to have confidence in himself. "I think I can get back to where I was; I really think I can. I've learned a lot from all these experiences. It'll help me from getting into trouble again. I don't want more trouble."

Then he takes a longer, deeper look: No sponsors, no financial backing, and right now he alone knows where the money comes from that is supporting himself and the Buick. There is a certain desperation in his voice when he says, "It's really a scary thing. I was 32 last March. You sit back and you realize it's hard to begin a whole new career at 32."

Maybe the new career will be driving race cars for a living. Breedlove recently has been taking race driving lessons at a California school and he has shown fantastic aptitude.

Very soon, probably, the long hair will be sheared off, conservative clothes will go back on, and Craig Breedlove will be starting out all over again. From the very bottom. His one-man rebellion will be over. His only advantage, and chance, is the memory of his earlier days when they laughed at him and called him a fool.

He had no money—and not much hope—then, either.

Outdoors

THE INCREDIBLE TRACKING DOG

By Don D. Ellis

From Outdoor Life

Jim Burman started out by himself from his home in Kamloops, where I was then stationed as a British Columbia game warden, on the morning of September 19, 1943. He intended to hunt in rough country above Savona, at the west end of Kamloops Lake. It was an area he was not familiar with, but he told his wife not to worry, that he'd stay close to the road.

Mrs. Burman phoned me late the next afternoon, a very anxious woman. Her husband had planned to be home by dark the first day. He was now 20 hours overdue, and she was sure he'd had an accident or was lost. I had to agree.

Would I lend a hand? That was part of my job.

I loaded Reo, the tracking Doberman Pinscher that I owned and had trained, into my car and drove to the Burman place. Mrs. Burman told me what she could. I'd be looking for a man in his early 40's, with some experience as a hunter, who worked for the Kamloops Public Works Department. He had left home carrying a big lunch and a bottle of pop in a packsack.

Mrs. Burman gave me a sock that her husband had worn. That was all Reo would need to pick up the track.

I found Burman's car parked at the end of the lake, two miles west of Savona. There was no snow on the ground. The job would be entirely up to the dog. I gave him a good smell of the sock and the car and attached his harness and leash. I never buckled that harness onto Reo unless he was supposed to track someone down, and he knew its meaning as well as I did. We were ready to go.

Reo lined out without a second's delay, going straight north, in the direction Burman had said he intended to hunt. But it was plain from the start that the man had not followed his plan of keeping near the road. He hadn't even stayed near a trail.

The country was open sagebrush hills for about two miles. Then we came to timber. By that time I realized that the missing man had started for the Cooper Creek road but failed to reach it. And Reo and I were not far into the timber when I discovered the reason. Jim Burman had become confused and started to travel in a big circle about four miles across. At that point he was really lost, and his tracks showed that he was running.

Just before dark I could see that he was dragging something on the ground.

Reo found and picked up three empty cartridges as we followed the track. The brass cases were some distance apart, which meant that they had not been fired as a signal. Two of them were in places where no deer would have been sighted, and I had no idea what the man was shooting at. But I was sure of one thing. I was dealing with a panic-stricken lost hunter. He had been out for two days and a night, with a second night coming on. It was a safe bet that Reo and I would find him in bad condition.

The dog and I stayed on the track all night. Just as day was breaking I heard a shot not far ahead. Reo was tugging hard on his rope now. We were closing in. Then, on the slope of a hill, I saw what we were looking for.

He was stumbling along, holding his rifle by the barrel and dragging the butt on the ground, obviously exhausted. I called his name.

He wheeled and gave me a wild stare. "Jim," I called, "it's Ellis. The game warden."

He started to run away, stumbled and fell, got up and staggered a few steps, and went down again. He was plainly a man demented, and I didn't want to rush him. Instead I turned up a draw, got out of his sight, and ran to head him off. When I looked over the top of the hill he was sitting on a log, watching back where he had last seen me, and he had the rifle across his knees, ready for use. The search for a lost man was turning into a hunt for one berserk instead.

If I called his name again he'd be likely to take off, and if I tried to run him down I stood a good chance of getting shot. I tied Reo to a tree and started a sneak, stalking Burman as I'd stalk a deer.

When I was only a few feet away I spoke his name in a low voice. He bounded to his feet to run but was so tired that he went down in a heap, and before he could get up I had the rifle and was talking to him very quietly.

The first thing he asked for was a drink. He needed it desperately. I gave it to him—opening the bottle of pop that was still in his packsack. He had touched neither it nor his lunch.

We sat and talked for a long time before he began to come back to reality. He told me that wolves had come for him while he was trailing a wounded deer, and had followed him all night. He had shot all but one of his shells at them but couldn't drive them off, he said. He was not even in wolf country.

I finally walked him slowly back to his car, but when we got there he didn't recognize it.

One more day and night in the woods would probably have been too much for Jim Burman. Reo had added another name to the list of lost people—men, women and children—who owed their lives to his incredible ability to track. I had Reo for 11 years, and the list grew long.

I worked as a game warden for the British Columbia Fish and Wildlife Branch from 1938 to 1965, when I retired. I was stationed first at Kamloops and then at Kelowna, where I live now. Of the many people with whom I had dealings in those 27 years, I am sure that not more than a handful ever knew that I owed the job in the first place to a keen-nosed fantastically intelligent dog, the most remarkable animal I have ever known.

The chain of adventures started in 1936, while I was working for the city of Kelowna as a truck driver. That fall a little four-year-old girl wandered away from her home on the Bear Lake road 12 miles out of Kelowna.

She was lost in country with no deep canyons and no water that a child could drown in. But although 400 men combed the area for days and cougar hounds were brought in (in case she had been carried off by a cougar or bear), no trace of her was ever found.

A few days after that tragedy I was talking about it with a friend, George Sutherland, and I remarked that it was too bad the local game warden, the provincial police, or someone else didn't have a tracking dog for use in such cases.

The suggestion took hold with Sutherland. That was in the hungry 30's, and we had no money for buying a trained dog, even if we could have located one. But George did have a few bucks in the bank, and he took me up on the idea.

"You've trained dogs for hunting," he said. "You know how to go about it. If you can find a young dog that you think would make a good tracker, I'll put up the money. You train it, and if it turns out O.K. we'll give it to Mac Maxson, the game warden."

That was how I came to own Reo. I got the name and address of a man in Vancouver who was raising a very good strain of Dobermans, and George and I arranged to buy a six-month-old male for $50.

The name on the dog's papers was Reo von Papen, but before he died 11 years later he was known all over British Columbia as Don Ellis's Reo.

I started the dog's training the morning after he arrived, taking him in my truck and getting acquainted with him. I realized from the outset that I was dealing with an exceptionally intelligent dog, one that seemed to understand every word that was said to him.

Before long Reo developed his tracking instincts to such a point that I'd come home from work and offer my kids a quarter if they could hide where Reo couldn't find them. In those lean days a kid would do most anything for a quarter, but very rarely did I have to pay off.

I fitted the dog with a harness and a light leash of rope, using them only when he was on a tracking job. He learned very quickly what that harness meant, and he loved the work.

I had to discipline him only once. That time, he left a man track for a fresh coyote track. I paddled him, and he never forgot the lesson. From then on he hated the very smell of coyote. In fact he reached the point of refusing to take any track but a human's.

Reo got his first workout by accident. When I'd had him about two months I took him to George Sutherland's home to show him off. George had two daughters, Ella and Mabel, who were eight or nine (they're grown and married now), and as I left that night one of them said, "If we go and hide next Sunday, will you come with Reo and find us?"

I said sure, thinking they'd forget all about it. Then I proceeded to do the forgetting myself. The next I heard of it was the following Sunday evening. I arrived home about 9 o'clock and was no sooner in the house than the phone rang. It was Mrs. Sutherland, and she was worried and mad.

Ella and Mabel had been as good as their word. They had taken a lunch and gone up Knox Mountain, counting on me to keep my end of the bargain. It was now dark as a black cat, the girls had not come home, and their mother had been trying for hours to reach me. It was my turn to be worried—and good!

Knox Mountain is rough and rocky and covered with cactus, a hard place to search for lost children. I hotfooted it for the Sutherland place, got a slipper belonging to one of the girls, and let Reo have a smell. He went at the job as if he had been doing it for years, straining on his rope and half-dragging me up the mountain.

Near the top he slowed down and started to whine. I found out later that all four of his feet were stuck so full of cactus spines that I had to carry him down. But he didn't quit.

He led me to a cave just big enough for a man to crawl into, and when I shone my flashlight inside I saw the two little girls huddled together at the far end, crying quietly. I felt like doing a little crying myself, for the whole thing was my fault.

Reo went up to them and licked their faces, and we started for home. What Mrs. Sutherland said to me when we got there sounded a lot like, "You and your big mouth!" And I didn't blame her. But at least I knew I had a tracking dog.

Before that summer was over, Reo, young as he was, turned in another performance that gave me a lot of satisfaction and did much to establish his reputation.

Another child turned up missing, again a four-year-old girl from Kelowna. A family named Ryder had just suffered the loss of a two-year-old boy, and the parents were not sleeping well. One hot moonlit evening they and their little daughter drove out to Hydraulic Creek for a picnic, and after eating they decided to take a nap in the car. They put the tot on the front seat. When the parents awoke at midnight they found that she had opened the car door and wandered away.

They made a quick, frantic search, and then the father raced to town to get me, leaving the mother at the scene.

Reo smelled a coat that the child had left behind and picked up the track at once, heading up the creek. A mile from the picnic ground he led me to a hole in the bank, where a big tree had blown down. The girl was curled up there, sobbing.

When I'd had Reo for a year, there came the day that I had been dreading.

"Don't you think it's about time you turned him over to the game warden?" George Sutherland asked me one day. I had to agree. The only roadblock I could think of was that Reo seemed to be strictly a one-man dog and I didn't know whether Maxson could handle him.

The next day I took him around to the warden's house, ready for the parting. Mac Maxson was in the yard skinning a coyote, which Reo hated. The warden came over to the truck and put his hand through the door to pat the dog. Reo smelled coyote and sank his teeth into the hand. Naturally, Maxson wanted no part of him after that. I couldn't have had better news.

That fall I trained a bird dog for Gordon Wismer, British Columbia's Attorney General. He had heard of Reo's exploits, and when he came to pick up his dog he said, "We could use you and that dog of yours. How would you like a job with the game department?"

I started work the first of May, 1938, and that was the beginning of more than a quarter-century on the most interesting and challenging job I could have found—thanks to Reo.

At first I was assigned to drive a truck for a fish hatchery, but I didn't get much chance to do that. We had no phone at the hatchery, but time and again the inspector would drive in to say that they needed my dog and me for a tracking job.

Reo brought off one of his most amazing feats that summer. A woman picnicking at Penantan Lake, two miles from the hatchery, lost a valuable diamond ring in six-inch-high grass and came to us for help.

I didn't have much hope for success, but I took Reo to the lake, let him smell another of the woman's rings, covered his eyes (as I did when I threw something for him to search for), removed the blindfold, and told him to find.

I had given up and was having a cup of coffee in the lodge when the dog came trotting up to me with the ring in his mouth. The search had taken him two hours.

One of Reo's lost-man exploits that I remember best was the tracking of two young hunters. They had gone hunting in rough country west of Kamloops—an area of willow, timber, creeks and swamps—and had become confused and as so often happens, had started to walk in a circle. I got the call for help from the mother of one of the hunters, and Constable Hall of the British Columbia Provincial Police came with me.

We found their car in midmorning, and Reo had no trouble with the track. We followed it for the rest of that day, stopping at noon and again just before dark to boil tea in a billycan and to eat.

It took a good man to stay with Reo on a long search like that. But most of the time he pulled me along on his leash, especially going uphill, and maybe because of the excitement of what we were doing I never seemed to feel tired until the job was finished.

Hall and I went on in the darkness, using our flashlights to get over logs. We were about ready to give up and camp under a tree until morning when the dog made a sharp turn to the right and lunged ahead in his harness. The lost hunters were curled up under a big fallen tree, trying to keep each other warm.

It was after midnight when the constable and I made the find. We had been on the track since 8 A.M. The hunters had been out for two days, a night, and half of the second night when we caught up with them.

Before the four of us got back to the highway both boys were assuring us that they had not been lost. They had just run out of time and couldn't make it out to the road, they explained.

I can recall only two occasions when the person Reo tracked down did not come out alive. One was a woman, known to be in a very depressed frame of mind, who left her husband's car and disappeared while he was in the house talking with the owner of a neighboring ranch.

I got the call at midnight of an ink-black night, during a hard rainstorm.

The unfortunate woman had left her hat on the car's seat, and that was enough for Reo. He tracked her across the ranch, through two fences, and to the shore of a nearby lake. She had left her handbag and coat there, and her body was floating facedown 150 yards out. A cowboy from the ranch rode his horse into the lake and brought her ashore.

The second person we didn't find in time was also a suicide, a young woman who drowned herself in the Thompson River. Reo tracked her to a big eddy where the water boiled under a logjam. Then he sat down, staring at the swirling current.

"Where is she, boy?" I asked, and he dived in headlong, and if it hadn't been for his leash, that would have been the end of him.

It took men with pike poles to get the girl's body out. How Reo knew she was there under the logjam, I'll never understand. An extra sense that dogs have, I guess.

All his life Reo excelled at three things: finding lost people, sniffing out game-law violations, and tracking down men wanted by the police. He was as good at one as at another, combining an incredibly keen nose with an almost human understanding of what was required.

Some of his encounters with violators were so amusing that even the men who paid the fines got a kick out of his performance.

Checking duck hunters one morning, I stopped a car with Vancouver license plates and asked the four men in it for a look at their hunting licenses and kill. They acted nervous, explaining that they were hurrying home to be on time for work.

"I won't hold you up long," I promised.

They had six ducks. Their licenses and everything else seemed to be in order. But when they were ready to drive off I missed Reo.

"Hold it a minute till I see where my dog is," I said.

He was under the car, chewing on a leather shoestring with which the men had tied an illegal blue grouse to the frame. He brought the grouse out, went back, and retrieved three more, one at a time. The hunters didn't get back to work in Vancouver that day, but they took their punishment with complete good nature.

Another time, I was checking anglers on Jackpine Lake, and while sitting in my car eating lunch I heard shooting. Grouse season was not open, so I investigated. I found six fishermen eating around a campfire and saw one coming across the lake in a boat. When the boatman saw me he turned around, beached the boat, jumped out, and ran. He came back to the boat in a few minutes and rowed across and joined his party at the campfire.

I took him and Reo back to where he had beached the boat, and put Reo on his track. The dog was back in nothing flat with a grouse. He brought me two more, and the best excuse the embarrassed violator could think of was, "Well, I only shot three."

Of the 50-odd searches on which I used Reo during his 11 years, the longest was a three-day and three-night manhunt for an armed prison escapee in 1941.

We didn't have much to go on, just faint scent from a blanket the man had used. And heavy rain fell much of the time. But right after dawn on the fourth morning the dog led the posse to where the convict had holed up in a shallow depression in the ground.

The man started shooting, and Reo went for him, something the dog never did to a lost person. When that happened and the posse started to return the fire, the wanted man changed his mind and stood up with his hands in the air.

Reo's attitude toward the people he tracked down was, under ordinary circumstances, very unusual. Though he was never friendly to strangers, I have seen him jump up on someone he had found, wagging all over with friendliness, as if he wanted to be thanked.

I've had three tracking dogs since Reo, and one of them was

very good at it. But if you didn't watch him he'd attack the person he had found, and I believe he would have killed if he had got the chance.

One of Reo's most spectacular performances involving crime was finding an empty cartridge alleged to have been used in a murder. He was blindfolded and allowed to smell another cartridge that had been handled by the suspected murderer. It took him four hours to make the find in a pile of wood chips near the cabin in which the killing had taken place.

Perhaps Reo's most unbelievable achievement happened in connection with the robbery of a store at Chase.

One of the bandits dropped his hat in the store, and the dog had no trouble picking up the track. But the robbers had made their getaway in a car, and the trail soon ended.

Two weeks later, as Reo and I were walking the street in Kamloops, we met a stranger, and as he passed, the dog got his scent, turned on him and growled. A policeman nearby took the man into custody. It's hard to believe, but the stranger turned out to be the owner of the dropped hat.

Once more, Reo had found his man.

I lost Reo in 1947. He was restless that night, refusing to lie down on the rug at the foot of my bed where he slept, coming back time after time for a customary pat on the head. The end came quietly. Sometime after midnight I felt him dragging my blanket off. By the time I turned the light on he was dead.

As a newspaperman friend of mine put it, in the tribute he wrote to Reo, a gallant dog had gone west. I have never known another like him.

General

A DECADE FOR ALL SEASONS

By Steve Cady

From The New York Times

O. J. Simpson was 12 years old and throwing stones at busses in a San Francisco ghetto when the decade began. He'll finish it next Wednesday with a first-year gross of $1 million from pro football and other business enterprises, a classic symbol of the Super Sixties.

"Money means everything to ghetto kids," says O. J. "Willie Mays was my boyhood hero, but not because he was a great baseball player. Because he had a big house."

Sociologists and historians eventually will get around to looking through microscopes at the sports decade just ending, a decade of dizzying expansion and topsy-turvy change. Until then, simpler labels will have to do.

But how do you explain Clark Kent becoming SuperJet and SuperMet instead of Superman? What happened in the 60's makes the histrionics of the conventional comic strip look tame.

Call it the Super Sixties, meaning "very large" and also "excessive" or "extreme." Or color it green, change the S's to dollar signs and call it the $uper $ixties. At a Kentucky horse auction, a former truck driver with a chain of supermarkets bid $405,000 for an untested yearling filly, turned to his trainer and said, "Do you think people will know who Wendell P. Russo is now?" At the Super Bowl, the television announcer said, "And now a word from our sponsor." The one-minute word cost $135,000.

Yet the Big Spenders were matched by millions of Little Spenders, fiercely seeking escape from a tense and tumultuous world in the sanctuary of the ball park, the racetrack, the football stadium, the basketball or hockey arena. More often than not, the spending meant placing a bet and tensely watching the outcome on television.

At times, the watchers seemed to be staring themselves goggle-eyed as seasons overlapped and one big game after another merged into a split-screen, stop-action, isolated-camera orgy of home runs, touchdowns, key baskets and bone-rattling hockey collisions. But just when the doctor would get ready to pronounce America a nation of passive, flabby watchers, the doers would contradict him.

Entries in the annual Boston Athletic Association Marathon proliferated to an outstanding total of 1,152 for this year's 73rd running. Most of the blister-prone contestants were amateur disciples of jogging, the most popular of the physical fitness fads in the Sixties. Their goal: jog the entire distance of 26 miles, 385 yards from the rocky pastures of rural Hopkinton to downtown Boston.

"Where you finish doesn't matter," said Dr. George Sheehan, a 50-year-old cardiologist and father of 12. "The tragedy is when you have to walk in."

Elsewhere on the do-it-yourself front, officials had to limit the sailing fleet in the biennial Newport-Bermuda ocean race to 151 yachts. Other unpaid yachtsmen found time to make three successful defenses of the America's Cup.

Recreational sporting activities, such as boating, golf, fishing, tennis, hunting and skiing, increased spectacularly.

"They're really pouring it in," said an observer of the leisure-time sports market. "When the little guy suddenly gets a little money, he spends it." In some of the Northern states, the family with only one snowmobile in the garage had become a rarity: most ski-country families now had two or more snowmobiles.

With more money to spend and more leisure time to spend it, the nation's growing population made the 60's a roaring bull market for both participant and spectator sports.

In a renaissance such as this, it was only fitting that the era's most lavish creation should be called the Super Bowl. It was equally fitting that it should be won in 1969 by a team that hadn't been born at the start of the decade, the New York Jets, and that the Jets should be led by a brash and controversial swinger named Joe Willie Namath.

This was the decade of the Super Star, the Super Salary, the Super Stadium, the Super Horse, the Super Synthetic, the Super Upset, the Super Controversy. It was a time when the Big O meant Oscar Robertson; the Big A stood for Aqueduct, where horseplayers bet as much as $6 million at one track on one day, and the Big E meant either Elvin Hayes or the Big Exacta, depending on whether a fan was talking about the basketball star or the strike-it-rich wagering gimmick designed to lure people to racetracks.

The forces with the biggest initials, though, were NBC, CBS and ABC—the major television networks that poured increasing millions of dollars into sports subsidies in apparently justified efforts to improve their ratings, polish their images and hold their subscribing stations. By the late 1960's, television gold had become so important that program directors routinely signaled referees when to call time out for a commercial; sudden-death golf play-offs began not at the first hole but at whichever hole was most convenient for the TV camera crew, and the President of Mexico could be told politely to cool his heels for half an hour while the closing ceremonies of the Mexico City Olympics were delayed to coincide with prime television viewing time.

Athletes, often with appearance fees in mind, turned first to the television commentator, not to the sports writers who for generations had helped make folk heroes out of their predecessors. Sometimes, regulations got trampled in the rush to the microphone.

Last May, for example, Bill Hartack kept the stewards at Pimlico waiting while he calmly (and in direct violation of racing rules) told a national television audience he didn't think the foul claimed against his horse in the Preakness was justified. Occasionally, writers fought back against the TV cameras and cables that enveloped the sports scene. During a rain delay at a baseball game, an appeal to the commissioner resulted in the ousting of television crews from the dugouts—traditionally off limits for sports writers during games. After a play-off game leading to this year's World Series, a baseball writer swung in frustration at a tangle of lights and cables blocking his path to an interview. In the ensuing scuffle, a TV light was toppled and the writer was burned on the hand.

Unquestionably, television forced a change in the writing habits of most sports reporters. In the 60's, the "why" became increasingly important in the writer's standard list of five W's. In many cases, television already had answered the when, where, what and who.

Often, the "why" was most eagerly sought by people who had bet on the game. With the proliferation of teams came a proliferation in wagering. Enormous sums of money were bet illegally each year on professional sports. Some estimates put the total as high as $50 billion, 10 times as much as was waged legally at the nation's thoroughbred and harness-racing tracks.

It was a profitable decade for the bookie, a dangerous one for the compulsive gambler. With all the major leagues (baseball, football, basketball and hockey) expanding into every corner of the United States, new teams with strange names flooded the pages of newspapers with box scores and summaries: Bucks, Rockets, Colonels, Caps, Suns, Pacers, Floridians, Flyers, Seals, North Stars, Penguins, Kings, Astros, Angels, Buccaneers, Nets, Supersonics, Cougars, Falcons, Saints, Bengals, Bills and, of course, the Mets and the Jets.

Sports, more than ever before, constituted a major industry. And the advertising media, particularly television, seized the reins to sell products and services. However, as television raised the stakes to giddy heights, major problems developed. Athletes organized and demanded a bigger slice of the pie. Behind-the-scenes power struggles boiled in nearly every sport. It was the decade of the boycott, the threatened boycott, the deferred payment, the fatter pension plan.

Saturday's hero had become a seven-day-a-week possibility, and some of the brashest of the lot did their playing on Sunday. Even the antifootball housewife knew the difference between a blitz and a blintz.

In less complicated times, a champion fighter used to mumble through bloodied teeth: "I'd just like to say hello to my mother. Hi, ma. I'm fine."

Nowadays, star athletes reaching the microphone would be more apt to say: "I'd just like to say hello to my attorney, my business partner, my ancillary adviser, my theatrical agent and my publisher. Hi, boys. We're doing fine."

This was a decade when a jockey (Braulio Baeza) could gross more than a quarter of a million dollars in one year of horseback riding, when a golfer (Billy Casper) could earn more than $200,000 in one year from purses alone, when the payroll for the employees in the business empire of another golfer (Arnold Palmer) totaled $1 million annually, when a basketball player (Wilt Chamberlain) could earn $250,000 a year, when new stadiums cost as much as $50 million each, when a thoroughbred sire could be syndicated for $5 million and when television paid professional football $27 million a year so armchair quarterbacks could say "Ooooh!" or "Lookit that!" or "Dummy, he shoulda run the draw."

Don't attempt to explain why the two most violent pro sports, football and hockey, enjoyed the sharpest surge in popularity. Or why one of the least violent sports, soccer, flopped as a pro spectacle. Or why safety-valve watching of violence on the playing fields failed to prevent a steady rise of much worse violence outside the world of sports. The sociologists will get around to that.

Just say it was the era of the "Monsterman" linebacker, the blood-lusting hockey defenseman, the torn knee cartilage and bruised rib cage, a decade when the meek may have inherited the television set and the point-spread, but the big and the bold inherited the sports earth.

Athletes in the Super Sixties ran faster, jumped farther, tackled better, leaped higher, collided harder, expressed themselves oftener (frequently on controversial subjects), drew bigger salaries and were watched and wagered on by more people than ever before. In keeping with the tempo of the times, the performers often took on the larger-than-life proportions of Michelangelo's heroic figures.

Sometimes, it even seemed as if Clark Kent had ducked behind a locker and emerged in a sports uniform instead of in his customary Superman tights. The fact that Superman kept having to change his skin color as well as his clothes reflected another important aspect of the 60's: the emergence of the black athlete as a force, first as a mercenary, now in a position of domination.

There goes Superman as Bob Beamon, long-jumping 29 feet, 2¼ inches at the 1968 Olympics—almost two feet farther than anybody else in track and field history. There he is as Maury Wills, stealing 104 bases in one season to break Ty Cobb's supposedly unbreakable record. Now he's Wilt the Stilt, scoring 100 points in a game, or Bill Russell, dominating pro basketball for the Boston Celtics, or Lieut. Arthur Ashe, beating the pros in the first $100,000 United States Open tennis tournament. He's Lew Alcindor, winning his third player-of-the-year award in college basketball. He's Cassius Clay, knocking out big, bad Sonny Liston and announcing that the new world heavyweight boxing champion will henceforth be known as Muhammad Ali.

He's rubbing sweat from his eyes on the pitcher's mound, Bob Gibson fast-balling the St. Louis Cardinals to a World Series championship. He's on the college football field, O. J. Simpson of the University of Southern California knocking down would-be tacklers and setting up a fat pro contract as No. 1 pick in the football draft.

But Superman was white as well as black in the Super Sixties. He reappears as Roger Maris of the New York Yankees, hitting 61 home runs and breaking Babe Ruth's one-season record, but having to settle for an asterisk beside the 61, denoting a longer season. Now Superman takes the form of Sandy Koufax, aching with pain but pitching no-hitters in four consecutive seasons for the Los Angeles Dodgers. There he is as Bobby Hull, scoring his 58th goal of the season as the $100,000-a-year star of the Chicago Black Hawks. It's the 1964 Tokyo Olympics and Superman is Don Schollander, winning four gold medals in swimming. It's the 1968 Olympics and he's 32-year-old Al Oerter, out-psyching younger and supposedly stronger rivals to win a record fourth gold medal in the discus.

Now Superman changes into tennis shorts to become Rod Laver and win as a pro in open competition the same grand slam he won as an amateur. At Churchill Downs, he's Hartack, winning his fifth Kentucky Derby in 10 attempts as he guides Majestic Prince to the blanket of roses. In foot-racing, Superman looks like Jim Ryun, setting a world mile record of three minutes 51.1 seconds. In yachting, he's Bus Mosbacher, sailing *Intrepid* for the America's Cup.

He can even change himself into a horse:

Kelso, winning five straight horse-of-the-year titles; Dr. Fager, running a world-record mile of 1:32 1-5 with 134 pounds on his back; Nevele Pride, trotting a world record mile of 1:54 4-5, Bret Hanover pacing a world-record mile of 1:53 3-5.

The decade enters its final year, and Superman becomes SuperJet and SuperMet, winning the Super Bowl for the astonishing New York Jets, the World Series for the even more astonishing New York Mets. Neither team existed in 1960, a time when the New York Yankees dominated baseball and the New York Giants represented championship football.

In the new order, the Yankees and Giants were also-rans, inspiring pity instead of fear. That's the kind of crazy, upside-down decade it was.

The rise of the Mets from laughingstock to world champion and the decline of the once mighty Yankees underscored the chameleon nature of the era. In a decade of buckshot expansion, the balance of power could shift overnight.

From the two-league, 16-team setup it had operated for 60 years, baseball added two teams in 1961, two in 1962 and four in 1969. The play-off, that contrived but wildly successful stimulant for gate receipts and fan interest, entered the baseball picture in the form of divisional semi-finals in each league leading to the World Series.

While the playing careers of such stars as Ted Williams, Stan Musial, Mickey Mantle, Whitey Ford, Yogi Berra and Koufax ended, baseball developed profitable new markets despite a relative decline in prestige as the national pastime. Under the spur of local political pressures, new ball parks were constructed in eight cities. The group included the world's first indoor stadium, Houston's Astrodome, with its translucent domed roof, its artificial grass and its constant, air-conditioned, 72-degree temperature.

Meanwhile, the "Damn Yankees" of Broadway notoriety slipped to the point where they didn't even qualify as "Darn Yankees." Purchased by the Columbia Broadcasting System for $14.2 million in 1964, the Yankees that year won their fifth straight American League pennant, their 13th in 15 years and 29th in 44 years. One year later, the Yankees finished sixth. In 1966, they wound up last. They have not been contenders since.

In another switch that reflected the quick-change mood of the decade, Casey Stengel was dismissed by the Yankees in 1960 after winning his 10th pennant in 12 years—and promptly hired by the Mets in 1961. Going from baseball's greatest team to its worst, he created the Met mystique that set the stage for the emotional binge that accompanied the club's 1969 World Series conquest under Gil Hodges.

Despite the annual "dying sport" diagnosis, baseball continued to generate vastly higher income during the 60's. In 1962, the Mets and Houston Astros paid "entry fees" of $2 million apiece to stock their new franchises with players. By 1969, when Montreal and San Diego joined the National League, the entry fee had soared to $10 million.

Rapid expansion took place in other professional sports, too. Football mushroomed to 26 teams in two major leagues, basketball to 25 teams in two warring leagues, the National Hockey League to 12 teams. Doubling its size, the NHL placed the six new teams in one division so that an expansion club would be certain to gain the Stanley Cup final.

Along with expansion, the 60's produced controversies that kept the sports world in turmoil:

The continuing power struggle between the Amateur Athletic Union and the National Collegiate Athletic Association for control of American amateur sports.

Charges of payoffs in cash and merchandise to 1964 Olympic athletes by equipment manufacturers.

The disputed 1968 Kentucky Derby, precipitating a still-unresolved court case over whether first-place Dancer's Image ran with an illegal medication in his system.

Exercise girls at racetracks, winning their crusade to be licensed as jockeys and compete against male riders.

A recent court ruling that allowed baseball umpires to vote on unionization.

Control of golf and tennis prize money.

Namath's battle with Pete Rozelle, football commissioner, over the quarterback's ownership of a Manhattan bar where "undesirables" congregated.

The banning of turbine engines at Indianapolis.

A boycott by horsemen that closed down Aqueduct for nine days.

Ara Parseghian ordering Notre Dame to run out the clock for a 10–10 tie with Michigan State in their 1966 "game of the decade," rather than risk an interception, a decision that prompted Irish alumni to groan, "He tied one for The Gipper."

Roberto de Vicenzo losing the 1968 Masters golf tournament by signing an incorrect scorecard.

The successful Wally Butts-Bear Bryant law suit over a magazine article charging rigging of college football games.

First a proposed boycott of the 1968 United States Olympic team by black athletes, then the black power salutes during the playing of "The Star-Spangled Banner" at Mexico City.

Like his white teammate, the black athlete of the 60's was more socially aware than before. And on many fronts, he translated his awareness into challenges to what he regarded as a basically racist sports management.

By the end of the decade, black athletes were conspicuous in every baseball, football and basketball lineup—but conspicuously absent in nonplaying jobs. Baseball's 24 major league teams, for example, had no black field manager, no black general manager, only one black umpire, four black coaches and few full-time black scouts.

"We can sweat," noted one black spokesman, "but apparently not as managers, administrators, scouts or sports writers."

Black candidates for managerial jobs had only a prediction by Bowie Kuhn, new commissioner of baseball: "There is no doubt in my mind that baseball will have a black manager in the near future."

Disparity between black power on the playing field and lack of blacks in the front office was only one of the paradoxes of the 60's.

Another was the "mini-retirement" of the Super Star, usually announced at a tearful press conference. American sports fans had been told that "winners never quit and quitters never win." In the 60's, though, a lot of winners quit—and came back to win again.

Ryun, the Super Miler, walked off the track in the middle of the AAU national mile championship.

"I was disgusted with myself," he explained later. "I had never learned how to lose."

Larry James quit the Villanova track team, but came back to win an Olympic gold medal. Others who retired or threatened to retire and then unretired themselves included Namath, Wills, Ken (Hawk) Harrelson, Donn Clendenon of the Mets, Hull, Pancho Gonzales, Coach Vince Lombardi, Palmer and Jerry Quarry.

Jean-Claude Killy, France's triple gold medalist in Olympic skiing, provided a possible clue to the American athlete's soul-searching:

"The sports hero must always be on top," he said. "If he goes down, he becomes a loser. I quit when I was on top, and the business opportunities came."

Yet Ryun and the others could find a 60's parallel in Richard M. Nixon, a major political loser who fought his way out of retirement into the Presidency of the United States.

If the Super Sixties produced gold from gate receipts and television, there were those who felt the golden age had been tarnished by too much commercial greed. The promoters who pulled sports franchises out of loyal cities to make an extra buck in fresher territory were likened to carpetbaggers. Racetracks, whipped and spurred by revenue-seeking politicians, let their plants be turned into glassed-in hothouses for winter racing—making a travesty out of their sport. "Grab the money today, forget about tomorrow." Too often, that seemed to be the philosophy.

There was concern, too, about the proliferation in sports gambling. Jimmy the Greek, establishing odds and point-spreads from Las Vegas, had become the Last Great Scorekeeper of Grantland Rice's verse, and the paraphrased refrain went: "It matters not who wins or loses, but how you cover your points."

The "good" teams were teams like the Boston Patriots and Atlanta Falcons, clubs that rarely won but almost always managed to lose by fewer points than the bookies had established. The "bad" teams were teams that may have won often, but not by as many points as they were supposed to win by.

It was a decade when horse racing's traditional morning line was overshadowed by the point-spread, the probable pitchers, the vigorish (a bookie's two-way commission), the takeoff (removing a suspicious game from the betting card), the push (a no-bet tie on the point-spread) and hitting the middle.

Bettors trying to hit the middle would wager on both teams in the same game with different bookies offering different point-spreads. Hitting the middle meant they had won both bets.

All this worried people such as John Brennan, the former Federal Bureau of Investigation executive who kept an eye on harness racing as president of Harness Tracks Security, Inc. He noted that the decade had begun with the second major postwar "fix" scandal in college basketball.

"The major concern in sports today," said Brennan, "is to keep the angle guys, the termites, from ingratiating themselves with the athletes."

As the 60's gave way to the 70's, Brennan saw the need for a national surveillance staff to protect all the sports that generated substantial betting.

"We're talking about a multi-billion-dollar gambling business," he warned. "We need an all-sports protective agency, not just a few part-time agents. It's either that or, I'm afraid, some Super Scandals in the 70's."

THE GREAT SWIM HOAX

By Hal Lebovitz

From the Cleveland Plain Dealer

For a fellow who once reveled in practical jokes—there was this time we sent a note to a college classmate, "Please report to the psychology lab at 10 A.M. tomorrow to compare your intelligence with that of a normal human being," and he went—I can't work up an anger over the hoax that was pulled on us in last Sunday's *Plain Dealer.*

As a matter of fact, I must admit some admiration for "The Culprits," as they called themselves in the anonymous apology they mailed us a few days later.

Shortly before deadline last Saturday night, a call came in from the "Lakewood High-Akron Firestone swim meet." George Zimmer, our scholastic swim specialist, handled it.

The information George took down, and subsequently rewrote, gave us one of the best reading stories in our Sunday paper. These two unbeaten teams—"titans of scholastic swimming" he called them—had battled to a 44–44 tie. The deadlock in itself was remarkable and the story noted "it was the first time in recent memory a dual meet ended in a draw."

But even more remarkable was the manner in which the meet ended:

"Tied at 44–44 going to the 400-yard freestyle relay, Bob Carr of Lakewood and Greg Lane of Firestone, swimming the last leg of the event, were both disqualified for jumping too soon. Each drew the other offside. Thus both teams remained unbeaten . . ."

I remember reading it myself Sunday morning and being intrigued by the weird finish.

Great story, except that not a single word of it was true.

The next day the Lakewood coach called to politely inform us there had been no such meet and that, in fact, Lakewood isn't even scheduled to oppose Akron Firestone in a dual meet this season.

"The Culprits," some unidentified young men in Lakewood with a vivid imagination and a keen sense of the practical joke, had taken us in.

One can picture them sitting there, concocting the whole thing. They had done their homework well. They knew the names of all the swimmers on both teams and their best swim times. Zimmer could not have known by the results the "correspondent" gave him that the whole thing was a put-on.

Even though we had to write a retraction the next day we did so admiringly. The put-on was so well done we actually enjoyed it.

Naturally, we're wary of phony stories. We have a way of screening "hole-in-one" calls. We double-check information we consider questionable. And had Zimmer checked the Lakewood swimming schedule he would have known his leg was being pulled. But he didn't have time. The deadline was at hand and the story was too big. The "correspondent" had identified himself and the name sounded genuine.

In retrospect, it's amazing we aren't taken in more often since we cover more than 150 school events each weekend. The fact that we aren't is a tribute to the manner in which Dan Coughlin and Dick Zunt have organized the scholastic staff.

Zimmer, of course, is kicking himself now. Being close to the swim scene he says, "I should have known better."

T'ain't necessarily so. May we remind him how many readers were taken in by Bill Hickey's marvelous fictional accounts of "Pusan State's" football team and it's phenomenal, unstoppable star, "Won Sok Hung"?

Before Bill airily became the radio and TV editor, he was a member of our overworked sports staff. His creative but tired mind concocted the delightful stories about "Won Sok," his teammates Ho Lee Gee, Pusan State's great coach Nu-Roc-Nee, the announcer Gib Chann Lee and other characters so obviously put-ons it didn't seem necessary to label this pleasurable reading as "fiction."

Yet, when Bill finally worked Pusan State into "Saki Bowl" our sports department switchboard was flooded with calls that New Year's Day, seeking the outcome of the game.

A copy boy in our own sports staff was so carried away by Hickey's accounts, he took a 50-1 bet on Pusan State when offered those odds by one of the sharpies in our staff department.

Perhaps the greatest sports story hoax of them all came from the fertile brain of a New York advertising man named Morris Newberger.

Back in 1941, all by himself, he created an unbeaten football team. In his small Manhattan office he conjured up Plainfield State Teachers College.

Then he gave his team a schedule. In order, Plainfield was to play Scott, Chesterton, Fox, Randolph Tech, Ingersoll, Benson, Appalachian and in the finale—and homecoming, naturally—it was to meet it's archrival, good old Harmony College. Sound real, don't they?

Newberger's mimeograph machine was busy rolling out releases for all the papers in the New York area. At that time there were seven dailies in metropolitan New York alone.

In the opener, Plainfield State beat Scott, a much bigger opponent, 20–0. Newberger called this score, and the details, into *The New York Times,* New York *Herald Tribune,* the Associated Press, the other metropolitan papers and wire services and they dutifully carried brief accounts of the "upset."

The following Saturday, Plainfield overcame tough Chesterton. Next week, Fox College was knocked off. Newberger called in these scores and sent out weekly mimeographed releases containing more detailed information. Plainfield, it developed, had a miracle player, John Chung, a full-blooded Chinese fullback (no relation to Won Sok Hung), who averaged 9.3 yards per carry and ate rice between halves.

Thanks to Chung's wizardry, Plainfield State ran off bigger scores each week as it continued its unbeaten ways.

When Newberger phoned in Plainfield's 35–0 victory over Randolph Tech, a sports department rewrite man asked, "Where's Plainfield State? In Plainfield, New Jersey?"

"Just outside," replied Newberger, and hung up. The answer apparently satisfied the writer, for the account of the game was duly published.

By the time Plainfield won its sixth straight, Chung was on his way toward becoming All-America, well, at least Little All-America. Herb Allan, then a sports writer for the New York *Post,* picked up one of Newberger's publicity releases and rewrote it into a glowing feature about this star who ripped off yards after eating rice.

A few days later he wished he could have eaten the copy, rice and all. Caswell Adams, of the *Herald Tribune,* seeking to do a personal interview tried to locate Chung. He couldn't even find Plainfield Teachers.

Plainfield never did get to play Appalachian and Harmony. Adams, failing to find the school, discovered Newberger instead. He exposed the entire put-on. Newberger and Plainfield retired undefeated.

So, George, if the sophisticated New York writers could laugh off the hoax of nonexistent Plainfield Teachers, you shouldn't be so disturbed at being taken in by "The Culprits." Lakewood High and Akron Firestone do exist.

Slippery Rock Teachers? Yes, George, take the score. There really is a school by that name.

THE RISK TAKERS

By Robert Daley

From Playboy

Watch the death-defying high-diving daredevil clinging to his tiny platform near the ceiling of the arena. His toes grip the edge. Drums roll. He dives into the void. The mob gasps.

He plunges five stories before the rope around his ankle stops him short and yanks him back part of the way he has come. Upside down, he swings back and forth, his head only eight feet from the ground. He then unhitches himself, stands and accepts the crowd's tumultuous applause. He is a grinning 24-year-old Pole named Sitkiewicz, and he is the featured aerialist with this year's Ringling Bros. and Barnum & Bailey Circus. He is a very amiable chap, always laughing. He says good morning to people, even at night. He speaks no language anyone else around speaks, the last word in alienated man. By learning one trick no one else will try, he has set himself apart from the rest of the world; and for performing this trick 13 times a week, he earns something over $200. The elephants are not the only circus performers who work for peanuts. Sitkiewicz's career is good for about ten years, if the rope doesn't break. After ten years, if he wants to stay employed, he had better find a new and more dangerous trick.

Watch the death-defying, snake-wrestling daredevil. His name is Kurt Severin. He calls himself "author . . . world traveler . . . photo journalist . . . adventurer." His specialty is snakes. In the past, it has also been sharks, crocodiles and the puberty rites of Latin-American jungle tribes. Today, wading through the Amazon jungle, he comes upon an anaconda thicker through the middle than a man's thigh. About 18 feet long, the anaconda dangles from a tree. Severin decides to grab it by the head while his guide photographs him and it, both grinning.

An instant later, the huge constrictor has flung Severin to the ground and is coiled around him, crushing the life out of him.

"Keep snapping," gasps Severin, who sees a great series of photos in this.

He has the anaconda by the throat with both hands, but the anaconda has him by the throat, too. Its tail is wrapped around Severin's windpipe and is sliding around in a second loop. Severin, contemplating how long the series of photos should be, fights for time. But soon his face goes red. He can't breathe or talk. He manages to pry the anaconda loose enough so that he can say, "Remove the necklace."

Three men, struggling, at last get the snake off Severin.

"Did you get a lot of photos?" gasps Severin, fingering his swollen throat.

Yes.

Severin is happy. "I've had much closer calls than that with cobras," he says.

Watch the death-defying daredevil Jose Meiffret pedaling a special bike in a windbreak behind a racing car at speeds of over 108 miles per hour, the former world record, which was set in 1941. In the 60's, Meiffret first raised the record to 109.6, then to 115.9. These are records no one gives a damn about. They are worth absolutely nothing commercially. Each attempt costs Meiffret—a short, bald, 50-ish gardener with a concave dent in his skull from an earlier crash—thousands of dollars of his own money.

Now watch Meiffret on an autobahn in Germany leaning forward over the handlebars, straining to make the oversize sprocket go around. Somewhere close to 60 miles an hour, he ducks in behind the windbreak jutting upward from the rear of the racing car. The mob tensely leans forward along both sides of the measured kilometer. The spectators stare down from the overpasses. Now the racing car, with Meiffret tucked into the windbreak, is speeding along at 100 miles per hour . . . 115 . . . 125. Inside the windbreak, Meiffret is straining to keep his front wheel one inch from a roller bar. If he touches the roller bar, he knows it won't roll, it will fling him off his bike and kill him. If he drops back out of the windbreak through loss of a pedal, or fatigue or a heart spasm, the wind will throw him off the bike and kill him. If he hits a crack in the road, or a pebble, he is a dead man.

Out of the measured kilometer rockets the racing car. Jose Meiffret is still in the windbreak, upright, alive. Ladies and gentlemen, a new absolute speed record for miles per hour pedaled in a windbreak behind a racing car: 127.98 mph, by the death-defying Jose Meiffret, daredevil of international cycling!

This article is concerned with death and with those who risk it deliberately, gratuitously and perhaps compulsively.

But that's not fair, you say. Each of the three men mentioned so far sounds like some kind of nut. The Pole is in a circus, exactly where he belongs, indistinguishable from the other freaks there. Severin has gone to the Far East to see some snakes. Good, because we don't want him around here. Meiffret is frantically and unsuccessfully trying to find backers for a new record attempt, for he has no money left to pay for it himself. Glad to hear it. We are not interested in crackpots acting out death wishes.

But wait. I have some more daredevils for you. The boundary line gets fuzzy.

Watch the war photographer at Khesanh. His name is David Douglas Duncan and he is famous for photographing the art treasures of the Kremlin and Picasso's secret hoard of his own work. Duncan does not have to go to war. He is over 50 years old and he has been to too many wars already: World War Two, Palestine, Greece, Korea, Indochina. But he recently went into the Marine outpost at Con Thien, got his photos and came out alive. Now he flies into Khesanh, runs from the plane, which is being bombarded on the landing strip, and begins snapping a grim record of everyday terror and death. A C-130, machine-gunned while landing, skids the length of the runway and blows up. Duncan, running, braves the heat, the recurring explosions, and photographs live Marines pulling charred dead ones out of the blaze. A direct hit blows up part of the main ammo dump, leaving hundreds of scorched but unexploded artillery shells to be disposed of. Duncan photographs Marines gingerly handing scores of live, damaged shells down into a hole to be buried. An enemy rocket explodes fuel hoses that lead like fuses to the main gasoline dump. Marines fight the blaze; Duncan's cameras click. A single stray spark and they will all be instantly immolated. Duncan, at his age, knows the danger better than they do.

After nine days, Duncan flies out of Khesanh. In New York, he shepherds his pictures into *Life* magazine and onto ABC television. Then he turns around and flies back to Vietnam, back into the middle of bursting shells, terror and death. He might be photographing artsy scenery for *McCall's,* which once paid him $50,000 for some shots of Paris. But he chooses to go back into combat. Why?

"Death wish?" snorts Duncan. "I have no death wish. I have too much going for me. But it's the most important story of our time, perhaps in the entire history of our country."

Watch the ironworker fastening ribs to the skeleton of a skyscraper 30 or more stories above the street. His name is Edward Iannielli, Jr. Watch him, if you can stand to watch him, scamper across the void on an eight-inch beam, to get to a cup of coffee someone has sent up on an exposed dumbwaiter. Watch him scamper back across the eight-inch beam while studying the coffee carefully so as not to spill it. Listen to Eddie Iannielli talk.

"You're more of a crazy man up there at first, then it gets to be habit. You only focus on your feet, never on the ground. You have to have a sense of speed. You always start out on a beam at the same speed you're gonna finish. You can't change speeds in the middle. Of course, big beams you can walk out on with your eyes closed. You never start out on a beam unless you inwardly have said to yourself you can make it."

The son of an ironworker, Eddie once visited his father on a job, saw a ladder and climbed it, higher and higher: "Finally, I'm on the top, standing on this steel beam way up there, and I'm all alone and looking all around up there, looking out and seeing very far, and it was exciting; and as I stood there, all of a sudden I am thinking to myself, 'This is what I want to do!' " Eddie was then 13 or 14.

When he was an apprentice, climbing a ladder while balancing about 20 cups of coffee for the men, he fell backward two flights, landed on some canvas and got scalded and nearly drowned by the coffee. Working on the First National City Bank Building in New York, he fell into the void but landed on a beam three stories down and, though hurt, held on. The older workers told him he'd never live to see 30.

Working on the Verrazano-Narrows bridge approach, he got one finger crushed and another amputated—the surgeon removed the crushed finger but sewed the amputated one back on in a crooked position, so Eddie could use it to hold onto beams. One day, high on the bridge, he turned to find a buddy clinging to a wire, feet dangling into emptiness, voice pleading, "Help me, Eddie."

Eddie had a grip on the man's clothes but couldn't hold him. The man fell 350 feet to his death. Eddie watched him fall, naked back showing as the shirt flapped in the wind.

"I nearly got killed three times since the bridge," says Eddie.

"Sure, I've been thinking about it. But I couldn't quit. I love it too much. I wake up thinking today might be my last day. But that doesn't mean I'm going to stay in bed."

Watch the diver 140 miles east of Miami—and 432 feet below the surface of the sea. His name is Robert Stenuit. Inside the capsule that has taken him to the bottom, he takes a deep breath of pressurized gas, holds it and swims down into the water. Across from him in the gloom is the rubber house in which he will live for two days. Above him is 432 feet of water. Wearing only a swimsuit, holding his breath, he pauses to look straight up toward the sun he cannot see and to realize that, at that depth, if anything goes wrong, he will have no chance of reaching the surface—none.

So he swims over to the rubber house and climbs in. The gas in there tastes to him as fresh as mountain air. "What calm in this other world," he thinks. "What silence. What peace."

He hurries to connect the gear. His colleague, Jon Lindbergh, swims in. They find that their dehumidifying apparatus doesn't work. Their lights implode, spraying slivers of glass into the rubber walls. In dark and cold, they wrestle into place the four-foot aluminum cylinders that will purify their rubber house of the rapidly accumulating carbon dioxide. But one cylinder is flooded and the other has the wrong cover on it and is useless. They are panting from exertion and the carbon dioxide level in the rubber house is already dangerous.

So they wait while a new cylinder is sent down. When it comes, they wrestle it into the rubber house. They work frantically. At last they hear it working—gas rushes in the way it is supposed to. They are, momentarily, safe. That night, on the bottom of the sea, they eat corned beef, drink canned water and carrot juice. In the morning, they work outside on the bottom.

After 49 hours on the bottom—the longest deep dive ever—and four days decompressing, they come out into the sunlight again.

"Our successors," exults Stenuit, "will stay in the depths that long or longer. They will colonize the sea floor, cultivating its resources instead of pillaging them."

You are against nuts, you say, but you tend to be for war photographers, ironworkers and divers, if they don't take too many chances. You are for bravery, where it seems to pay off, though you are not entirely clear on what bravery is or how much payoff is necessary. Maybe you would like to believe that the daredevils you approve of display a higher quality of bravery than the ones you don't, or that you can measure the meaning of risk in terms of the good it may do—for someone else. You are against the death wish, whatever that is. You think nobody has a right to risk his life very much. We have a lot of laws against suicide and that kind of thing.

So let us see what you think about certain athletes.

Watch the daredevil bullfighter, El Cordobes, in Madrid. His first bull of the day gores him three inches deep under the arm. He springs up, ignores both his own wound and the bull's horns and plays and kills it so skillfully that, in the general delirium, he is awarded both ears.

Ducking into the infirmary, he allows his armpit to be sewed up without any anesthetic, then hurries outside to face his second bull. This one hooks him at once. He springs to his feet, runs back to it and it spears him again, throws him, wheels and is on top of him. Its horn rips part of his costume off, he lies with his back bloody and exposed and the horn digs for him. His men drag him free and try to carry him off, but he breaks loose, scoops up his bloody cloth and gives the bull a hair-raising series of molinetes, passing the animal behind his back. His costume is half gone, he is covered with blood, his eyes are as glazed as a fanatic's and he is passing the bull again and again behind him.

People are screaming, "No, no, no!" A man near me is shouting, "Get him out of there. He doesn't know what he's doing." El Cordobes is being paid over $16,000 today to give us thrills, but such insane bravery as this is not pretty to watch. "Get him out of there," we scream.

At last the fearful passes end. He kills the bull with a stroke. Now we cheer ourselves hoarse for him and award him an ear. Men jump down to parade him out the main gate on their shoulders.

Watch the daredevil racing driver, Jackie Stewart, on the 14-mile, 175-curve Nurburgring. Listen to his reaction to the Fuchsrohre, a windy downhill plunge into a dip, then a steep uphill climb into a sharp left-hand turn, followed by a right, a left and another right.

Stewart says: "The first time you go down that hill, you're in fourth gear, and you decide you should be able to make it in sixth gear flat out. So the next time around, that's what you try; you go downhill in sixth gear at 163 miles an hour, switching back and forth from one side of the road to the other, the trees and hedges going by. You can't see anything but greenery and you think: 'Christ, I'm going too fast. It's bloody terrifying.' You think: 'I'm not going to have enough time to do everything.' In the dip at the bottom of the hill, the g forces are tremendous; you're squashed down in your seat, the suspension isn't working and you realize you can't control the car anymore. You think: 'It is going to take its own line up the hill, whatever that line may be.' You can't get your foot off the accelerator onto the brake accurately—you only get a corner of it, and the car is going up the hill like on tram tracks. You're struggling to steer it and, at the same time, you're trying to come down two gears and get it slowed enough for the left-hander, and then there is a right, left, right coming—I tell you, it's bloody terrifying.

"But the second time you do it, your mind and body are synchronized to the elements you're competing against, and it is all clear to you, like in slow motion.

"It won't terrify you again until next year, when there will have been some improvements to the car and tires, and you go down there a little bit faster."

Or watch the daredevil mountain climber, Walter Bonatti, the Superman of the Alps, whose specialty is climbing sheer north faces in winter—alone. See him on the north face of the Matterhorn, climbing without gloves for a better grip, while the helicopters and light planes buzz about him all day. Every year or so up to now, he has made one of these fantastic climbs, selling his story and photos in advance to various European magazines. Every climb is much the same. Leaving his 70 pounds of gear behind, he climbs a little way up some sheer rock wall, hammering in pitons. Then he climbs down to get his gear and climbs up again, removing the pitons as he goes, for he will need the same pitons again higher up.

Each night, he hooks his sleeping sack to pitons planted more or less solidly in a fissure in the rock, curls himself into it in a fetal position, lights his spirit heater on his knees and cooks himself some bouillon or tea out of chunks of ice broken off the wall. He eats some dried chamois meat and some nougat candy. Then he hangs there all night, trying to sleep but kept awake, usually, by cold and terror.

Meanwhile, back in their warm, safe homes, Europeans watch that day's part of the climb on television, thank God they are not Walter Bonatti and ask themselves what the hell he is doing up there alone.

He has been up there as long as seven days in the past. The Matterhorn climb takes only four. There is a huge cross atop the Matterhorn, raised there long ago by climbers who came up the easy way; and on the final afternoon, Bonatti at last spies the cross, with a halo of setting sun behind it. The cross seems incandescent and miraculous all at once, and Bonatti feels blinded. He climbs the final meters between himself and safety and approaches the cross with open arms. When he feels it against his chest, he embraces it, falls on his knees and begins to weep.

Do these people have a vision of life that is denied to most of us? Or are they all crazy? And what about the lives of spectators killed by stray racing cars or rescuers killed trying to get climbers off mountain walls? We also don't want to pay for any of the risk-taking via tax dollars. When a guy puts to sea in a 10-foot canoe, we don't want the Coast Guard going after him on our money. Should they be stopped? I don't know how you can stop most of them; you can't put police lines around every mountain or every sea. But would you want to stop them, if you could?

And let's look at this so-called death wish. Is there such a thing and, if so, is it everywhere and always deplorable? Or do we merely paste an easy label (because we do not understand) on what is really something else: courage, ambition and technique of such awesome perfection that it removes most of the danger we, from a distance, think is there? Is it possible, most of the time, that most of these people are safer than you and I are walking to work? Is it further possible that they have a perfect right, regardless of society's approval or disapproval, to risk their lives as much as they please? Is it also possible that you and I have an absolute need of such men around us, the useless as much as the useful, those who get away with it as much as those who, misjudging the length of the rope, regale us with brains upon the floor?

Let us look more closely.

You ask what kind of men are these who regularly choose to risk their lives. A few of the ones I have known appear to be what the world calls weirdos. I think Jose Meiffret, the speed cyclist, is a bit strange, and I think this principally because his insanely dangerous record attempts are worth nothing to anyone else and nothing to him commercially. He does it strictly for glory: "At such speeds, I belong no longer to the earth and not yet to death. At such speeds I am—me!" Meiffret, small, poor, stepped on all his life, suddenly found a way to make people take notice. In the windbreak, crossing into the measured kilometer at 127 miles per hour, he says his head was filled with only one thought: "Twenty seconds more and the record is mine anew. The record will be my revenge on life, revenge on the misery I have suffered." To get to that moment, he practiced strict chastity, slept on a board, ate only health foods. He had written hundreds of letters, trying to line up backers and cooperation and he had spent every sou he owned. His life was not important to him, compared with the record.

I think Donald Campbell, the former land- and water-speed record holder, was a bit strange. Campbell had all sorts of fetishes and superstitions and also believed he could communicate with the dead. Just before setting his final record, as he sat in his cockpit quivering with fear, his face suddenly went calm, and in a moment, he rocketed safely down the run at 403 miles per hour. He explained that his dead father's face had appeared to him, reflected in the windscreen, his dead father's voice had assured him he would be safe.

Other racing drivers claimed Campbell reeked of death. Stirling Moss once told me he was absolutely certain Campbell would shortly kill himself. Moss was right. Campbell's boat blew up as he tried for the water-speed record.

And talking to Florida-based Kurt Severin about snakes and about fear is certainly an unsettling experience. "I don't know fear," he says. "It is one thing I am not acquainted with. I get an uncomfortable feeling at times, but it is not fear." Was he not frightened with the anaconda coiled around him? "No. There were three people around to get it off me. I only wanted to have a picture of myself with the anaconda to send to my wife."

Severin has been in the water with sharks and with crocodiles. He has been in three wars and about 20 revolutions. He claims to have been the first parachutist to photograph himself in flight. He did that in 1934.

But I do not know if I believe him about lack of fear. To get a photo of a cobra striking, he decided, he would have to give it something to strike. Why not himself? Why not, indeed. He built a plastic shield around his camera, provoked the cobra and it came right through the shield and hit his hand, missing a grip on the hand but pumping out enough venom to kill approximately 22 people. Severin dropped the camera, which broke open, spoiling the film. Another, stronger shield was built, and this time, Severin got the shot he wanted.

"I'm not afraid of snakes or sharks or animals. I'm afraid of bugs, though. I'm afraid of disease. I once slept in the bed of a guy who had just died of yellow fever. I didn't know it at the time, of course. Later, I was scared for eight days. It is not a funny feeling to think something might be encroaching on you."

Severin speaks five languages, plays the violin and is interested in painting, ballet and classical music. When he talks, he makes excellent sense; it is only when you mull over, later, what he has said that you become awed, or appalled.

"Fear of snakes is all in the mind," he says. "Snakes are not slimy. As a matter of fact, they have a very pleasant touch. It's like plastic. It's really quite nice."

Whatever Severin may think about fear, most other habitual risk takers are often terrified, and they admit it. In fact, what most separates them from the rest of us is not that they risk death but that they subject themselves to frequent terror, an emotion most of us struggle to avoid at all costs.

Every racing driver, every time he loses control of a car and waits for it to hit whatever it is going to hit, is terrified. Every matador, when he is down and the bull is on him, is terrified. El Cordobes, gored by the first bull he ever faced in Madrid, lay on the sand with the horn rooting about in his intestines: "It wasn't the pain I was worried about, it was the fear. When I felt the horn inside me, I was so scared I thought my heart would stop and I would die of the fear."

Jose Meiffret on his record bike is scared—he carries his last will and testament in his jersey pocket. The ironworker, Eddie Iannieli, is scared by every accident: "When something happens, all your fear comes back, but you suppress it. You just put it out of your mind." He talks about his most recent accident. He was sitting on top of a beam about two stories up, and the bolts at the base of the uprights broke or pulled out and the whole thing fell over sideways. Eddie suffered a back injury that kept him out of work for many weeks. "No matter how much you're prepared for something like that to happen, it happens so fast you're not prepared for it. A lot of guys get killed, and I'm still alive and I'm very grateful."

The climber, Bonatti, has known as much terror as any man alive, perhaps more. Climbing K2 in the Himalayas, he was unable to find two other climbers higher up, as night fell. At 27,000 feet, unable in the darkness to go up or down, without any food, heat or shelter of any kind, he was forced to spend the night in the open on an ice shelf, beating himself with his arms all night to keep himself awake and alive. That was prolonged terror.

Innumerable times, Bonatti has found himself clinging to some sheer wall, certain (for the moment) there was no possible way to go either up or down. On the Lavaredo in Italy, he had to inch across a fragile ledge of snow. On the Dru in France, he had to lasso a jutting projection and swing across the void like Tarzan, while wondering if the rope would slip off or the projection snap. Once, he was caught in a storm with six other men on a narrow ledge on Mont Blanc. Lightning was attracted by the group's sack of pitons, ice axes and such. Bolt after bolt blasted and crackled around the group. The air was saturated with electricity. They could not get rid of the cursed sacks of steel—without them, they could get neither up nor down the mountain. They simply had to huddle there, terrified, waiting to be fried or blasted off the ledge. Again and again, lightning crashed about them. Bonatti found himself screaming.

I have known a good many people who habitually take risks; and although I have heard a number of them say they enjoy the danger, I have never heard one say he enjoyed the terror.

Habitual risk takers are able to do what they do, first because they suppress (or, in some cases, eliminate) certain fears that are normal in all of us: fear of height, fear of the depths of the sea, fear of excessive speed, fear of bullets and bombs, fear of wild beasts, fear of snakes. All of these fears, in them as in us, are basically fear of the unknown. Once all the facts and details are known, the fears become much less fearsome and a reasonable man is often able to ignore them. As Severin says, snakes are not slimy, and once you know that, there is no reason to be afraid. In fact, he says, almost all feared creatures "will scram out of there at the approach of man. If sharks were as dangerous as written, most of our beaches would be unsafe."

In other words, at least part of Severin's bravery is only knowledge. Similarly, the bullfighter is not normally afraid of the bull, because he has spent years learning how to handle bulls, just as the racing driver has spent years learning how to control speed that would frighten most of us. The mountaineer knows rocks, knows which fissures will hold a piton and which won't; and he also knows that once anchored to a piton, he is absolutely safe, no matter what the height. David Douglas Duncan goes in to photograph wars knowing in advance approximately what he will find there—he was once a U.S. Marine trained for combat. He knows he won't be surprised by anything, he knows he won't panic and he knows instinctively now how to recognize places and moments that he judges overly dangerous; these he avoids. In other words, he knows when to stick his head up and when not to; he obeys certain rules, and these rules keep him alive. Occasionally, he will expose himself to get a picture; but by moving fast, he cuts the risk to a minimum. He is, of course, a brave man, but he is not a foolish one, and he accepts risk only when certain he understands it exactly and has put all odds in his favor. I once heard him tell Guy Lombardo that he would never drive one of Lombardo's speedboats: "I would be terrified. I'm not trained for that. I don't know anything about it." In combat, Duncan is obviously as vulnerable as each GI to some stray shell; but while in combat he runs no risk of being sideswiped by a taxicab, or mugged in the park, or hit on the head by a suicide on his way down from the roof. The odds can be said to come out almost the same, once you realize, as Duncan does, that life is not very safe.

In addition to possessing knowledge and technique, most of these risk takers approach each dangerous place only after having taken every possible precaution in advance. Bullfighters always have a surgeon present in the arena infirmary (indeed, surgeons are required by law in Spain) and the richer bullfighters often travel with their own personal horn-wound specialists—just in case. Sitkiewicz hangs around for an hour after his act; then, when the show ends and the audience empties out, he goes up and rerigs his rope himself for his next dive. No one else is allowed to touch it.

The racing driver, Jackie Stewart, feels that the modern, monocoque Grand Prix car is so strong that the driver can survive almost any crash. The only danger then is fire—so Stewart wears fireproof long underwear, fireproof coveralls, fireproof gloves, socks and shoes and a fireproof bandanna covering all his face except his eyes. Inside all this in a three-hour race he nearly suffocates, but he wears it. "I'm very safety conscious, as perhaps you've noticed," he told me once. "But in a fire, a man ought to be safe for thirty seconds, dressed that way; and by that time, somebody ought to be able to get him out. Thirty seconds is quite a long time, actually." That was the day of the 1966 Belgian Grand Prix. Stewart crashed in a rainstorm and the car crumpled around him so tight it was 15 minutes before they got him out. The fire suit wouldn't have saved him. The next year, he turned up for the same race wearing, in addition to his fire suit, a patch over his breast, giving any eventual surgeons his blood type. Precautions, Stewart feels—all risk takers feel—are important.

Why do men such as these seem to search out danger?

Psychologists will tell you that each of them first selects a difficult profession in order to separate himself from the mass of men. Later, each raises his stake up to and beyond the danger line, in order to separate himself further from other men within the same profession. Psychologists will give you many such explanations, overlooking what are, in most cases, the two basic ones: Most men who search out danger do it for money and for the pure pleasure of it. For the standouts, the money comes only one way: big. The pleasure usually comes big, too, sometimes even orgiastic, stupendous.

Start with money, the simplest of all human motives. Car racers and, even more so, bullfighters earn fantastic sums. Sitkiewicz may earn only a bit over $200 a week, but what else could he do, in Poland, to earn so much? Some photographers earn good pay also; but David Douglas Duncan, having taken the precaution (that word again) of selling his photos in advance to both *Life* and ABC television, will earn ten times as much by going into sticky combat zones most others want no part of.

By working high up on narrow beams where not many other men will go, Eddie Iannielli earns (counting bonuses and extra vacation time) roughly $20,000 a year, almost twice what laborers like himself earn below. He risks a quick death, yes, but his special skill is so rare that he never risks being out of work, a possibility that haunts—and terrifies—much of mankind all the time.

There is money in most danger and sometimes, paradoxically, even a little security. And there are pleasures, many pleasures. Start with the simplest of these.

To control anything—anything at all—delights man. He is delighted to control the way a plant grows or the shape of a bush or a dart thrown at a dartboard, or a car driven fast and well. So do not be surprised to hear that there is pleasure in controlling a very hot car, indeed, or a raging bull or one's feet on a beam. The controlled forces are tremendous, unpredictable, and therefore the pleasure of control is that much greater. A man thinks: "Look at me, fragile and puny human being that I am! Look what I am controlling!" This is never said aloud, because the fragile and puny human being in question would much rather have you believe him a hero. But this is the way he feels. He gets a kick out of controlling something hardly anybody else can control. It's nice that you down there are watching him and cheering his control, but he would feel pleasure whether you were there or not, for the principal applause he is listening to is his own.

There is pleasure in accepting challenge. At a world convention held in London, on undersea activities, the inventor Edwin Link spoke of sending a man to live at a depth of 400 feet. Listen to the diver Robert Stenuit: "All heads turned to me. Four hundred feet! The very idea made my insides itch. Did I really want to descend to that awful depth, to shiver night and day and perhaps to furnish headlines for the journals that specialize in catastrophe?

"I really did. Always I have found joy in danger lucidly accepted and prudently overcome. And when a reporter put the question to me, I heard myself answer: 'Of course. Yes.'

"To me, it was the most extraordinary adventure of which a diver might dream."

There is pleasure in provoking terror in others, too. The gasp Sitkiewicz hears when he dives from the roof is pure pleasure to him. Most of the risk takers I have known delight in talking about danger, delight in mentioning death casually, delight in watching listeners' eyes go wide. Eddie Iannielli says: "Windy days, of course, are the hardest. Like, you're walking across an eight-inch beam, balancing yourself in the wind, and then, all of a sudden, the wind stops—and you temporarily lose your balance. It's some feeling when that happens." Eddie always enjoys the admiration, the near worship, when he talks like this. All of these men are aware from such reactions, from the questions they are constantly asked ("But why do you do it, why?") and from the hypothesizing psychologists in the background that so-called normal people don't understand who they are or how they can accept such risk, and this is very pleasant. It is nice to feel so singular. The desire to feel singular is basic to the human personality; but the timid clerk at his desk may have to do without fulfilling this basic need every day of his long, safe life, subsisting on his Mittyesque fantasies.

There is also the simple pleasure of physical activity. All of the risk takers are easily bored. They go crazy in static situations and normally they go on taking risks however long they may live. Duncan and Meiffret are over 50. Kurt Severin is over 65 and on Medicare, and on a trip, as has been said, to the Far East to see more snakes: "I have always had an urge to do things, to be in all sorts of funny situations. It's curiosity, it's—I don't know. I want to see things others haven't seen, and that involves danger, because one goes into the unknown. I'm a senior citizen. People tell me I should sit on my big fat ass and digest what I have seen and not expose myself anymore. But I can't do it. I have to go out."

There is pleasure as well in the belief of most risk takers that they are contributing to the world by doing something dangerous that has to be done. Stenuit believes one day men will colonize the continental shelf, thanks to his pioneering dives. If he is wrong, he may be accused of having risked his life for nothing. Nonetheless, at the time, he believed he was contributing his best and most important talent to the world. So does Duncan believe he is contributing by bringing back photos that may throw some light on the awful struggle in Vietnam. So does Walter Bonatti believe that he and all mountaineers contribute: "We demonstrate in the most stunning way of all—at the risk of our lives—that there is no limit to the effort man can demand of himself."

Now we come to pleasures that are not so simple and, therefore, not so easy to describe.

"I think we appreciate life better, because we live closer to death," the late Marquis de Portago once wrote of racing drivers. Does this make any sense to you? Danger heightens all the senses. A man feels extraordinarily alert and alive. Up to a certain point, alcohol does this, too, and I suppose drugs do, although I do not know this personally. But I firmly believe that nothing stimulates a man as much as danger does, and it doesn't even have to be very much danger.

One extremely hot day last January, I was hunting quail on the King Ranch in south Texas. There were other shooters, most of whom I did not know, and I was worried about possibly getting my head blown off by accident, or blowing off someone else's, and this made me alert. I was watching everybody very carefully, and then the girl nearest me jumped back and blasted a rattlesnake.

She stood there trembling, unable to move. The rattler, tail buzzing, writhed brokenly near her feet, and I ran over and shot its head off.

At lunchtime, we gathered in a grove of oaks and dined on a stew made from kid goat and on broiled baby lamb chops and drank cold Rhine wine and talked of rattlesnakes. There were nine of us shooters in all, hunting in groups, and the total score in rattlesnakes so far was four. Much of the King Ranch was still under water from the fall hurricanes and the rattlers seemed to have come up onto the higher ground from all over; the sun had brought them out of their holes and it was plainly very dangerous to continue shooting. But nobody wanted to go home yet. Our excitement was too high.

In the afternoon, hunting through a grove of mesquite trees, I did not see what turned out to be the biggest rattler of the day, a six-footer, until I was within a stride of it. The diamondback rattler in that kind of country is almost impossible to see.

I gave it both barrels. This disturbance set off a bevy of quail, which flew all about me. People were shouting "Shoot!" but I was quivering too much even to reload.

But this emotion passed and we went on hunting, often through high, hummocky grass. "Some chance of seeing a rattler in here," I thought, but I plowed through it, anyway, eyeballs working over every blade, every shadow. I have never felt so alert in my life, presumably because my life depended on my alertness. I also have never felt so keenly aware of the sun on my back, or the smell of gunpowder, or the color of birds, or the buzzing of insects. I felt hungry and thirsty and tired in a very pleasant way, enjoying food and drink and rest in advance, while still slogging through fields, trying to flush quail.

When night fell, the groups came together at a dirt crossroads in the dark and drank gin and tonic mixed out of the trunks of the shooting cars. The total score was seven rattlers. We all agreed it was madness to have hunted in there that day. We were all glad we had done it. Ice tinkled in glasses. They were the best gin and tonics I have ever tasted. I was excited, alert, aware of all of the sights, sounds and smells of the night. This lasted until I fell asleep later back at the ranch, and even until the next morning, when I lay awake in bed, listening to the dew drip off the roof and feeling good all over.

This is one level of the excitement that exists in danger. There is another that is perhaps impossible to describe to someone who hasn't experienced it.

Years ago, in the streets of Jerusalem, Jewish terrorists waved David Duncan to take cover, then mowed down the three Arabs he was with. Duncan raced after the terrorists' car, photographing the whole show as police and bullets came from all directions. Later, Duncan cabled *Life*: "What a beautiful day to be still alive."

Now, some will assert that danger is a drug, that a man gets so he can't leave it alone; and this is true, though not in the way the speaker usually means. I have never heard a habitual risk taker articulate what the "drug" is, or what the sensation feels like; but to me, it is purely and simply the extraordinary exhilaration a man feels to find the danger gone and himself still alive. I have felt this exhilaration.

For many years, I have gone to the fiesta at Pamplona each July and run in the streets with the bulls most mornings, and this is not particularly dangerous. There are many tricks for keeping well clear of the horns, and normally the bulls, obeying their strong herd instinct run flank to flank and ignore the runners completely. The only real danger is a bull separated from the herd. A bull alone will gore anything it sees.

There was one morning I ran in front of the bulls and, when they were close, I leaped high up onto a window grating, hoisting my derriere out of danger. When the herd had gone by, I dropped down into the street again and sauntered between the barriers toward the arena into which the herd had disappeared. There were other men in the street with me and mobs of people crowding the barriers along both sides of the ramp that goes down to the tunnel under the stands.

Suddenly, the men on the fences started shouting: "Falta uno!" There was one bull still loose in the street.

The men in the street scattered and there I stood, face to face with the bull, who for a moment, could not decide what to do.

I searched for an empty spot on the fence. There was none. What to do? Where to run? I remember thinking: Be calm. Think it out carefully. If you panic, you are lost. I saw I was the only man in the street. The bull was 10 yards away. In the other direction was the ramp under the stands and the arena floor beyond. I thought: Can I beat the bull into the arena? If I could get into the arena, I could perhaps hurdle the barrera to safety. But I saw that the bull would catch me in the tunnel or before. I thought: It's the only chance you have; start running.

I ran.

The tunnel was 20 yards away . . . 10. I could hear the bull.

Suddenly, I spied a gap atop the fence. I leaped up there. The bull rushed by under my feet. A moment later, the wooden door slammed behind it. I was safe.

I felt none of the quivering one feels after losing control of a car or nearly stepping on a rattlesnake. Instead, I felt a flood of exhilaration. I did it! Look at me. I'm still alive!

It was one of the most stupendous feelings of my life, accompanied by much of the wonder of first sexual intercourse: So this is what all the talk has been about.

It wasn't a feeling of relief or of gratitude. It was exhilaration. I had faced real danger and got out of it on my own two feet and I was still alive and I felt great, absolutely great.

Then I thought: This must be the drug they speak of. It is a sensation I could get to love entirely too much; and the next day, I was afraid to run with the bulls (though I have run many times since), fearing that I might go for that extraordinary exhilaration again and this time, possibly, do something really stupid.

And so some of the habitual risk takers go for this feeling sometimes and some of them find it occasionally, but it must be rare. A feeling as glorious as that can't be common, and I suppose you can call it a drug, if you want to.

On a more practical level, you can't have a safe world and a progressive one. (Probably you can't have a safe world under any circumstances, so you might as well try for the progress, whatever the cost.) And you must admit that most progress comes from risk. This has always been the case. Five hundred years ago, Columbus risked his life and his ships and crews to discover a new world he didn't know was there, and that's why all of us are where we are today. The men of his time later called Columbus a hero. But there must have been a hundred other captains who never found the new world, because they looked in the wrong place; and some of them didn't come back, and no doubt "normal" people of the time called such men daredevils obeying some stupid death wish.

Or think of Edison fooling around with high voltage he didn't understand, high voltage that had killed several men before him and would kill many after him. Edison was obviously a daredevil. Was he acting out a death wish as well?

All of progress comes from pushing a little closer to the edge than the guy before you, and this involves risk. The world needs risk takers, needs an oversupply of them, and the spillover becomes the circus performers and daredevil athletes, all of whom have the same temperaments, basically, as all explorers and most inventors.

Cut off the right to risk one's life, and progress would end and society would atrophy and die. The right to watch men risk their lives on mountains, in car races, bullfights and circuses is equally important. We need to know where death is, if only to avoid it; and such men show us that and much more. Often accused of having a death wish, they make careers out of staying alive. And that is the simplest, most singular thing about them. It should not be overlooked.

WHATEVER HAPPENED TO GOOD SPORTSMANSHIP?

By Maury Allen

From Coronet

Baseball has been steadily slipping as America's National Pastime while football grows in importance each year. The Super Bowl has become the country's single most important sports event. There is a simple explanation for the rapid growth of football and the decline of baseball. In a word: violence.

Football has kept pace with the temper of the times. In a world filled with war, mayhem, riot, passion, football shows it in miniature each time two pro teams meet head-on for a Sunday afternoon of blood and battle. "Baseball," says no less an authority than Bill Veeck, who spent most of his life in the game, "is an 1890 game. It's a peaceful afternoon in the country. What baseball needs to compete is more violence."

The very nature of football is to hurt the other fellow. The nature of baseball is to avoid body contact; to hit the ball, run gracefully and finesse the opposition. Violence is rare and unrewarded. In football it is applauded and encouraged. "Football," says Vince Lombardi, the supersuccessful coach of the Green Bay Packers, who is now with the Washington Redskins, "is a game of hitting. You hit the other guy harder and faster than he hits you."

In a way, all of this leads to new emphasis, new dimensions, new attitudes in sports. Football and basketball players stress violence. Baseball, losing out, has to encourage the same sort of thing. The old concepts that sports, even professional sports, had elements of respect and good sportsmanship seem to be dying in a blaze of violence, action, fighting and viciousness.

A year ago a young third baseman for the New York Mets named Kevin Collins was holding a ball in his hand waiting to tag the runner who was out from here to your front porch. The runner was an infielder named Doug Rader for the Houston Astros. Rader came in hard! So hard, he cracked Collins in the jaw and sent him to the hospital. "I did my job," said Rader, "without any regrets. I was supposed to get into third base safely. If I couldn't do it before the ball I had to try something else."

The "something else" turned out to be a vicious elbow to the face. As often happens in these things, a field fight erupted and Rader wound up with a black eye.

The next time the two teams played in New York, the crowd was twice what it would normally be. The bloodthirsty fans were ready to see some more action. If they couldn't get it in the game, they would take it in a field fight or anything that might erupt.

Even Rader, who claimed the unsportsmanlike blow was an accident, was frightened by the violence he had encouraged. "I got a letter saying somebody would kill me if I stepped on the field tonight," he said. "Some of these people are sick."

Violence and bad sportsmanship would not occur if the owners of teams discouraged it or penalized their players. It is one thing to be a rough, tough football player. It is another to be a dirty football player.

The Oakland Raiders were champions of the American Football League two years ago. One of their strongboys was a mustachioed defensive lineman named Ben Davidson. He stood 6-feet-7 and weighed about 275 pounds—all muscle. Oakland was playing the New York Jets. New York's celebrated quarterback Joe Namath went back for a forward pass. He looked downfield for his man, lifted his arm and . . . that's all he remembered. Davidson had landed on him like a ton of bricks. The Oakland end had cracked Namath with a hard forearm right in his face. The cheekbone was crushed, and Namath had all winter to think about the injury.

"If you are going to play football," Namath said, "you are bound to get hurt, but a blow in the face is not a good place for a single guy like me to get injured.

"I had to check my face out every morning in the mirror," said Namath. "When we won the league championship, all the married guys on the club had to thank their wives for putting up with all the stress and strain all season. I had to thank all the single broads in New York. It just showed that Davidson didn't end my career."

Even in a game as supposedly nonviolent as professional basketball, the bad sportsmanship is beginning to show. When Doc

Naismith invented basketball at Springfield College he was aiming for a calm way of exercising the football and baseball players in the winter. The game was supposed to be a noncontact sport, all speed, grace, and finesse.

Now it is mostly a bruising game under the boards where super-giants like Wilt Chamberlain, Bill Russell, Wes Unseld, Willis Reed and Nate Thurmond wrestle for the basketball. Charles Darwin, if he were around, might characterize it "survival of the fittest." The action under the baskets has got rougher, wilder, more physical as the game goes on. This is what young Lew Alcindor will be getting himself into when he becomes a professional player. Of course, for a million dollars or so, Alcindor has to expect to take some punishment. He might also be expected to give it since there will be some 250 pounds next year on his seven-foot frame.

Even the smaller men get into some pretty physical competition. Seattle was playing the New York Knickerbockers last winter in Madison Square Garden. Joe Kennedy of Seattle and Cazzie Russell of New York were guarding each other. There was a little more than the usual pushing, shoving, holding and elbowing between the two. Both were resorting to one of basketball's favorite tricks, holding the opponent's shorts when he goes up for a shot. One day soon, I am sure, an opponent will go up for a shot and his shorts won't.

This one night, Russell went up for a shot. Kennedy brushed him. Then the ball came off the basket, Russell dove for it and Kennedy dove for Russell. "The ball was going out of bounds," said Russell later. "There was no need for the man to dive on me."

"I was just going for the ball," said Kennedy, "I certainly wasn't trying to hurt anybody." Whatever the truth, Kennedy did dive across Russell's knee. The New York player let out a loud scream. Russell was finished for the season. He had suffered a fractured ankle.

"Kennedy says it was an accident," Russell said later, "but I know I was scoring off him. When you are doing that, they try something to stop you."

It does seem that a dangerous trend is setting in with most sports. Ball players are beginning to accept the fact that anything is all right if you can get away with it. In a way, sports are no more than a mirror of everyday life. As values of right and wrong have changed in all our daily performances, so have they changed in sports. "Winning isn't the best thing," says Vince Lombardi, "it's the only thing."

In his highly readable book, *Instant Replay,* Jerry Kramer of the

Packers points out that Lombardi would often abuse a man on his team in an effort to stimulate him. The individual never mattered; only the team mattered; only winning mattered. Maybe, in a way only Lombardi mattered. His job was to win! If you could help the Packers win, you would stay. If you couldn't, he would abuse you or trade you or release you without much consideration for personal worth and dignity.

What is really happening in American sports is that sportsmanship and fun and fair play have disappeared in favor of violence and winning and selfishness. The recent baseball hassle over pensions was strong evidence of this. Major-league baseball players formed an association. All major-leaguers were members. The association through its elected player-representatives voted to call a boycott of spring training. They asked the players not to report as a threat to gain larger pension benefits.

Twenty years ago just about every ball player would have honored such a request. There was a closeness among ball players. There was an allegiance to each other, a one-for-all, all-for-one sort of relationship. This February, a few teams stuck it out but most had a clubhouse full of scabs. The standard answer by the players who reported was, "I owe my allegiance to the club."

What they really were saying, in effect, was that they agreed with the pension demands of their teammates, that they would take the increased pension benefits, but that somebody else had better do the fighting for them. Some teams did present a unified front. The successful teams, the pennant-winning Detroit Tigers and the St. Louis Cardinals, the traditionally close Yankees and the Los Angeles Dodgers, showed almost perfect loyalty to their association. "The teams that stayed together," said Tim McCarver of the Cardinals, "may be the teams that play together."

Selfishness seems to be one of the strongest motivations in the pension issue. The players who were more worried about their individual contracts and careers, instead of the greater good of the team and all the players, rushed to sign. "I don't think any of those guys who reported quickly will turn down any of the pension money we were able to win from the owners," said McCarver. The evil dollar seems to have driven most ball players away from the closeness and the good sportsmanship of the old days to the refrain heard most around ball parks these days, "What's in it for me?"

"There will come a day when some of these fellows draw that pension money years from now," said McCarver, "and they will probably have completely forgotten how they earned it. They got it because a lot of guys stuck out their necks." The result of the pension hassle may create more bitterness and less sportsmanship, even among teammates.

"I don't think the players who fought for the improved pension will forget quickly which ones didn't," said Ed Kranepool of the Mets. "It's pretty hard to be friendly to a guy who didn't help in a tough fight."

Joe Torre of the St. Louis Cardinals, one of the leaders for the players in the improved pension, said the dispute could cause some hard feelings with teammates: "When a pitcher who is out there is in trouble and I'm catching, I'll remember what he did. If he wasn't with us, I'll probably yell, 'C'mon, scab, get the ball over the plate.' That might shake him up a little."

One of the major reasons sports have changed in emphasis and tone in the last ten years is the attitude toward pensions. Football players went on strike last summer before their bosses raised the pension. Basketball players delayed the start of an All-Star Game a few years back over their pension problems. Hockey players are on the verge of an insurrection.

"The first thing the kids asked in the old days," says one baseball owner, "is how fast can I get a chance to prove how good I am? Now the first thing they ask for is a look at the actuarial tables to find out how much money they will be drawing when they retire at 65."

The constant discussion about pensions, huge salaries, bonus deals, welfare benefits, hospitalization and the like are bound to have a terrible influence on the kids. They try to copy the batting stance of their heroes. They will probably start copying his pension stance. One day soon, a little-leaguer will march up to home plate, hold up his hand and announce, "I don't swing unless my milk allowance is raised."

A few years ago ball players spent their off hours going to movies and reading the sports pages of their local newspapers. Now they spend their time studying actuarial tables and following the stock market. There is more conversation in a baseball clubhouse about the Dow-Jones average than about girls.

"When I was a kid," said Bowie Kuhn, the new commissioner of baseball, "baseball was the biggest thing in my life. I worked as a 12-year-old on the scoreboard in Washington. Baseball was everything to me. Things have changed. I'd like to see the country get back to that." It is a noble thought but it is unlikely to happen as long as pension wrangles and bonus payments, hospitalization plans and maternity benefits dominate the sports pages.

Sportsmen must find ways to keep these pension problems and money problems out of the papers. They must find ways to emphasize the fun of playing ball and the joy of a base hit on a summer day at a country picnic. The time must come again when sportsmanship and fair play and enjoyment are the main reasons people play ball.

Kids have to have some basis for the old American dream of hitting home runs and scoring touchdowns and shooting baskets just to be a hero for a moment, just to have fun.

When the kids start reading the actuarial tables instead of the sports pages, another pleasant chunk of America will be forever lost.

COURAGE: A LOVELY WOMAN

By Stan Hochman

From the Philadelphia Daily News

Betty Meade is beautiful.

They went years without letting a woman attend the Philadelphia Sports Writers Banquet and then they invited Betty Meade, who is beautiful. For years, men have been standing up at these banquets mumbling platitudes about why people play games.

Then they invited Betty Meade, who is beautiful. She stood there with her blonde hair glinting like a halo in the spotlight. She came out there in her gray dress with the fur trim, and her net stockings, and the artificial leg in the right stocking, and she told it better than it had ever been told before.

"Competing in athletics helps you to face problems," she said, and guys who had been babbling drunkenly all evening were struck silent. "In sports, you have to fight for everything you get. Nobody is going to hand you anything.

"You learn to lose. The first five or six years I played tennis I did a lot more losing than winning. Athletic competition helps you to learn to face anything in life. When I lost my leg, it was another loss. I'd have to face life, to learn to walk again, to run again."

At banquets, everybody always talks about winning. Then they invited Betty Meade and she gave them a lesson in humility and faith and courage. That's why they invited her, to honor her as the year's Most Courageous Athlete.

She won the national squash singles last year. And the doubles. And the mixed doubles. And two days after she won the singles, her legs were smashed in an auto accident. They were able to mend the left leg, which was broken in two places. They had to amputate the right leg below the knee.

"I was near hysterics," her husband Newton Meade remembered. "She looked up at me and said, 'Don't worry about me, I'll be okay. Take care of yourself.' I knew damn well she wasn't going to be okay. But that shows her attitude, right there."

She had been active all her life, touch football with the farm kids growing up in Great Valley, softball and basketball and tennis and squash. Attitudes have a way of getting shattered when the ether wears off.

"Three days after the accident," she recalled before last night's banquet, "a girl from South Philadelphia called and asked if she could come to see me. She had lost a leg nine years before. She came up there and unscrewed her artificial foot and walked for me and told me I'd be able to dance again.

"I didn't care about dancing. All I wanted to do was run and play squash and tennis. But I realized I'd never play the same again. I'd been number one in the Middle States tennis rankings and I'd won the nationals in squash three times. If the accident had to come, it came at the right time."

There were visitors and calls and letters, including one from a teen-age boy who played squash at the Cynwyd Club and who promised to dedicate every winning squash match to her.

And when the ether wears off and the flood of visitors recedes and it is time to hobble home again, even the toughest attitude can shatter if it isn't bolstered by faith.

Betty Meade's father was a minister. "You believe when you're growing up," she said quietly. "And you go off to college and maybe you begin to doubt it. Then you find something to believe in again.

"The thing that was such tremendous strength to me was that so many people were praying for me. That's the main reason I wasn't depressed, why I didn't go into a tailspin.

"People who had never prayed before prayed for me. A man who always said he was an agnostic wrote me that he got down on his knees. When I read that I thought that maybe this accident was for the best.

"I had played so much and accomplished so much. I was older. Maybe it was easier for me to adjust. When you play sports you learn to win and to lose. You become accustomed to losing without taking it home with you and making everyone miserable. When it's over, it's over.

"Athletes seem to have a much healthier attitude. There's a difference between a good loser and learning how to lose. I was never a good loser, but losing teaches you something."

She is back playing squash. She has played eight rounds of golf including a round of 102. Her husband bet her $100 she wouldn't break 100 before the year ended, but he knows he does not have to invent challenges.

"She's working with weights to strengthen her upper leg," he said, beaming at her. "And she'll start on sprints soon, six or seven steps at a time. Before, her shot-making and determination made the difference. She can still beat 50 percent of the squash players in her present condition. Nothing she does will surprise me. I'm just proud to be part of her."

She stood there last night, her serenity flooding the big room like some kind of torch. The poker players in the raucous crowd recognized that she was willing to play the cruel hand she was dealt. There was faith and humility and courage for even the fuzziest eyes to see. Betty Meade, you're beautiful.

THE AVANT-GARDES OF "MUSIC"

By Leonard Koppett

From The New York Times

The marching band, brassy and brisk whether or not it is led by an amazing baton-twirler of either sex, is an essential feature of major college football. Its pregame entrance and half-time maneuvers represent a distinctive, indigenous American pop art form.

In the Ivy League in recent years, however, these traditional routines have been abandoned for a much more sophisticated entertainment—essentially satiric, in style a parody of the precision-proud quasi-military bands, in substance a social comment on politics, sex and other campus concerns. These bands are the avant-garde (or at the very least the off-Broadway) of intermission intellectuality.

At most football colleges, the half-time shows have passed beyond simple human spellouts and crisp marching to college and martial airs, to fancy formations and show tunes. But the basic approach remains the same: a spectacular display, in the spirit of the Radio City Music Hall Rockettes, aimed at dazzling the eye and arousing patriotic (toward nation, region or college) feelings.

But such productions require considerable rehearsal time, large numbers of players and a predilection for conformity. The Ivies have gone their own way for practical as well as intellectual reasons.

Columbia, for instance, "marches" about 35 men (and a couple of Barnard girls). Whether they could keep in step or not, the Columbia men don't particularly want to, and don't think their audience would be thrilled if they did. Therefore, they have sought distinctions by displaying unusual instruments such as:

1. "The only E-flat double-reed contrabass marching Sarrusophone in Civilization."

2. An authentic Australian Aborigine Didgereedoo (whose spelling is in dispute). This is a hollow-log, two-note super-kazoo.

3. "The world famous Lenthopipe," a horizontal construction of aluminum tubing, a funnel and a rubber shower hose.

4. The world's largest triangle (about eight feet per side), intended to downgrade Harvard's famous big bass drum-on-wheels.

The sarrusophone, in fact, is a legitimate instrument. It can be described as the offspring of an inebriated contrabassoon and a baritone saxophone of easy virtue. However, few people—and no Columbians—have been able to play it. Last year, the Rutgers band rented it, came to Baker Field with it and announced, "We not only have one, but we have someone who can play it." The Columbia band answered (home bands get last licks): "We still have the only one in *civilization.*"

That's a fair sample of the level of insult the Ivy-type shows generate. Their stock in trade is a parodying of formations, backed up by a script full of double meanings.

One of the Harvard shows dealt with Chicago and Mayor Daley and the Democratic Convention of 1968. The themes were "Beat the Press" and "Mace the Nation"; the band played "Chicago" while lining up to spell "Dick"—which promptly shifted into "Oink." Subtlety is not a prime goal of these student script writers.

Peace has been a popular subject with all the Ivy bands, with Harvard hitting it perhaps most frequently. Yale, at this year's Brown game, dealt with troop withdrawals from Vietnam: from its band of about 100, two people "withdrew"—and promptly returned. The Harvard band, at its Dartmouth game, made a stick figure with a pentagon-shaped head, which flew into fragments during a commentary about "not losing our heads."

And when "creeping Communism" seemed to be a pre-election issue in 1968, the Yale band devised a creeping formation while playing "Marche Slav."

An idea of the technique used can be gained from a portion of the script used by Princeton at its Columbia game this year. The subject was the meat-packing industry, and the commentary must be taken by ear, rather than read, to get the true effect:

Meat-packers, Princeton noted, "have been putting chicken in hot dogs to make them cheap. And speaking of meat-packing, the band observes that Wall Street secretaries have been shaking the very foundations of the financial district by shunning the traditional brassiere. By provoking a rising interest rate, this practice has understandably contributed to a bear market. Noting that the businessman has always favored fewer restraints, we form a 'laissez-faire' economy and salute him and his newly liberated secretary."

To which the band played "Born Free."

What Princeton men consider a coup of sorts occurred in 1967, when the game with Harvard was televised nationally by the American Broadcasting Company.

Understandably nervous about possible content, ABC didn't intend to televise the half-time show. After consultation, it agreed to put the formations on camera, but not the patter or music. So Princeton began the show by spelling out "ABC," telling the spectators present: "In a blatant attempt to get television exposure from ABC, the band forms a plug on the field." But immediately afterward, with the cameras presumably committed, the "A" turned into an "N" and the band played "Who's Sorry Now?"

These scripts are devised, and the routines worked out, by student groups. There is, inescapably, a veto power over material exercised by school authorities, and the most persistent battle is against over-explicit sexual terms and other impolite expressions. (The Columbia band regularly forms the symbols for male and female and merges them, which is acceptably abstract; but one of its birth-control scripts had to be confiscated at Dartmouth a couple of years ago when the athletic director happened to glance at a copy.)

But the basic motivation, it seems clear, is in the tradition of college humor—a desire to show off cleverness and wit rather than a desire to shock for the sake of shock. What is relatively new, since the mid-1950's, is the broadened sphere of subject matter, and the emphasis on written script.

None of the bands has yet attempted a parody of *Oh! Calcutta!*, but when it does one can expect that an early-season game will be chosen for reasons of climate.

THAT OLD GLOVE HAD SOME LIFE

By Ray Fitzgerald

From the Boston Globe

The old glove is dead.

The Richie Ashburn model for left-handers, veteran of 10,000 baseballs, has expired at the age of 23.

Present when death came were its owner, who writes this column, and his two sons, who were mainly responsible for the glove's demise.

Services tomorrow will be private and burial will be early next week at the Scituate dump.

Ah, there was a glove. The kids in the neighborhood made fun of it, with its four stubby fingers, funny-looking thumb and inadequate webbing.

"How can ya catch anything with that hunk of leather?" they'd say, waving their super-trap, $40, hand-tooled Reggie Smith models in the air.

What do the kids know? They weren't around that spring day in 1947, when the man in the South Bend, Indiana, department store handed the glove over, for $18, cash.

Brand new the mitt was then, with the leather oiled and shiny, the button that held the wrist strap pure gold.

"Richie Ashburn" was written strong and clear across the heel of the glove, and though a fleeting thought at the time was that Richie Ashburn wasn't much of a fielder, the thought was immediately dismissed.

The glove had major league potential, but its owner didn't. It went through college, grabbing a line drive here and a pop fly there, but the glove couldn't hit the ball for the guy who owned it.

There were some big moments—an over-the-head catch in a summer league in Glens Falls, New York, a diving backhander in another summer league in Brattleboro.

But little by little, the glove began spending more time on the front closet shelf, under a shoe box and a ladies' umbrella.

Once it came out of retirement, when the owner, who by this time was writing about baseball for a living, took it on a road trip. He thought it would be fun to work out with the team.

But the players laughed at the glove. They giggled and threw the ball hard, to see what would happen. The owner caught the ball casually, as though the glove made catching baseballs easy, but that wasn't so.

His right palm ached for a week, and he put the glove back on the shelf.

In recent years, the Richie Ashburn model has been in disrepute. The leather is dryer than a starlet's bathing suit, and a rip inside the thumb has become larger, spewing large quantities of stuffing.

The glove has had to stoop to the indignity of family outings, class reunions, pick-up softball games and backyard games of catch.

A year ago, the leather thongs that held the webbing together snapped. Having worked overtime for 22 years, and having been ignored all that time, they were entitled.

Since then the webbing has been secured with shoestring, tied in a square knot. It's been a makeshift arrangement, and yesterday the end came.

One of the few surviving members of the Society for the Preservation of Richie Ashburn models has urged a transplant.

"Bring it over to Fitzie in the Red Sox clubhouse," he said, "he'll sew it up for you."

But that would only prolong the agony. The webbing would be okay, but the thumb would go. This way, a nice clean death, is better.

A man gets attached to certain things in his life—a dog, a favorite putter, an old wallet.

That's the way it was with the Richie Ashburn glove. It was a link with the past, when a man felt that with a little break here and there, he could be anything he wanted to be.

Now he has to face the fact. That dream about standing on the mound at Yankee Stadium with the bases full and striking everybody out is just not going to come true.

The glove is gone and its owner feels a lot older than he did yesterday.

For the Record

CHAMPIONS OF 1969

ARCHERY

World Champions

Men—Hardy Ward, Mount Pleasant, Tex.
Women—Dorothy Lidstone, Vancouver, British Columbia.

United States Champions

Men—Ray Rogers, Muskogee, Okla.
Women—Mrs. Doreen Wilber, Jefferson, Iowa.

U.S. Professional Champions

Men—Vic Berger, Springfield, Ohio.
Women—Ann Butz, Suffern, N.Y.

National Field Archery Champions

Pro Free-Style—Wendell Davis, Johnson, Tenn.
Amateur Free-Style—Jamie Silkirk, Canton, Ill.
Women's Pro Free-Style—Peg Southern, Cockeysville, Md.
Women's Amateur Free-Style—Diane Vetrecin, Chula Vista, Calif.

AUTOMOBILE RACING

World Road Racing—Jackie Stewart, Scotland.
World Manufacturers—Porsche.
Canadian-American Cup—Bruce McLaren, N.Z.
U.S.A.C.—Mario Andretti, Nazareth, Pa.
Indianapolis 500—Mario Andretti.
NASCAR—David Pearson, Spartansburg, S.C.
Le Mans—Jackie Oliver, England, and Jackie Ickx, Belgium (Ford GT).
Grand Prix of U.S.—Jochen Rindt, Austria.

BADMINTON

United States Champions

Men—Rudy Hartono, Indonesia.
Women—Miss Minarni, Indonesia.
Men's Doubles—Ng Boon Bee and Gunalan, Malaysia.
Women's Doubles—Miss Minarni and Ratno Koestijah, Indonesia.
Mixed Doubles—Erland Kops and Miss P. M. Hansen, Denmark.

BASEBALL

World Series—New York Mets.
National League—New York (East), Atlanta (West), New York (play-offs).
American League—Baltimore (East), Minnesota (West), Baltimore (play-offs).
All-Star Game—National League.
Leading Batter (N.)—Pete Rose, Cincinnati.
Leading Batter (A.)—Rod Carew, Minnesota.
Pacific Coast League—Tacoma (North), Eugene (South), Tacoma (play-offs).
American Association—Omaha.
Eastern League—York, Pa.
National Collegiate—Arizona State.
Eastern Intercollegiate—Dartmouth.

BASKETBALL

National Association—Boston Celtics.
American Association—Oakland Oaks.
National Collegiate—U.C.L.A.
N.C.A.A. College Division—Kentucky Wesleyan.

National Invitation—Temple.
Ivy League—Princeton.
Yankee Conference—Massachusetts.
West Coast A.C.—Santa Clara.
Southern Conference—Davidson.
Southeastern Conference—Kentucky.
Big Ten—Purdue.
Ohio Valley—Murray State-Morehead State.
Western Athletic—Brigham Young-Wyoming.
Big Eight—Colorado.
Missouri Valley—Drake-Louisville.
Mid-American Conference—Miami (Ohio).
Southwest Conference—Texas A. and M.
Atlantic Coast—North Carolina.
N.A.I.A.—Eastern New Mexico.

BILLIARDS

U.S. Amateur (3-cushion)—Gerry Glenn, N.Y.A.C.
U.S. Open (3-Cushion)—Larry Johnson, Cambridge, Mass.

BOBSLEDDING

World Champions

Two-Man—Italy.
Four-Man—West Germany.

North American Champions

Two-Man—U.S. Navy.
Four-Man—Canceled.

National A.A.U. Champions

Two-Man—U.S. Navy.
Four-Man—Cleveland Bobsled Club.

BOWLING

American Bowling Congress Champions

All-Events (Classic)—Larry Lichstein, Hartford.
All-Events (Regular)—Ed Jackson, Cincinnati.
Singles (Classic)—Nelson Burton, Jr., St. Louis.
Singles (Regular)—Greg Campbell, St. Louis.
Doubles (Classic)—Jim Stefanich, Joliet, Ill., and Don McCune, Munster, Ind.
Doubles (Regular)—Bob Maschmeyer and Charles Guedel, Indianapolis.
Team (Classic)—Dick Weber-Wrist Masters, Santa Ana, Calif.
Team (Regular)—P.A.C. Advertising, Lansing, Mich.

Other Champions

All-Star Men—Billy Hardwick, Louisville.
All-Star Women—Dorothy Fothergill, North Attleboro, Mass.
A.B.C. Masters—Jim Chestney, Denver.
P.B.A.—Mike McGrath, El Cerrito, Calif.
Tournament Earnings—Billy Hardwick.

BOXING

World Professional Champions

Flyweight—Bernabe Villacampo, Philippines, and Efren Torres, Mexico.
Bantamweight—Ruben Olivares, Mexico.
Featherweight—Shozo Saijyo, Japan, and Johnny Famechon, Australia.
Junior Lightweight—Hiroshi Kobayashi, Japan, and Rene Barrientos, Philippines.
Lightweight—Mando Ramos, Long Beach, Calif.
Junior Welterweight—Nicoline Loche, Argentina.
Welterweight—Jose Napoles, Mexico.
Junior Middleweight—Freddie Little, Las Vegas.
Middleweight—Nino Benvenuti, Italy.
Light-Heavyweight—Bob Foster, Washington.
Heavyweight (WBA)—Jimmy Ellis, Louisville.
Heavyweight (5 states)—Joe Frazier, Phila.

National A.A.U. Champions

106-Pound—Dennis Mince, Kanner, La.
112-Pound—Caleo Long, Army.
119-Pound—Terry Pullen, Metairie, La.

125-Pound—Joe Bennett, Joilet, Calif.
132-Pound—Juan Ruis, Air Force.
139-Pound—Rudy Bolos, Braddock, Pa.
147-Pound—Armando Muniz, Army.
156-Pound—Larry Carisle, Marine Corps.
165-Pound—Larry Ward, Milwaukee.
178-Pound—Dave Matthews, Akron, Ohio.
Heavyweight—Ernie Shaver, Warren, Ohio.

CROSS-COUNTRY

National A.A.U.—Jack Bachelor, Florida.
National A.A.U. Team—Pacific Coast Club.
National A.A.U. Women—Doris Brown, Seattle.
N.C.A.A.—Gerry Lindgren, Washington State.
N.C.A.A. Team—Texas (El Paso).
I.C.4-A.—Art Dulong, Holy Cross.
I.C.4-A. Team—Villanova.
Heptagonal—Keith Colburn, Harvard.
Heptagonal Team—Harvard.

CYCLING

World Champions

PROFESSIONAL

Sprint—Patrick Sercu, Belgium.
Pursuit—Ferdinand Bracke, Belgium.
Motor Paced—Jaap Ouderk, Netherlands.
Road—Harm Ottenbros, Netherlands.
Tour de France—Eddy Merckx, Belgium.

AMATEUR

Sprint—Daniel Morelon, France.
Pursuit—Xavier Kurmann, Switzerland.
Motor Paced—Al Boom, Netherlands.
Road—Leif Mortenson, Denmark.
Women's Road—Mrs. Audrey McElmury, La Jolla, Calif.

United States Champions

Sprint—Tim Mountford, Sherman Oaks, Calif.
10-mile—Jackie Simes 3d, U.S. Army.
Road—Alan De Fever, San Diego, Calif.
4,000 Meter—John van de Velde, Glen Ellyn, Ill.
Women's Track—Mrs. Audrey McElmury.
Women's Road—Donna Tobias, Aurora, N.Y.
Junior (Track)—Gary Campbell, Paramount, Calif.
Junior (Road)—Don Westell, Huntington, L.I.

FENCING

World Champions

Foil—Friederich Wessel, West Germany.
Epée—Bohdan Andrzejewski, Poland.
Saber—Alex Orban, New York.
Women's Foil—Elena Novikova, Soviet Union.
Foil Team—Soviet Union.
Epée—Soviet Union.
Saber Team—Soviet Union.
Women's Foil Team—Rumania.

United States Champions

Foil—Carl Borack, Hollywood, Calif.
Epée—Stephen Netburn, New York.
Saber—Alex Orban, New York.
Women's Foil—Ruth White, Baltimore.
Foil Team—Salle Csiszar, Philadelphia.
Epée Team—Mori Fencing Academy, L.A.
Saber Team—New York Athletic Club.
Women's Foil Team—Salle Santelli, N.Y.

National Collegiate Champions

Foil—Anthony Kestler, Columbia.
Epée—James Wetzler, Pennsylvania.
Saber—Norman Braslow, Pennsylvania.
Team—Pennsylvania.

Intercollegiate Association Champions

Foil—Walter Krause, N.Y.U.
Epée—James Davidson, Navy.
Saber—Rafael Keifitz, C.C.N.Y.
Foil Team—Princeton.

Epée Team—Navy.
Saber Team—C.C.N.Y.
Three-Weapon Team—Princeton.

FOOTBALL

Intercollegiate Champions

National—Texas.
Eastern (Lambert Trophy)—Penn State.
Eastern (Lambert Cup)—Delaware-Wesleyan.
Eastern (Lambert Bowl)—Kings Point.
Ivy League—Princeton, Dartmouth, Yale.
Big Ten—Michigan and Ohio State.
Yankee Conference—Massachusetts.
Middle Atlantic (University)—Delaware.
Middle Atlantic (College, North)—Wilkes.
Middle Atlantic (College, South)—Johns Hopkins, Lebanon Valley and Ursinus.
Southeastern Conference—Tennessee.
Atlantic Coast Conference—South Carolina.
Southern Conference—Davidson and Richmond.
Mid-American Conference—Toledo.
Big Eight—Missouri and Nebraska.
Missouri Valley Conference—Memphis State.

National League

Eastern Conference—Cleveland Browns.
Western Conference—Minnesota Vikings.
League—Minnesota Vikings.

American League

Eastern Division—New York Jets.
Western Division—Oakland Raiders.
League—Kansas City Chiefs.

Super Bowl

Kansas City Chiefs

Canada Professional

Grey Cup—Ottawa Rough Riders.

GAELIC FOOTBALL

World—Kerry.
Irish—Kerry.
World Hurling—New York.
Irish Hurling—Kilkenny.

GOLF

Men

National Open—Orville Moody.
National Amateur—Steve Melynk.
P. G. A.—Ray Floyd.
British Open—Tony Jacklin.
British Amateur—Michael Bonallack.
Masters—George Archer.
Canadian Open—Tommy Aaron.
Canadian Amateur—Wayne McDonald.
N.C.A.A.—Bob Clark, Calif. State (L.A.)
N.C.A.A. Team—Houston.
World Cup—United States.
World Cup Individual—Lee Trevino.
Ryder Cup—United States and Britain (tie).
World Series of Golf—Orville Moody.
U.S.G.A. Senior—Curtis Person.
U.S. Senior—William Scott, Jr.
Walker Cup—United States.
U.S.G.A. Public Links—John Jackson, Jr.
World Senior Amateur—David Goldman.
World Senior Pro—Tommy Bolt.
U.S. Senior Pro—Tommy Bolt.

Women

National Amateur—Catherine Lacoste.
National Open—Donna Caponi.
British Amateur—Catherine Lacoste.
Canadian Amateur—Mrs. Marlene S. Streit.
Eastern Amateur—Mrs. Mark Porter.
U.S.G.A. Junior—Hollis Stacy.
U.S.G.A. Seniors—Mrs. Philip Cudone.
U.S. Senior—Mrs. Allison Choate.
Intercollegiate—Jane Bastanchury.
Western Amateur—Jane Bastanchury.
Southern Amateur—Mrs. John Rathmell.
Ladies P.G.A.—Betsy Rawls.

GYMNASTICS

National A.A.U. Champions

All-Round—Mauno Nissinen, Seattle.
Long Horse—Paul Tickenoff. Northwestern La.
Free Exercise—Toby Towson, Mich. State.
Parallel Bars—Yoshi Hoyasaki, Seattle.
Side Horse—Dave Thor, Reseda, Calif.
Horizontal Bar—John Elias, Northwestern La.
Rings—Robert Emery, Penn State.
Team—Husky Gym Club, Seattle.

Women

All-Round—Joyce Tanac, Seattle.
Side Horse—Joyce Tanac.
Free Exercise—Joyce Tanac.
Balance Team—Joyce Tanac.
Uneven Parallel Bars—Joyce Tanac.
Team—Downtown Y.W.C.A., Seattle.

National Collegiate Champions

All-Round—Mauno Nissinen, Washington.
Free Exercise—Toby Towson, Mich. State.
Side Horse—Keith McCanless, Iowa.
Long Horse—Dan Bowles, California, and Jack McCarthy, Illinois.
Rings—Paul Vexler, Penn State, and Ward Maythaler, Iowa.
Parallel Bars—Ron Rapper, Michigan.
Horizontal Bar—Bob Manna, New Mexico.
Team—Iowa.

HANDBALL

U.S. Handball Association 4-Wall Champions

Singles—Paul Haber, Milwaukee.
Doubles—Lou Kramberg-Lou Russo, N.Y.
Masters Doubles—Ken Schneider-Gus Lewis, Chicago.

National A.A.U. 1-Wall Champions

Singles—Steve Sandler, New York.
Doubles—Steve Sandler-Marty Decatur, N.Y.
Masters Doubles—Al Goldstein-Nat Schifter, Brooklyn.

HARNESS RACING

Horse of Year—Nevele Pride.
2-Year-Old Trotter—Victory Star.
2-Year-Old Pacer—Truluck.
3-Year-Old Trotter—Lindy's Pride.
3-Year-Old Pacer—Laverne Hanover.
Aged Trotter—Fresh Yankee.
Aged Pacer—Overcall.
Leading Money-Winner—Overcall.
Leading Driver (Heats)—Herve Filion.
Leading Driver (Earnings)—Del Insko.
Hambletonian—Lindy's Pride.
Yonkers Futurity—Lindy's Pride.
Kentucky Futurity—Lindy's Pride.
Dexter Cup—Lindy's Pride.
Colonial—Lindy's Pride.
Messenger Stakes—Bye Bye Sam.
Cane Pace—Kat Byrd.
Little Brown Jug—Laverne Hanover.
Adios—Laverne Hanover.

HOCKEY

Stanley Cup—Montreal Canadiens.
National League—Montreal (East), St. Louis (West).
American League—Hershey.
Eastern League—Clinton.
International League—Dayton.
Central League—Dallas.
Allan Cup—Galt Hornets.
National Collegiate—Denver.
Memorial Cup—Montreal Canadiens.
Ivy League—Cornell.

ICE SKATING

FIGURE

World Champions

Men—Tim Wood, Bloomfield Hills, Mich.
Women—Gabriele Seyfert, East Germany.
Pairs—Aleksei Ulanov-Irina Rodina, U.S.S.R.
Dance—Diane Towler-Bernhard Ford, Britain.

United States Champions

Men—Tim Wood.
Women—Janet Lynn, Rockford, Ill.
Pairs—Cynthia and Ronald Kauffman.
Silver Dance—Candace Johnson and Bruce Bowland, West Orange, N.J.
Gold Dance—Judy Schwomeyer, Indianapolis, and James Sladky, Rochester.

SPEED

World Champions

Men—Dag Fornaess, Norway.
Women—Lasma Kauniste, Soviet Union.

United States Champions

Men's Outdoor—Pete Cefalu, West Allis, Wis.
Men's Indoor—Bill Lanigan, Bronx.
Women's Outdoor—Sally Blatchford, Northbrook, Ill.
Women's Indoor—Mary Blair, West Allis, Wis.

United States Open Champions

Men's Indoor—Bill Lanigan.
Women's Indoor—Cathy Crowe, St. Louis.
Men's Outdoor—Rich Wurster, Ballston Spa, N.Y.
Women's Outdoor—Sue Bradle, Peekskill, N.Y.

LACROSSE

Club—Long Island A. C.
Intercollegiate—Army and Johns Hopkins.
North-South—South.

MOTORBOATING

Unlimited Hydroplanes

Dixie Cup, Guntersville, Ala.—Miss Budweiser.
Kentucky Cup, Owensboro, Ky.—Miss Budweiser.
World Championship, Detroit—Miss U.S.
Indiana Cup, Madison, Ind.—Myr's Special.
Atomic Cup, Tri-Cities, Wash.—Myr's Special.
Seafair, Seattle—Miss Budweiser.
Gold Cup, San Diego—Miss Budweiser.
High-Point Champion—Miss Budweiser.
High-Point Driver—Bill Sterett.

World Offshore Races

Bahamas 500—Don Aronow, Coral Gables, Fla.
Wills Int'nal—Vincenzo Balestrieri, Italy.
Naples—Francesco Cosentino, Italy.
Roseto Split—Vincenzo Balestrieri.
Sam Griffith—Bill Wishnick, New York.
Viareggio—Don Aronow.
N.Y. Grand Prix—Peter Rittmaster, Miami.
Lez Embiez—Don Aronow.
Oregrund—Leonard Ebbeke, Sweden.
Long Beach—Don Aronow.
Cowes-Torquay—Don Aronow.
Deauville—Tommy Sopwith, England.
Miami-Nassau—Don Aronow.
Miami-Key West—Bill Wishnick.
World Champion—Don Aronow.

RACQUETS

Tuxedo Gold—G. H. (Pete) Bostwick, Jr., Locust Valley, L.I.

ROWING

United States Champions

Open Quarter-Mile—Jim Dietz, New York A.C.
Pairs With Coxswain—Tony Johnson, Larry Hough and Jim Stone, Potomac, B.C.
Pairs Without Coxswain—Johnson and Hough.
Fours With Coxswain—Union Boat Club, Boston.
Fours Without Coxswain—Vesper B.C., Philadelphia.
Eights—Union B.C.-Ecorse B.C., Michigan.
Single Sculls—Bill Maher, Detroit.

Double Sculls—John Van Blom and Tom McKibbon, Long Beach (Calif.) R.A.
Quadruple Sculls—Vesper B.C.
Team—Potomac Boat Club, Washington.

Intercollegiate Champions

Intercollegiate R.A.—Pennsylvania.
Dad Vail Trophy—Georgetown.
Eastern Sprint—Harvard.
Harvard-Yale—Harvard.
Oxford-Cambridge—Cambridge.
Western Sprint—Washington.

SHOOTING

United States Rifle Champions

Small-Bore Prone—Thomas Whitaker, U.S.A.F.
Women's Small-Bore—Margaret Murdock.
Small-Bore 3-Position—Maj. Lones Wigger.
Women's 3-Position—Margaret Murdock.
Service—Sgt. Willie D. Jordan, U.S. Army.
High Power—Theodore Fasy, Long Beach, Calif.
Women's High Power—Marina A. Geipel, Bedminster, N.J.

United States Pistol Champions

National—P.O. 1 Donald Hamilton, U.S. Navy.
Police—Tommy Gaines, U.S. Border Patrol.

Trapshooting Champions

Grand American—Bernard Bonn, Jr.
Women's Grand American—JoAnn Nelson.
North American Clay Target—Dean Stoy.
Women's N. Amn. Clay Target—Ruby Jenner.
Champion of Champions—John Imbt.
Women's Champion of Champions—Loral Delaney.

United States Skeet Champions

All-Round—Bob Shuley, Roselle, Ill.
Women's All-Round—Margaret Burdett, Angus, Ont.
12-Gauge—Walt Badorek, Klamath Falls, Ore.
28-Gauge—Kenny Barnes, Bakersfield, Calif.
.410-Gauge—Don Johnson, Mount Royal, Que.

SKIING

World Cup

Men—Karl Schranz, Austria.
Women—Gertrud Gabl, Austria.

United States Champions

ALPINE

Slalom—Bobby Cochran, Richmond, Vt.
Women's Slalom—Barbara Cochran, Richmond, Vt.
Giant Slalom—Hank Kashiwa, Old Forge, N.Y.
Women's Giant Slalom—Barbara Cochran.
Downhill—Vladimir Sabich, Kyburz, Calif.
Women's Downhill—Ann Black, Seattle.
Combined—Malcolm Milne, Australia.

JUMPING

Men—Adrian Watt, Minneapolis.
Veterans—Don Hurst, Ispheming, Mich.
Junior—Greg Swor, Duluth, Minn.

National Collegiate Champions

Slalom—Paul Rachetto, Denver.
Downhill—Mike Lafferty, Colorado.
Alpine Combined—Paul Rachetto.
Cross-Country—Clark Matis, Colorado.
Jumping—Odd Hammerness, Denver.
Nordic Combined—Georg Krog, Denver.
Skimiester—Ed Damon, Dartmouth.
Team—Denver.

SOCCER

United States Champions

Open—New York Greek-Americans.
Amateur—British Lions, Washington.
Junior—St. Philip Neri, St. Louis.
North American League—Kansas City Spurs.
National Collegiate—St. Louis.

Other Champions

English Division One—Leeds United.
English F.A. Cup—Manchester City.
Scottish Division One—Glasgow Celtic.
Scottish F.A. Cup—Glasgow Celtic.
European Champions Cup—A. C. Milan.
World Club—A. C. Milan.

SOFTBALL

Amateur Association

FAST PITCH

Men—Raybestos, Stratford, Conn.
Women—Lionettes, Orange, Calif.

SLOW PITCH

Men—Copper Hearth, Milwaukee.
Women—Converse Dots, Miami.
Industrial—Avco-Lycoming, Stratford, Conn.

SQUASH RACQUETS

United States Champions

Amateur—Anil Nayer, India.
Amateur Doubles—Samuel P. Howe 3d, Philadelphia, and Ralph E. Howe, New York.
Open North American—Sharif Khan, Detroit.
Women's Doubles—Joyce Davenport and Carol Thesieres, Philadelphia.
Professional—Mohibullah Khan, Boston.
Veterans—Henri R. Salaun, Boston.
Senior (Over 50)—Edward J. Hahn, New York.
Intercollegiate—Anil Nayer, Harvard.

SWIMMING

Men's National Long-Course Champions

100-Meter Free-Style—Don Havens.
200-Meter Free-Style—Hans Fassnacht.
400-Meter Free-Style—Hans Fassnacht.
1,500-Meter Free-Style—Mike Burton.
100-Meter Backstroke—Mitch Ivey.
200-Meter Backstroke—Gary Hall.
100-Meter Breast-Stroke—Jose Fiolo.
200-Meter Breast-Stroke—Mike Dirksen.
100-Meter Butterfly—Doug Russell.
200-Meter Butterfly—Mike Burton.
200-Meter Individual Medley—Gary Hall.
400-Meter Individual Medley—Gary Hall.
400-Meter Medley Relay—Phillips 66.
400-Meter Free-Style Relay—Los Angeles A.C.
800-Meter Free-Style Relay—Phillips 66.
One-Meter Dive—Jim Henry.
Three-Meter Dive—Win Young.
Platform Dive—Dick Rydze.
Team—Phillips 66, Long Beach, Calif.

Men's National Short-Course Champions

100-Yard Free-Style—Don Havens.
200-Yard Free-Style—Frank Heckl.
500-Yard Free-Style—Hans Fassnacht.
1,650-Yard Free-Style—Mike Burton.
100-Yard Backstroke—Fred Haywood.
200-Yard Backstroke—Gary Hall.
100-Yard Breast-Stroke—Brian Job.
200-Yard Breast-Stroke—Brian Job.
100-Yard Butterfly—Ross Wales.
200-Yard Butterfly—Mike Burton.
200-Yard Individual Medley—Dave Johnson.
400-Yard Individual Medley—Gary Hall.
400-Yard Medley Relay—Yale.
400-Yard Free-Style Relay—U.S.C.
800-Yard Free-Style Relay—U.S.C.
One-Meter Dive—Jim Henry.
Three-Meter Dive—Win Young.
Platform Dive—Dick Rydze.
Team—University of Southern California.

Women's National Long-Course Champions

100-Meter Free-Style—Sue Pedersen.
200-Meter Free-Style—Sue Pedersen.
400-Meter Free-Style—Debbie Meyer.
1,500-Meter Free-Style—Debbie Meyer.
100-Meter Backstroke—Susie Atwood.
200-Meter Backstroke—Susie Atwood.
100-Meter Breast-Stroke—Kim Brecht.
200-Meter Breast-Stroke—Kim Brecht.
100-Meter Butterfly—Virginia Durkin.
200-Meter Butterfly—Lynn Colella.
200-Meter Individual Medley—Lynn Vidali.
400-Meter Individual Medley—Debbie Meyer.
400-Meter Medley Relay—Lakewood A.C.
400-Meter Free-Style Relay—Santa Clara S.C.
800-Meter Free-Style Relay—Arden Hills S.C.
One-Meter Dive—Cynthia Potter.
Three-Meter Dive—Lieut. Micki King.
Platform Dive—Lieut. Micki King.
Team—Arden Hills S.C., Sacramento.

Women's National Short-Course Champions

100-Yard Free-Style—Wendy Fordyce.
200-Yard Free-Style—Linda Gustavson.
500-Yard Free-Style—Vicki King.
1,650-Yard Free-Style—Debbie Meyer.
100-Yard Backstroke—Susie Atwood.
200-Yard Backstroke—Susie Atwood.
100-Yard Breast-Stroke—Sharon Wichman.
200-Yard Breast-Stroke—Kim Brecht.
100-Yard Butterfly—Ellie Daniel.
200-Yard Butterfly—Ellie Daniel.
200-Yard Individual Medley—Lynn Vidali.
400-Yard Individual Medley—Lynn Vidali.
400-Yard Medley Relay—Santa Clara S.C.
400-Yard Free-Style Relay—Santa Clara S.C.
800-Yard Free-Style Relay—Arden Hills S.C.
One-Meter Dive—Cynthia Potter.
Three-Meter Dive—Cynthia Potter.
Platform Dive—Beverley Boys.
Team—Santa Clara S.C.

National Collegiate Champions

50-Yard Free-Style—Dan Frawley, U.S.C.
100-Yard Free-Style—Francis Heath, U.C.L.A.
200-Yard Free-Style—Mark Spitz, Indiana.
500-Yard Free-Style—Mark Spitz.
1,650-Yard Free-Style—Hans Fassnacht, Long Beach.
100-Yard Backstroke—Fred Haywood, Stanford.
200-Yard Backstroke—Charles Hickcox, Ind.
100-Yard Breast-Stroke—Don McKenzie, Ind.
200-Yard Breast-Stroke—Mike Dirksen, Ore.
100-Yard Butterfly—Mark Spitz.
200-Yard Butterfly—John Ferris, Stanford.
200-Yard Ind. Medley—Charles Hickcox.
400-Yard Ind. Medley—Hans Fassnacht.
400-Yard Medley Relay—Indiana.
400-Yard Free-Style Relay—U.S.C.
800-Yard Free-Style Relay—U.S.C.
One-Meter Dive—Jim Henry, Indiana.
Three-Meter Dive—Jim Henry.
Team—Indiana University.

TABLE TENNIS

United States Open Champions

Men—Dal Joon Lee, Cleveland.
Women—Patty Martinez, San Diego.
Doubles—Lee and Glen Cowan, Los Angeles.
Women's Doubles—Patty Martinez and Wendy Hicks, Santa Barbara, Calif.
Mixed Doubles—Patty Martinez-Dal Joon Lee.
Junior Men—Glen Cowan.
Senior Men—Wm. Cross, New Brunswick, N.J.

TENNIS

International Team Champions

Davis Cup—United States.

Wightman Cup (Women)—United States.

Federation Cup (Women)—United States.

Wimbledon Champions

Men—Rod Laver, Australia.

Women—Mrs. Ann Haydon Jones, Britain.

Men's Doubles—John Newcomb and Tony Roche.

Women's Doubles—Margaret Court and Judy Tegart.

Mixed Doubles—Fred Stolle and Ann Jones.

United States Grass-Court Champions

Men—Stan Smith, Pasadena, Calif.

Women—Mrs. Margaret Court, Australia.

Men's Doubles—Dick Crealy and Allan Stone.

Women's Doubles—Mrs. Margaret Court and Virginia Wade.

United States Clay-Court Champions

Men—Zeljko Franulovic, Yugoslavia.

Women—Mrs. Gail Chanfreau, France.

Men's Doubles—Bill Bowery and Clark Graebner.

Women's Doubles—Mrs. Gail Chanfreau and Lesley Bowery.

United States Indoor Champions

Men—Stan Smith.

Women—Mary Ann Eisel, St. Louis.

Men's Doubles—Stan Smith and Robert Lutz.

Women's Doubles—Mary Ann Eisel and Valerie Ziegenfuss.

U.S. Open Champions

Men—Rod Laver.

Women—Mrs. Margaret Smith Court.

Men's Doubles—Fred Stolle and Ken Rosewall.

Women's Doubles—Françoise Durr and Darlene Hard.

Other Foreign Open Champions

Australian Men—Rod Laver.

Australian Women—Mrs. Margaret Smith Court.

Italian Men—John Newcombe, Australia.

Italian Women—Julie Heldman, New York.

French Men—Rod Laver.

French Women—Mrs. Margaret Smith Court.

THOROUGHBRED RACING

Thoroughbred Racing Assns. Champions

Horse of the Year—Arts and Letters.

Older Horse—Nodouble.

3-Year-old Colt—Arts and Letters.

3-Year-Old Filly—Gallant Bloom.

2-Year-Old Colt—Silent Screen.

2-Year-Old Filly—Fast Attack and Tudor Queen.

Steeplechase—L'Escargot.

Older Filly or Mare—Gamely.

Turf Course—Hawaii.

TRACK AND FIELD

Men's National Senior Outdoor Champions

100-Yard Dash—Ivory Crockett.

220-Yard Dash—John Carlos.

440-Yard Run—Lee Evans.

880-Yard Run—Byron Dyce.

One-Mile Run—Marty Liquori.

Three-Mile Run—Tracy Smith.

Six-Mile Run—Jack Bachelor.

3,000-Meter Steeplechase—Mike Manley.

120-Yard High Hurdles—Willie Davenport and Leon Coleman.

440-Yard Hurdles—Ralph Mann.

High Jump—Otis Burrell.

Pole Vault—Bob Seagren.

Long Jump—Bob Beamon.

Triple Jump—John Craft.

Shot-Put—Neal Steinhauer.

Discus Throw—Jon Cole.

Hammer Throw—Tom Gage.

Javelin Throw—Mark Murro.

Team—Southern California Striders.

56-Pound Weight Throw—George Frenn.

15,000-Meter—Garry Bjorklund.
50 Miles—Jim McDonough.
Two-Mile Walk—Ron Laird.
10,000-Meter Walk—Ron Laird.
15,000-Meter Walk—Ron Laird.
20,000-Meter Walk—Ron Laird.
25,000-Meter Walk—Ron Laird.
35,000-Meter Walk—Ron Laird.
40,000-Meter Walk—Ron Laird.
50,000-Meter Walk—Byron Overton.

Men's National Senior Indoor Champions

60-Yard Dash—Charlie Greene.
60-Yard High Hurdles—Willie Davenport.
600-Yard Run—Martin McGrady.
1,000-Yard Run—Herb Germann.
One-Mile Run—Henryk Szordykowski, Poland.
Three-Mile Run—George Young.
One-Mile Relay—Sports International.
Two-Mile Relay—U. of Chicago Track Club.
Sprint Medley Relay—Grand Street Boys.
High Jump—John Rambo.
Pole Vault—Peter Chen.
Long Jump—Norm Tate.
Triple Jump—Norm Tate.
Shot-Put—George Woods.
35-Pound Weight Throw—Al Hall.
Team—Pacific Coast Club, Long Beach, Calif.

National Collegiate Outdoor Champions

100-Yard Dash—John Carlos, San Jose State.
220-Yard Dash—John Carlos.
440-Yard Run—Curtis Mills, Texas A&M.
880-Yard Run—Byron Dyce, New York U.
One-Mile Run—Marty Liquori, Villanova.
Three-Mile Run—Ole Oleson, U.S.C.
Six-Mile Run—Frank Shorter, Yale.
120-Yard Hurdles—Erv Hall, Villanova.
440-Yard Hurdles—Ralph Mann, Brigham Young.
3,000-Meter Steeplechase—Jim Barkley, Oregon State.
440-Yard Relay—San Jose State.
One-Mile Relay—U.C.L.A.
High Jump—Dick Fosbusy, Oregon State.
Pole Vault—Bob Seagren, U.S.C.
Long Jump—Jerry Proctor, Redlands.
Triple Jump—Pertti Pousi, Brigham Young.
Shot-Put—Karl Salb, Kansas.
Discus Throw—John Van Reenen, Washington State.
Hammer Throw—Steve DeAutremont, Oregon State.
Javelin Throw—Mark Murro, Arizona State.
Team—San Jose State.

Intercollegiate A.A.A.A. Outdoor Champions

100-Yard Dash—Don Martin, Yale.
220-Yard Dash—Roy Pollard, Morgan State.
440-Yard Run—Larry James, Villanova.
880-Yard Run—Byron Dyce, N.Y.U.
One-Mile Run—Marty Liquori, Villanova.
Three-Mile Run—Jerry Richey, Pittsburgh.
3,000-Meter Chase—Tom Donnelly, Villanova.
120-Yard High Hurdles—Erv Hall, Villanova.
440-Yard Hurdles—John Hanley, Rutgers.
440-Yard Relay—Yale.
One-Mile Relay—Villanova.
High Jump—Joe David, Maryland.
Pole Vault—Jim Williamson, Maryland.
Long Jump—Walter Jones, Cornell.
Triple Jump—Hartley Saunders, Morgan State.
Shot-Put—John Hanley, Maryland.
Discus Throw—Dick Drescher, Maryland.
Javelin Throw—John Bacon, Maryland.
Hammer Throw—Dick Narcessian, Rhode Island.
Team—Maryland.

Women's National Outdoor Champions

100-Yard Dash—Barbara Ferrell.
220-Yard Dash—Barbara Ferrell.
440-Yard Run—Kathy Hammond.
880-Yard Run—Madeline Manning.
1,500-Meter Run—Mrs. Doris Brown.
100-Meter Hurdles—Chi Cheng.
200-Meter Hurdles—Pat Hawkins.
440-Yard Relay—Mayor Daley Y. F., Chicago.
880-Yard Medley Relay—Tennessee State University.
One-Mile Relay—Angel T. C., Seattle.
High Jump—Eleanor Montgomery.
Long Jump—Willye White.
Javelin Throw—Kathy Schmidt.
Discus Throw—Kathy Frost.
Shot-Put—Maren Seidler.
Team—Tennessee State University.

VOLLEYBALL

National A.A.U. Champions

Men—United States Armed Forces.
Women—Rebels, Mayor Daley Y. F., Chicago.

U.S. Volleyball Ass'n. Champions

Men—Downtown Y.M.C.A., Los Angeles.
Women—Shamrocks, Long Beach, Calif.

WATER POLO

A.A.U. Outdoor—Corona Del Mar, Calif.
A.A.U. Indoor—De Anza, Cupertino, Calif.
N.C.A.A.—U.C.L.A.

WEIGHT LIFTING

World Champions

114-Pound—Vladislav Krischishin, U.S.S.R.
123-Pound—Mohamed Nassiri, Iran.
132-Pound—Yoshiyuki Miyake, Japan.
148-Pound—Waldemar Baszanowski, Poland.
165-Pound—Viktor Kurentsov, Soviet Union.
181-Pound—Masachi Ohuchi, Japan.
198-Pound—Kaarlo Kangasniemi, Finland.
242-Pound—Jan Talts, Soviet Union.
Heavyweight—Joe Dube, Doctor's Inlet, Fla.

National A.A.U. Champions

123-Pound—Fernando Baez, Puerto Rico.
132-Pound—Gary Hanson, York, Pa.
148-Pound—Steve Mansour, Highland Park, Mich.
165-Pound—Fred Lowe, York, Pa.
181-Pound—Mike Karchut, Chicago.
198-Pound—Frank Capsouras, York, Pa.
242-Pound—Bob Bednarski, York, Pa.
Heavyweight—Ken Patera, Portland, Ore.
Team—York (Pa.) Bar Bell Club.

WRESTLING

World Free-Style Champions

105.5-Pound—Javadie Ebrahim, Iran.
114.5-Pound—Rick Sanders, Portland, Ore.
125.5-Pound—Tanaka Tadamichi, Japan.
136.5-Pound—Marita Takeo, Japan.
149.5-Pound—Abdullah Mohaved, Iran.
163-Pound—Zarbeg Beriashvilli, U.S.S.R.
180.5-Pound—Fred Fozzard, Stillwater, Okla.
198-Pound—Boris Gurevitch, Soviet Union.
220-Pound—Chota Lomidze, Soviet Union.
Unlimited—Aleksandr Medved, Soviet Union.

National A.A.U. Free-Style Champions

105.5-Pound—Dale Kestel, Michigan, W. C.
114.5-Pound—Yasou Katsumura, Nebraska O.C.
125.5-Pound—Tashio Nakano, Japan.

136.5-Pound—Dan Gable, Iowa State.
149.5-Pound—Fumiaki Nakamura, New York A.C.
163-Pound—Lee Detrick, Michigan, W. C.
180.5-Pound—Len Kaufman, U.S. Army.
198-Pound—Buck Deadrich, Chicago.
220-Pound—Jess Lewis, Oregon State.
Unlimited—Dale Stearns, Iowa.

National Collegiate Champions

115-Pound—John Miller, Oregon.
123-Pound—Wayne Boyd, Temple.
130-Pound—David McGuire, Oklahoma.
137-Pound—Dan Gable, Iowa State.
145-Pound—Mike Grant, Oklahoma.
152-Pound—Gobel Kline, Maryland.
160-Pound—Cleo McGlory, Oklahoma.
167-Pound—Jason Smith, Iowa State.
177-Pound—Chuck Jean, Iowa State.
191-Pound—Tom Cline, California Poly.
Unlimited—Jess Lewis, Oregon State.
Team—Iowa State.

YACHTING

Distance Events

Trans-Atlantic (Newport-Cork, Ireland)—James Kilroy's Kialoa II, Newport Beach, Calif.
Trans-Pacific (San Pedro-Honolulu)—Jon Andron's Argonaut, Santa Barbara, Calif.
Annapolis-Newport — Ted Turner's American Eagle, Atlanta.
Southern Ocean Racing Conference—Jack Powell's and Wally Frank's Salty Tiger, Madeira Beach, Fla., and Darien, Conn.
Chicago-Mackinac—Pat Haggerty's Bay Bea, Houston.
Bayview-Mackinac—Peter Stern's Diavolo, Chicago.
Marblehead-Halifax—Irwin Tyson's sloop Summertime, White Plains, N.Y.
Storm Trysail Club Block Island—Conrad Jones's sloop Ergo, Marion, Mass.
Block Island Race Week (best over all)—Conrad Jones's sloop Ergo, Marion, Mass.
Miami-Montego Bay—Ogden Reid's Flyway, New York.
World's single-handed circumnavigation—Robin Knox-Johnston's Suhaili, Britain.
Fastnet Cup (England)—Richard Carter's Red Rooster, U.S.

International

Canada's Cup—Manitou, Royal Canadian Y.C.
Scandinavian Gold Cup (5.5-Meter)—Gordon Ingate's Pam, Australia.
One-Ton Cup—Chris Bouzaid's Rainbow II, New Zealand.

North American Champions

Mallory Cup (men)—Graham Hall, N.Y. State Maritime College.
Adams Cup (women)—Mrs. Jan Chance O'Malley, Montoloking (N.J.) Y.C.
Sears Cup (junior)—Manton Scott, Noroton (Conn.) Y.C.
Prince of Wales Bowl (Match Racing)—Edward M. Burt, Quisset Y.C., Falmouth, Mass.
O'Day Trophy (Single-handed)—Gordon Bowers, Wayzata, Minn.

One-Design Champions
National Unless Otherwise Indicated

Atlantic—Joe Olson, Niantic, Conn.
B Lion (North American)—Don McNair, Niantic, Conn.
Blue Jay—Todd Field, Port Washington, L.I.
Comet (Int.)—Talbott Ingram, Oceanport, N.J.
Comet (North American)—Carl Chapman, Avalon, N.J.
Cottontail—Bruce Kennedy, Amityville, L.I.
Dragon (World)—Bob Mosbacher, Houston.
Ensign—Albert Weiser, Fall River, Mass.

Etchells 22—Timothea Larr, Oyster Bay, L.I.
Finn (World)—Joerg Bruder, Brazil.
Finn (North American)—Gordon Bowers, Wayzata, Minn.
5-0-5 (North American)—Dennis Surtees, Los Altos, Calif.
5-0-5 (World)—Vic Deschamps and Larry Marks, England.
5.5-Meter—Ted Turner, Atlanta.
5.5-Meter (World)—J.-M. Le Guillou, France.
Flying Dutchman (North American)—Roger Green, Toronto.
Flying Dutchman (World)—Rodney Pattison, England.
420 (World)—Z. Karmel, Israel.
Highlander (Int.)—Tome Smith, Hoover, Ohio.
Jet 14—Hans Bonn, Lavallette, N.J.
Lightning (North American)—Tom Allen, Buffalo.
Luders 16 (World)—Graham Ross, Chicago.
Moth—Doug Halsey, St. Petersburg, Fla.
One-Design—Bert Domner, San Francisco.
110—Mike Cuddy, Providence, R.I.
Penguin (Int.)—Bob Johnstone, Skokie, Ill.
Raven—Bill Pagels, Sayville, L.I.
Rhodes 19—Richard Saltmarsh, New Bedford.
Shields—Patrick O'Neal, Larchmont, N.Y.
Snipe—Earl Elms, Mission Bay, Calif.
Snipe (World)—Earl Elms.
Soling (N. Amn.)—John Dane, New Orleans.
Soling (World)—Paul Elvstrom, Denmark.
Star (North American)—Barton Beek, Los Angeles.
Star (World)—Pelle Petterson, Sweden.
Sunfish (N. Amn.)—Carl Knight, Mamaroneck, N.Y.
Tempest—Andrew Kostanecki, Noroton, Conn.
Tempest (World)—Cliff Norbury, England.
Thistle—Jim Miller, Oyster Bay, L.I.
Triton—Gene Yates, Sausalito, Calif.
210—Douglas MacGregor, Hingham, Mass.
Windmill (World)—Ed Laviano, Bellport, L.I.

WHO'S WHO IN BEST SPORTS STORIES—1970

THE PRIZE WINNERS

WELLS TWOMBLY (The Impossible Dream), a first-time winner with his crackling story of the 1969 Super Bowl, was called by *Newsweek* one of the ten new sports columnists who is changing the whole style of sports writing. The story with which he is represented in this volume appeared in the *Detroit Free Press,* but he is now a sports columnist for the *San Francisco Examiner,* which just about completes a geographic circle for him. He broke in with the *Willimantic* (Conn.) *Daily Chronicle,* went west to the *Pasadena Star News,* then the *North Hollywood Valley Times Today,* and then south to the *Houston Chronicle* before the *Free Press.* He has appeared frequently in Best Sports Stories.

ROBERT LIPSYTE (The Medal), who took this year's news-feature award with his moving piece on Dick Tiger, is now a four-time winner in *Best Sports Stories.* In 1964 and 1967 he won the news-feature award with his studies of baseball rookies. In 1965 his report of the Clay-Liston fight won him the news-coverage award. He is a graduate of Columbia College and the Columbia Graduate School of Journalism. He has been with *The New York Times* for over 12 years and is the author of many books. This year Harper & Row is bringing out his book for young people, *Assignment: Sports,* largely drawn on his *Times* features. In 1966 he won the Mike Berger Award for distinguished reporting.

ROGER KAHN (Willie Mays, Yesterday and Today) now has won three magazine awards in *Best Sports Stories,* the first in 1960 and the second in '69 with his story on Glenn Hall, the St. Louis hockey player. He began working for the *New York Herald Tribune* as a sports reporter and then went to *Newsweek* as sports editor. Later he became the sports editor of *The*

Saturday Evening Post and was a senior editor of that publication when it folded. He has been free-lancing since, and is the author of *The Passionate People,* a book about the Jews in America. He is a graduate of New York University and a frequent choice in this series of sports stories.

OTHER CONTRIBUTORS (In Alphabetical Order)

BOB ADDIE (The Last of the Autocratic Umpires) won *Best Sports Stories* feature award in 1963 with his moving account of blind children at a baseball game. He was graduated from the University of Alabama and began his career with the now defunct *New York Journal-American,* from which he went to *The Washington Post,* where he is a sports columnist. Although his beat is the baseball scene, he is versatile enough to write about all major sports. He was president of the Baseball Writers Association in 1967. He has made frequent appearances in this anthology.

MAURY ALLEN (Whatever Happened to Good Sportsmanship?), sports reporter for the *New York Post,* began his sports-writing career with the *Seymour* (Ind.) *Times* after Army service and then moved to the *Levittown* (Pa.) *Times.* In 1959, he joined *Sports Illustrated* and went from there to the *New York Post* in 1962. His main assignment is baseball. He is the author of five books, including one on the Mets called *Now Wait a Minute, Casey.* His latest book is entitled *The Record Breakers.* This is his third appearance in *Best Sports Stories.*

NEIL AMDUR (The Second Grand Slam) was born in Wilkes-Barre, Pennsylvania, attended the University of Missouri and received a Bachelor of Journalism degree. He spent six years on the sports staff of the *Miami Herald* and received the Florida Sportswriters Association award for general excellence in 1966. Amdur joined the staff of *The New York Times* in 1968 and has been covering college football, tennis and track and field. This is his first appearance in *Best Sports Stories.*

BOB BARNET (The Regal Red Comet from Out of the West) was born in Muncie, Indiana, began working for the *Muncie Star* directly after his high-school graduation and later became its sports editor. He also writes a Sunday editorial page column on any subject he chooses. He has held a myriad of civic and professional positions: former president of the Indiana Sports Writers and Radio Broadcasters Association, director of the Indiana Trotting and Racing Horse Association, executive secretary-treasurer for the Indiana Association of Fairs and holder of the 1965 George A. Barton Award for greatest contributions to the national Golden Gloves program. Prentice-Hall published his book *Winning High School Basketball,* which was coauthored by Jay McCreary.

SMITH BARRIER (The Special Level of Lew Alcindor) is the executive sports editor of the *Greensboro* (N.C.) *Daily News* and *Record* and the president of the United States Basketball Writers Association. He is also the past director of the Atlantic Coast Conference Service Bureau. His alma mater is the University of North Carolina, and he is the author of *On Carolina's Gridiron,* a history of football at his college. This marks his second appearance in *Best Sports Stories.*

IRA BERKOW (Citation Is Still a Ladies' Man) is 28 years old. He was graduated from Miami (Ohio) University in 1963 and received an M.S.J. from Northwestern's Medill School of Journalism in 1965. From there he went to the sports department of the *Minneapolis Tribune* and to the Newspaper Enterprise Association in 1967 as sports columnist. He was recently appointed NEA sports editor. This is his first appearance in *Best Sports Stories.*

FURMAN BISHER (Purgatory, with 18 Holes) sports editor of *The Atlantic Journal,* has received numerous honors for his perceptive writing. *Time* magazine named him one of the five best sports columnists in 1961. He was elected president of the Baseball Writers Association of America in 1960. His work has appeared in many major magazines and within the last few years he has had two books published: *Miracle in Atlanta* (World Publishing) and *Strange but True Baseball Stories* (Random House). He has appeared many times in this anthology.

SI BURICK (He Whipped the Establishment) is a perennial favorite of the readers of *Best Sports Stories,* having made many appearances in this continuing anthology. He became a sports writer for the paper he now works for, *The Dayton Daily News,* at the tender age of 19. In his 40 years of reporting he has covered just about everything that comes under the term "sports." He has been selected as Ohio's Sports Writer of the Year six consecutive years (1963–68). He is also a member of the board of directors of Dayton Newspapers, Inc.

ROBERT L. BURNES (The Mets Complete the Miracle) is one of the fine veteran reporters of the Midwest who has been with the *St. Louis Globe-Democrat* since 1935. He has been writing his column, "The Bench-warmer," since 1943, and in 1966 he was named executive sports editor. For 17 years he has had a daily 45-minute question-and-answer audience participation program on KMOX-CBS radio. He has had one book, *Fifty Golden Years of Sport,* published and has done articles for almost all major sport publications. He has had three previous articles in *Best Sports Stories.*

STEPHEN (STEVE) CADY (A Decade for All Seasons) has been a member of the sports staff of *The New York Times* since 1960. He was born in Boston, Massachusetts, and received a BA from Harvard in 1949 after his Army service. He was sports editor of his college paper (*The Harvard Crimson*) and a college stringer for the *Boston Herald-Traveler*. His first full-time job after graduation was with the *Providence* (R.I.) *Journal-Bulletin*. At *The New York Times* he began by specializing in pleasure boating and horse racing, but he now covers all important sports events. His work has appeared many times in *Best Sports Stories*.

LOU CHAPMAN (The Mets Go Into Orbit) has been with the *Milwaukee Sentinel* for more than 20 years. He has covered two major-league sports—the baseball Braves and pro basketball Hawks and now the Bucks. He was graduated from Marquette University and won six writing awards from the old Hearst organization. He contributed to *The Saturday Evening Post* and the *American Weekly* and has coauthored a paperback book on the Braves. This is his first appearance in *Best Sports Stories*.

BILL CONLIN (The "56 Scissors") has been with the *Philadelphia Daily News* for six years after four years with the *Evening Bulletin*. He appeared in *Best Sports Stories* in '63 with a basketball piece and shared the reporting prize with Bob Lipsyte in '65 for his story on the Penn State upset of Ohio State. He covers the Phillies, Penn State football and Big Five basketball. In addition to conducting a Philadelphia radio sports show, he also does basketball announcing.

ROBERT DALEY (The Risk Takers) is a former European correspondent of *The New York Times*. He has published several books on various sports, including *Only a Game*, a 1967 best seller, *The Swords of Spain* and *The Cruel Sport*, which was the basis for the film *Grand Prix*. Mr. Daley is an avid sportsman whose own experience serves as research for his books and whose dad, Arthur Daley, is the much respected sports columnist for *The New York Times*. This is his first appearance in *Best Sports Stories*.

RAY DIDINGER ("Too Weak an Ethic for Me to Follow") is a graduate of Temple University and has been a member of the sports staff of the *Philadelphia Evening* and *Sunday Bulletin* since June '69, handling the area's high-school sports and various feature assignments. After graduation in June '68, he spent a year writing news, features and a weekly column for the *Delaware County Daily Times* in Chester, Pa., before moving to the *Bulletin*. This is his first appearance in *Best Sports Stories*.

FRANK DOLSON (It Was a Devil of a Weekend) is making his third appearance in *Best Sports Stories*. He was graduated from the University of Pennsylvania in 1954, spent six months with *Sports Illustrated*, and then moved to *The Philadelphia Inquirer* in 1955. In 1959 he began to write occasional columns for that paper and since 1966 he has been a regular sports columnist for the *Inquirer,* covering a wide range of sports topics.

Don D. Ellis (The Incredible Tracking Dog) is a retired British Columbia game warden who landed the job with the help of his tracking dog and held it for 27 years. Now 71, he lives at Kelowna, in the Okanagan Valley, where he has worked the last 12 years as a warden. His two sons follow in his footsteps, the older as an operator of a hunting and fishing camp, and the other as a conservation officer for the British Columbia Fish and Wildlife Branch. Ellis is a several-time contributor to *Outdoor Life* magazine and makes his first appearance in *Best Sports Stories.*

Ray Fitzgerald (That Old Glove Had Some Life) is a graduate of the University of Notre Dame. He has been writing sports for the past 18 years, the last four at *The Boston Globe.* He lives in the seaside town of Scituate, Massachusetts, and is the only one in the village who doesn't own a boat. He was named Massachusetts Sportswriter of the Year in '63. This is his first appearance in *Best Sports Stories.*

Joe Gergen (Baseball Lives at Wrigley Field) has been associated with *Newsday* for the past 15 months and in that time has covered baseball (Mets and Yankees) and football (Giants). He previously worked for five years for United Press International in New York, covering a variety of sports. He was born in Brooklyn and attended Brooklyn Prep and Boston College (class of '63), where he served as sports editor of the newspaper and yearbook. This is his first appearance in *Best Sports Stories.*

Jim Hawkins (The Awful Anachronism) was graduated from the University of Wisconsin in 1966. He began his sports writing at the *Milwaukee Sentinel* and moved to the *Wilmington* (Del.) *News-Journal.* For the past two years he has been with *The Evening Sun* of Baltimore, Maryland, where he covers college football and basketball, as well as golf, and does features on pro teams—the Colts, Orioles and Bullets. This is his first appearance in *Best Sports Stories.*

Joe Heiling (An Army Cook Did It on a Pass) is a graduate of Victoria College in Texas. He spent four years in the Air Force and then worked on newspapers at Gulfport, Mississippi, and the *Daily Herald,* the *Caller-Times* and the *American-Statesman,* all in Texas. At present he is a baseball writer for *The Houston Post.* This is his first appearance in *Best Sports Stories.*

Mickey Herskowitz (The Longhorns Silence Those "Sooooooie" Pigs) is now the editor of *Jock,* the new regional sports magazine in New York. He began his career with *The Houston Post* and rose to an executive position there. He received the 1968 National Headliners Award, the Texas Headliners Award for sports and political reporting and also an AP press award for a column on the Apollo moon shot. He has been selected several times as sports writer of the year in Texas. He now makes his fourth appearance in *Best Sports Stories.*

STAN HOCHMAN (Courage: A Lovely Woman) was born in Brooklyn, received his MA from New York University and taught school briefly. He did brief stints with newspapers in Augusta, Georgia, and in Brownsville, Corpus Christi, and Waco, Texas. He then went west to San Bernardino, California, and returned East to the big league in 1959, when he went to work for the *Philadelphia Daily News.* He has recently branched out into writing television documentaries. He has appeared many times in *Best Sports Stories.*

JERRY IZENBERG (Race War Is Alive and Well at Madison Square Garden) is a syndicated columnist for the *Newark Star-Ledger,* his column appearing in six major daily newspapers. He has received awards from the National Golf Writers and the National Harness Writers. He is the author of *Championship: The Complete NFL Title Story,* has written TV shows for two major networks and has been published by top magazines throughout the country. He wrote and produced the TV documentary on Grambling College, "100 Yards to Glory." His work has merited many inclusions in *Best Sports Stories.*

KAYE KESSLER (Beaten at Their Own Game) started writing for the *Columbus Citizen* while in high school in 1940. After a three-year Army stint, he earned a degree in journalism from Ohio University. At present he is an assistant sports editor on the *Columbus Citizen-Journal* and a free-lance contributor to major sports magazines. He has received awards from the Golf Writers Association and the American Association of College Baseball Coaches, and in 1961 was named the outstanding basketball writer by United Press International. This is his third appearance in *Best Sports Stories.*

LEW KING ("Barbara Jo Rubin Is a Good Bet") is night sports editor of the *Philadelphia Bulletin.* He previously was assistant sports editor of the *New York Journal-American* and the *New York World Journal Tribune.* He is a former minor-league baseball player. He was graduated from the University of Missouri School of Journalism in 1948. This is his first appearance in *Best Sports Stories.*

DAVID KLEINBERG ("There's the Mental Thing") was graduated from the San Francisco State College in 1969 with a BA in international relations. He has served the *San Francisco Chronicle* periodically since 1962. He spent

14 months in Vietnam as an Army combat correspondent. This is his first appearance in *Best Sports Stories.*

Leonard Koppett (The Avant-Gardes of "Music") has had an extensive background training in the metropolitan area. He was reared in the Bronx, close to the Yankee Stadium, and it was this proximity plus his love of sports that impelled him to become a sports writer. After graduation from Columbia University in 1946, he joined the staff of the *New York Post* and in '63 he went to *The New York Times,* where he still is. He is at home writing in all the major sports, but his main interest in baseball led him to research and write his excellent book, *A Thinking Man's Guide to Baseball* (E. P. Dutton & Co., Inc., 1967). He is also author of *Twenty-Four Seconds to Shoot, An Informal History of the NBA* (Macmillan, 1968) and a history of the Mets to appear in 1970.

Hal Lebovitz (The Great Swim Hoax), the sports editor of the *Cleveland Plain Dealer,* has just coauthored a series of high-school science texts generated by his former teaching experience. He has also completed 31 years of football officiating and in between has been a baseball and basketball official. He does an editorial opinion column, "Hal Ask," and on alternate days a column, "Ask Hal," which elicits from his reading public as many as 7,000 questions a year. His writing has merited many appearances in *Best Sports Stories.*

George Leonard (Six at Tom Black Track) has been a member of *The Nashville Banner*'s sports staff for 28 years. He coauthored with *Banner* sports director Fred Russell a book called *Big Bowl Football.* He was Tennessee Sports Writer of the Year in 1968. He is a graduate of the University of Alabama and a World War II veteran. In 1964 he won the news-coverage award in *Best Sports Stories* with his story on the Alabama-Auburn game. This is his third appearance in *Best Sports Stories.*

Al Levine (The World's Tallest Chemist) at 24 is the youngest award-winning sports writer in Florida. He won second place in columns in 1965 and second in features in 1966 in the state sports-writing contest. He was with the *Miami News* for over four years and then in 1967 went to the *St. Petersburg Times,* returning to Miami in 1968. He was educated at Miami-Dade Junior College and the University of Miami. This is his first appearance in *Best Sports Stories.*

Roy McHugh (Quarry's Mistake) started his career with the *Cedar Rapids* (Iowa) *Gazette* after graduation from Coe College. He covered all sports for the *Pittsburgh Press* from 1947 to 1961, and then went to the *Evansville* (Ind.) *Sunday Courier and Press* as columnist and sports editor. He returned after two years to the *Pittsburgh Press* and last April became its sports editor, continuing to write a column five times a week. This is his second appearance in *Best Sports Stories.*

JACK MANN (Jim Bouton, Reliever) broke into sports writing with Long Island's *Newsday,* where he became sports editor in 1956. He then went in 1963 to the sports desk of the *New York Herald Tribune* and then in 1965 to *Sports Illustrated.* He moved in 1969 to the *Washington Daily News,* after having free-lanced for many of the major national magazines. He has appeared in *Best Sports Stories* on many occasions.

JESSE OUTLAR (A Sergeant Outshoots the General) is a graduate of the University of Georgia with a BS in journalism. He spent three years, from 1943 to 1946, with the Marines, and then became the managing editor of the *Camp Lejeune Globe.* He moved to the *Waycross* (Ga.) *Journal-Herald* for one year and then on to *The Atlanta Constitution.* He has been there for over 21 years, 11 of them as its sports editor. This is his first appearance in *Best Sports Stories.*

PHIL PEPE (Agee Makes the Orioles Sick Birds) is a graduate of St. John's University who in 1957 became a member of the *New York World-Telegram* staff, covering the Yankees and college sports. In 1966 he moved to the *World Journal Tribune* as a three-days-a-week columnist and general assignment reporter in sports, then free-lanced until in November, 1968, he joined the staff of *The News.* He is the author of five sports books, including the autobiography of Bob Gibson, *From Ghetto to Glory.* This is his third appearance in *Best Sports Stories.*

SHIRLEY POVICH (The Unlikely Heavyweight Champion) attended Georgetown University, chose journalism and at the age of 20 became sports editor of *The Washington Post,* perhaps the youngest sports editor of any metropolitan daily. His story on Don Larsen's perfect World Series game against the Dodgers was awarded first prize in coverage in *Best Sports Stories 1957.* He has also won numerous other awards, including the National Headliners Award and the Grantland Rice Award. His latest book, *All These Mornings,* was published in 1969 by Prentice-Hall. He has appeared in *Best Sports Stories* on numerous occasions.

MARTIN RALBOVSKY (A Profitable Bag) is making his first appearance in this anthology. Born in Schenectady, N.Y., he joined the *Union-Star* newspaper of that city and remained there eight years as assistant sports editor. In 1968 he went to Newspaper Enterprise Association for a year in Cleveland and now is with that news organization in New York City.

GENE ROSWELL (Allie Hears the Last Good-bye) is a native New Yorker and a graduate of New York University. He worked as a stringer for the wire services and New York dailies, joined the old *Bronx Home News* and then moved to the *New York Post,* working up from night sports editor to golf, basketball, tennis and football expert. His son, a North Carolina student, is the sports editor for the college newspaper. This marks Roswell's first appearance in *Best Sports Stories.*

JOE SCALZO (Breedlove) was born in Southern California 28 years ago. He began newspaper writing at 18. He wrote columns and free-lance magazine stories until the age of 22, when he took up motorcycle racing as a profession. He raced nationally for the Yamaha factory during 1964 but in '65 he quit racing and resumed writing. Currently he is employed by Bond Publishing Co. This is his first appearance in *Best Sports Stories.*

NICK SEITZ (Frank Beard Is Dull . . .) is making his fifth appearance in *Best Sports Stories.* He majored in philosophy at the University of Oklahoma, became sports editor of the *Norman* (Okla.) *Transcript* at the age of 22, and then was named sports editor of the *Oklahoma Journal.* He is now associate editor of *Golf Digest* magazine and a free-lance writer for other magazines, including *Sport* and *Parents.* He has won numerous prizes in golf and basketball writers' association contests.

LEONARD SHECTER (The Most Hated Winner in Football) is sports editor of *Look.* Prior to that he was a copyboy for the *New York Post* and then a sports reporter there. During this time he did a great deal of free-lancing for the major magazines. After 20 years with his paper he turned to periodical writing. He also was a sports commentator for the Westinghouse Broadcasting Company. In '68 he won the magazine award in *Best Sports Stories* with his study of Vince Lombardi, "The Toughest Man in Pro Football," which appeared in *Esquire.*

BLACKIE SHERROD (Calling the Old Shots) has been the executive sports editor of *The Dallas Times Herald* since 1958. The *Fort Worth Press* had his services before that. He has received a host of awards, regional and national, including the National Headliners Award for his consistently outstanding sports column. He is a past president of the Football Writers Association of America and of the Texas Sportswriters Association. In 1965 he was honored as Man of the Year by his alma mater, Howard Payne College. He has appeared in *Best Sports Stories* on many occasions.

AL SILVERMAN (Gale Sayers: The Hard Road Back) began his professional career by going to work for *True* and later *Argosy* magazine. He then became a magazine free-lancer, and for the past nine years has been editor at *Sport.* He has written nine sports books, the most recent being *Joe Dimaggio, The Golden Year 1941,* published by Prentice-Hall. Silverman is at present doing a biography of Gale Sayers. He was born in Lynn, Mass., and was graduated from Boston University. This is his first appearance in *Best Sports Stories.*

RON SMITH (Baseball's Not-So-Jolly Green Giant) has been writing sports since his graduation from Michigan State, when he went to work for the *Saginaw* (Mich.) *News*. In 1960 he became sports columnist for the *Detroit Times* and then moved to the *Phoenix* (Ariz.) *Journal* as sports editor. At present he is executive sports editor and columnist of *The Philadelphia Inquirer*. He has been published by many leading magazines. This is his second appearance in *Best Sports Stories.*

ART SPANDER (Not with Power, but with Poise) is a graduate of UCLA, class of 1960, with a degree in political science. From 1960 through 1963 he worked at UPI as a general reporter-rewrite man, with time out (six months) for the Army. Then, from 1963–65, he was a sports writer for the *Santa Monica Evening Outlook*. In May, 1965, he went to the *San Francisco Chronicle,* where he covers golf as well as basketball and football.

AL STUMP (High-scoring Catastrophe) is a free-lance writer with a fine national reputation for magazine writing. His article on the last days of Ty Cobb, *The Fight to Live,* won the *Best Sports Stories* magazine award in 1962. He is a native of the West Coast and received his education at the University of Washington. As a teen-ager he went to work for his local newspaper and received the assignment of covering the Rose Bowl. He later joined the staff of the *Portland Oregonian*. He has collaborated with many great personalities in the writing of their biographies and has appeared frequently in *Best Sports Stories.*

BILL SURFACE (Gamblers Are in the Pro-Football Huddle) began writing about sports for the *Lexington* (Ky.) *Herald* while in college. He later worked as a sports writer for the *Louisville Courier-Journal* and *Chicago Tribune,* before leaving in 1960 to devote full time to magazine and book writing. He has written six books and frequent articles on a wide range of subjects for *Argosy, The New York Times Magazine* and *Reader's Digest*. He was president in 1968 of the 265-member Society of Magazine Writers. This is his second appearance in *Best Sports Stories.*

GEORGE VECSEY (Mantle's Road to Fame: Pain, Struggle, Frustration) is a graduate of Hofstra University and began his newspaper work with *Newsday*. After working on the Long Island paper for eight years, he went to *The New York Times* sports department, where he receives important assignments in all the major sports. He has written three children's books, one being *The Baseball Life of Sandy Koufax*. He is also a coauthor of *Naked Came the Stranger* and has just completed *Joy in Mudville,* an informal history of the Mets, for the McCall Publishing Company. This is his second appearance in *Best Sports Stories.*

DICK YOUNG (Dream of a Team) is with the *New York Daily News* sports department. His talent has earned him five prizes in *Best Sports Stories,* and in all the writing divisions. He has garnered two prizes in news-coverage, in 1959 and 1960, two for news-features, in 1957 and 1966, and a prize for magazine writing in 1955. In addition to covering baseball, he writes a column for the *Daily News* entitled "Young Ideas."

PHOTOGRAPHERS IN BEST SPORTS STORIES—1970

THE PHOTO WINNERS

Paul DeMaria (The Battery Is Fully Charged), winner of this year's action photo award, is a New York City boy who first studied photography in high school. For a short while after graduation he worked at a local camera store prior to employment as a copyboy at the *New York Daily News.* In April of 1956, *The News* made him a studio apprentice and in 1962 he became a full-fledged photographer. He has won several awards from the New York Press Photographers Association and has captured titles in the New York State AP contest.

Bob Doty (Tiny Seats), winner of the feature photo prize, is a longtime contributor to the *Best Sports Stories* annuals and is the winningest photographer in the series. This is his fourth award. Previous prizes came in 1956, 1963 and 1965. He broke into the photo business as an AP wirephoto man and in 1938 he joined the *Dayton Journal Herald,* where he is now chief photographer. He has won a large number of other awards, including 14 Freedom Foundation citations and a Headliner Award.

OTHER PHOTOGRAPHERS (In Alphabetical Order)

Mike Andersen (A Rather Pressing Affair) is a graduate of the University of Missouri with a BJ degree and double major in photo journalism and news-editorial writing. He worked as a sports writer for the *Beaumont* (Tex.) *Enterprise,* as news editor of the *Casa Grande* (Ariz.) *Dispatch,* and as photographer for the *Waterloo* (Iowa) *Courier* and the *Lawrence* (Kan.) *Journal-World* before taking his present job with the *Boston Record-American.*

ERNEST ANHEUSER (One Man Gang) studied art at the Chicago Art Institute and turned to photography as a profession during World War II. He is now on the staff of the *Milwaukee Journal* and is a member of both the national and Wisconsin Press Photographer Associations.

VERNON J. BIEVER (Starr's in His Eyes) is a free-lance photographer who lives in Port Washington, Wisconsin, and handles a wide variety of sports assignments. He covers the Green Bay Packers for the *Milwaukee Sentinel* and did the photos for Jerry Kramer's book, *Instant Replay.*

CHARLES E. BJORGEN (Don't Say It!) is a graduate of the University of Minnesota with a BA degree in photo journalism. He worked as a photographer for the South Dakota Department of Game Fish and Parks for four years, then for a commercial advertising studio for a year before joining the staff of the *Minneapolis Star* in 1966. This is his first appearance in *Best Sports Stories.*

JOHN CROFT (A High Save) has been on the photo staff of the *Minneapolis Tribune* since 1957. A native of Minneapolis, he attended high school there and then the University of Minnesota. In 1950 and 1951 he worked as a copyboy at the *Tribune* and, before joining its camera staff, was a photographer with WCCO-TV, Minneapolis, in 1953. This is his first appearance in *Best Sports Stories.*

JOHN DUPREY (Meet Cousin Leo) has been with the *New York Daily News* since 1946. He started as a copyboy and became a photographer six years later. He has had assignments throughout the world and has captured more than 30 prizes, including Best of the New York Photographers Show in 1963.

JIM GARRETT (The Boppers) is a native New Yorker who attended St. John's University and the City College of New York before joining the staff of the *New York Daily News* in 1960. He was in the editorial promotion department of the *News* and in the photo studio before joining the staff of photographers in 1965. This is his second appearance in *Best Sports Stories.*

JOHN GREENSMITH (The Big L vs. the Big E) has been a news photographer for more than 20 years, having started with the *San Diego Union Tribune* in 1957. This is his seventh appearance in *Best Sports Stories.* He majored in photography at Ohio University. He also writes for boxing, wrestling and thoroughbred racing magazines.

TOMMY HAWKES (Conga! Ole!!) is only 19 years old and is still a student at the University of Texas at Arlington. While in high school, he served for two years as photographer on the school annual and newspaper, later joining the staff of the *Arlington Citizen-Journal,* a bi-weekly, as a part-time photographer.

KENT KOBERSTEEN (A Girl Who Attracts Many Bows) was a journalism major at the University of Minnesota, class of 1964, and after a stint as copyboy with the *Minneapolis Tribune* became a staff photographer in 1965. This is his first appearance in *Best Sports Stories.*

JOSEPH C. KORDICK (Gotcha!) has been with the *Chicago Sun-Times* photographic staff for almost 30 years. For nearly all that time he has specialized in sports coverage and his photos have appeared in *Best Sports Stories* many times. His son is a news photographer, too.

JIM LARAGY (Etched in the Stretch) has worked for the *Rochester Democrat & Chronicle* for 11 years and before that was with the other Gannett paper there, *The Times-Union.* Before entering the newspaper business, he worked for Kodak. Last year he won top prize in the AP state photo contest for a portfolio of shots. It's his first appearance in *Best Sports Stories.*

DENNIS C. MAGNUSON (Most Accidents Happen at Home) has been a photographer for the *St. Paul Pioneer Press* for 15 years. He has covered all phases of photography, but most of his work is in sports, mainly with the pros. This is his fourth appearance in *Best Sports Stories.*

LARRY C. MORRIS (If at First . . .) won the *Best Sports Stories* feature photo award in 1964 and was a co-winner of the action photo award in 1965. He became a staff photographer for *The New York Times* in 1950. Among his many awards are those given by *Look* magazine, the New York Press Photographers Association and the Newspaper Guild's Page One.

CHARLES R. PUGH, JR. (Caught in a Squeeze) won the *Best Sports Stories* action photo award last year in his debut in the anthology. He started his photographic career with the *Johnson City* (Tenn.) *Press-Chronicle* and has been with the *Atlanta Journal* since 1956.

JOHN E. ROEMER (That Heady Feeling) has been a photographer for the *Green Bay Press-Gazette* since 1965. Prior to that he was a military photographer in Germany for five years. In 1967 he took first place in a Des Moines photo contest and last year he had two pictures considered for Wisconsin AP Picture of the Year. This is his first appearance in *Best Sports Stories.*

EARL SEUBERT (College Sport with a Twist) is an old hand at winning awards for outstanding photography. His photos have been placing in competition since 1948 and he has accumulated more than 100 national, regional, state and local awards, including the *Best Sports Stories* feature photo award in 1953. He was named Newspaper Photographer of the Year in 1955. He joined the *Minneapolis Tribune* in 1948 and became its chief photographer in 1961.

SEYMOUR SNAER ("Some Win—Some Lose") is a veteran photographer with the *San Francisco Examiner* and the recipient of many awards, including the California Press Photographers Association award as 1959 Photographer of the Year. He is one of the pioneers in newspaper color photography and his work has appeared in *Best Sports Stories* several times.

LYNN T. SPENCE (The Case of the Ambivalent Umpires) is 33 years old and grew up in St. Louis, Missouri. He operated the pilot plant of a petrochemical company before striking out as a free-lance photographer. He became a staff photographer for the *St. Louis Post-Dispatch* in 1966.

PAUL TEPLEY (Canvas Coming Up!) has been a staff photographer for the *Cleveland Press* for seven years after serving UPI as a photographer for the same length of time. A graduate of Cleveland State University, he is 38 years old. This is his second appearance in *Best Sports Stories.*

JIM VINCENT (You Don't Want It? I'll Take It!) has been a staff photographer for the *Portland Oregonian* for four years and for the 12 years before that was with the *Oregon Journal.* This is his third appearance in *Best Sports Stories.*

JOHN H. WHITE (6′5″ + 5′2″ = V) is a 24-year-old staff photographer for the *Chicago Daily News.* A North Carolinian by birth, he attended Central Piedmont Community College, was a sergeant in the U.S. Marine Corps, and after working in a photo studio in Charlotte, North Carolina, joined the *Chicago News* in 1969.

STAN WOLFSON (Scoring on the Rebound) joined the *Newsday* photo department in 1966 after three years with the *New York World-Telegram & Sun.* Born in Brooklyn, he now lives in East Northport, Long Island, N.Y.

THE BATTERY IS FULLY CHARGED by Paul DeMaria, *New York Daily News*. If, as the old cliché goes, a picture is worth 1,000 words, this one, the action winning photo of this year, is worth at least triple that. Need you be told that it presents one of the New York Mets, Jerry Koosman, the winning pitcher, jumping on his battery mate, Jerry Grote, after the final putout that gave the Miraculous Mets the World Series? And that's Donn Clendenon (22) rushing in to join the celebration? Copyright, ©, 1969, *New York News Syndicate Co., Inc.*

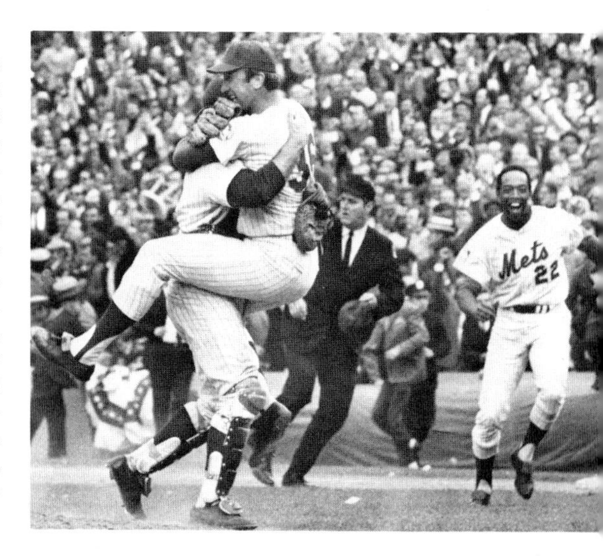

TINY SEATS

by Bob Doty, *Dayton Journal Herald*. How can this photo, winner of this year's feature award, be described other than to say that it was taken while Ray Floyd *(lower right)* was winning the National P.G.A. championship at the National Cash Register Golf Course in Dayton, Ohio? Any caption you may wish to supply will be perfectly appropriate. Copyright, ©, 1969, *Bob Doty*.

MOST ACCIDENTS HAPPEN AT HOME

by Dennis C. Magnuson, *St. Paul Pioneer Press*. Eddie Leon, Cleveland Indians, attempting to score from second, is out at home, tagged by Minnesota Twins catcher John Roseboro, who's sitting on home plate. Roseboro was cut in the face by cleats on Leon's shoe and had two stitches taken. Copyright, ©, 1969, *St. Paul Pioneer Press.*

THE CASE OF THE AMBIVALENT UMPIRES

by Lynn T. Spence, *St. Louis Post-Dispatch*. Umpires John Kibler (*left*) and Ed Vargo seem to have a difference of opinion on this play in the sixth inning of a game between the St. Louis Cardinals and the Los Angeles Dodgers in St. Louis. Bill Sudakis of the Dodgers is the runner and Mike Shannon of the Cards the fielder. Although the Dodgers protested, Kibler's judgment prevailed. Copyright, ©, 1969, *St. Louis Post-Dispatch.*

6′5″ + 5′2″ = V
by John H. White,
Chicago Daily News.
Pitcher Bryan Jacobs
(left), who's 6 feet 5
inches tall, getting a sign
of appreciation from
catcher Mitch Nelson, all
5 feet 2 inches of him,
after he'd pitched his
team to a 2-0 victory in
an Illinois High School
Association summer
league game at Niles
West, near Chicago. The
other enthusiastic gent is
third baseman Paul
Klipowicz. Copyright, ©,
1969, *Field Enterprises,*
Inc.

MEET COUSIN LEO

by John Duprey, *New York Daily News.* A black cat walks on to the field at Shea Stadium to greet Leo Durocher and the other Chicago Cubs in their dugout. Maybe that black-cat superstition has some merit. The Mets won, 7-1. Copyright, ©, 1969, *New York News Syndicate Co., Inc.*

STARR'S IN HIS EYES

by Vernon J. Biever, *Milwaukee Sentinel.* Alan Page (88), defensive end of the Minnesota Vikings, attempting to overwhelm Bart Starr, Green Bay Packers quarterback, in their game at Milwaukee. He did, too. Copyright, ©, 1969, by *Milwaukee Sentinel.*

GOTCHA!

by Joseph C. Kordick, *Chicago Sun-Times.* Mike McCoy (77) of Notre Dame trying to inundate little Jimmy Jones of Southern California (8) in their game at Notre Dame. Copyright, ©, 1969, *Chicago Sun-Times.*

ONE MAN GANG

by Ernest Anheuser, *Milwaukee Journal.* Dick Butkis, Chicago Bear linebacker, says nay as Jim Grabowski and other Green Bay Packers attempt to move the football over the goal line. He stopped the Packers again on the next play, forcing them to attempt a field goal. Copyright, ©, 1969, *Milwaukee Journal.*

YOU DON'T WANT IT? I'LL TAKE IT!

by Jim Vincent, *The* (Portland) *Oregonian.* Terry DeKraai (19) of USC recovering a fumble by Larry Rich (26) of Oregon State, after Rich makes a desperate attempt to retrieve his bobble. USC went on to win, 31-7, in game played at Parker Stadium, Corvallis, Oregon. Copyright, ©, 1969, *The Oregonian.*

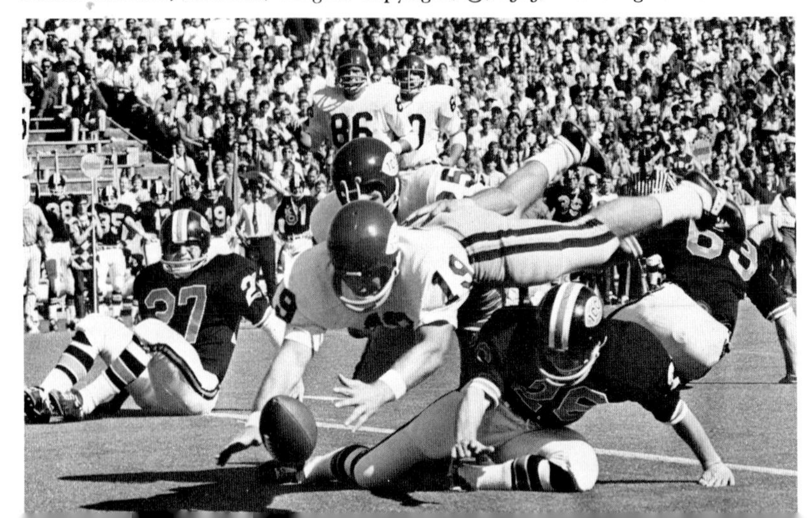

SCORING ON THE REBOUND

by Stan Wolfson, *Newsday*. Don Maynard, New York Jets' end, scoring a touchdown after he had bounced off Miami Dolphins' defensive back Dick Anderson (40). Play came in the fourth quarter at Shea Stadium and provided the tying score as Jets went on to win, 34-31. With the catch, Maynard became the first AFL player to gain over 10,000 yards. Copyright, ©, 1969, *Newsday, Inc.*

Caught in a Squeeze

by Charles R. Pugh, Jr., *Atlanta Journal.* The referee is racked up between two members of the Los Angeles Rams team in game with the Atlanta Falcons at Atlanta. But no one was hurt except the feelings of the Falcons, who lost the game. Copyright, ©, 1969, *Atlanta Journal-Constitution.*

Conga! Ole!!

by Tommy Hawkes, *Arlington* (Tex.) *Journal.* Eddie Stallings of University of Texas at Arlington (*left*) and John Lynch of Trinity of Texas (*right*) seem to be practicing the conga in their basketball game at Arlington, Texas. Trinity won, 103-99. Copyright, ©, 1969, *Citizen-Journal, Inc., Arlington, Texas.*

THE BIG L VS. THE BIG E

by John Greensmith, *San Diego Evening Tribune*. Lew Alcindor, now of the Milwaukee Bucks, arm to arm with his old foe, Elvin Hayes, now of the San Diego Rockets, in NBA game at San Diego. Alcindor scored on this one and the Bucks went on to win, 115-102, as Lew made 36 points and took off 19 rebounds. Copyright, ©, 1969, *San Diego Tribune*.

A Rather Pressing Affair

by Mike Andersen, *Lawrence* (Kan.) *Journal-World*. High-flying Pierre Russell of Kansas (44) fails to prevent Oklahoma's Bob Patterson from getting his pass away despite his extreme pressing defense. No. 40 is Dave Robisch of Kansas, which won the Big Eight Conference game played at Lawrence. Copyright, ©, 1969, *Lawrence Journal-World*.

THE BOPPERS

by Jim Garrett, *New York Daily News*. The technique may not be professional, but the action is spirited and (for once) the aim perfect as Ramon Sanchez (*right*) pops Richard Brady in the nose in the first round of a Golden Gloves bout in the Bronx, New York. Copyright, ©, 1969, *New York News Syndicate Co., Inc.*

CANVAS COMING UP!

by Paul Tepley, *Cleveland Press*. Ray Anderson heads toward a knockdown after a left thrown by Ted Gullick (note glove upper left) connected with the second-ranked light heavyweight in bout at Cleveland. Anderson got to his feet, but was knocked out some seconds later in the same round, the ninth. Copyright, ©, 1969, *Cleveland Press*.

Don't Say It!

by Charles E. Bjorgen, *Minneapolis Star.* You just know what Dave Gumlia, a local golf pro, is thinking after he'd missed a putt on the final hole of the Peters Open tournament in St. Paul, Minnesota. But he still won the tournament. Copyright, ©, 1969, *Minneapolis Star.*

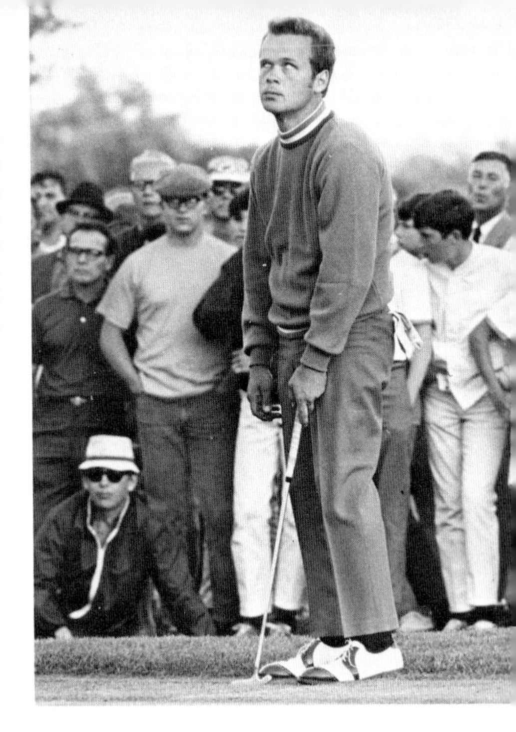

That Heady Feeling

by John E. Roemer, *Green Bay Press-Gazette.* Trying to head the ball, these soccer players, Zach Papanikalaou *(left)*, of the University of Wisconsin at Green Bay, and Desi McCullagh, a teammate, bump each other's heads as Bob Hagenow (4) of the University of Wisconsin at Parkside, the opposition, looks on. Papanikalaou recovered sufficiently to score six goals as Green Bay won, 10-1. Copyright, ©, 1969, *Green Bay Press-Gazette.*

IF AT FIRST . . .

by Larry C. Morris, *The New York Times.* Dr. Hugo Arrambide of Argentina being thrown by Adagio, which refused—for the second time—the eighth jump at the National Horse Show at Madison Square Garden in the international jumping event. Undaunted, Dr. Arrambide mounted again, but the horse balked once more, forcing elimination. Copyright, ©, 1969, *The New York Times Company.*

"SOME WIN—SOME LOSE"

by Seymour Snaer, *San Francisco Examiner.* Can you tell which bettor collected after a race at Bay Meadows Racetrack, near San Francisco? Copyright, ©, 1969, *San Francisco Examiner.*

A Girl Who Attracts Many Bows

by Kent Kobersteen, *Minneapolis Tribune*. A lady archer surrounded by some of her opponents as they line up for practice prior to tournament in suburban Minneapolis. Copyright, ©, 1969, *The Minneapolis Star and Tribune Company*.

College Sport with a Twist

by Earl Seubert, *Minneapolis Tribune*. There aren't too many varsity rodeo teams throughout the nation, but this is action in the national collegiate rodeo in Deadwood, South Dakota, last summer. Copyright, ©, 1969, *The Minneapolis Star and Tribune Company*.

A High Save

by John Croft, *Minneapolis Tribune*. This shot showing a goalie making a spectacular save was taken from a girder above the hockey arena at the Metropolitan Sports Center, in Bloomington, Minnesota. Action occurred during the 1969 state high-school tournament in a game between Roseau (Minn.) High and Harding High, of St. Paul. Copyright, ©, 1969, by *The Minneapolis Star and Tribune Company*.

ETCHED IN THE STRETCH

by Jim Laragy, *Rochester Democrat & Chronicle*. Black shadows against a lowering sky are caught by the photographer at a track meet between two high-school teams in Rochester, New York. Clearing the 120-yard high hurdle is Mike Erbelding of Bishop Kearney High with Tom Reneis of Monroe High chasing him. Copyright, ©, 1969, *Rochester Democrat & Chronicle*.